PEOPLE
A HISTORY OF OUR TIME

20th Century Greats Selected by The Associated Press

GALLERY BOOKS
An imprint of W.H. Smith Publishers Inc.
112 Madison Avenue
New York, New York 10016

© The Associated Press, 1986. All rights reserved.
ISBN 0-8317-6794-4

Project Director: Dan Perkes

Photo research by the Associated Press

Written by Geraldine Franklin, Jim Marks, Jennifer Regan

Design by Ryuichi Minakawa

Prepared and Produced by
Wieser & Wieser, Inc.
118 East 25th Street
New York, New York, 10010

Photos by the staff and member newspaper photographers of the Associated Press except as noted below:

Photos on page 58, page 116 (left), page 117 (upper left and right), page 118, page 126 (upper), page 127 (lower left and right), page 146 (upper and lower) and page 147 all THE GRANGER COLLECTION, New York.

Photos on page 59, page 117 (lower), page 118 (right), page 207 and page 208 (upper and lower) from CULVER PICTURES.

People: A history of our time.

   1. People—History—Pictorial works.   I. Associated Press.

ISBN 0-8317-6794-4

Printed in Hong Kong

Published by Gallery Books
A Division of W. H. Smith Publishers Inc.
112 Madison Avenue
New York, New York 10016

CONTENTS

GOVERNMENT AND POLITICS.............5

Anthony, Susan B.	Gandhi, Mohandas	Lindberg, Charles A	Roosevelt, Franklin D.
Begin, Menachem	George, Lloyd	MacArthur, Douglas	Sadat, Anwar
Chiang Kai-Shek	Hirohito	Mao Tse-Tung	Stalin, Joseph
Churchill, Winston S.	Hitler, Adolph	Mussolini, Benito	Sun Yat-Sen
Clemenceau, Georges	Ho Chi Minh	Nehru, Jawaharlal	Truman, Harry S.
De Gaulle, Charles	Keynes, John	Pope John XXIII	Wilson, Woodrow
Eisenhower, Dwight D.	King, Martin Luther	Rhodes, Cecil J.	
Gandhi, Indira	Lenin	Roosevelt, Eleanor	

SPORTS........................77

Ali, Muhammad	Hillary, Edmund	Nicklaus, Jack	Ruth, Babe
Bannister, Roger	Laver, Rodney	Owens, Jesse	Zaharias, Babe
Comanici, Nadia	Louis, Joe	Pele	
Gretzky, Wayne	Navratilova, Martina	Robinson, Jackie	

SCIENCE, INDUSTRY AND MEDICINE.....107

Bell, Alexander	Einstein, Albert	Lister, Joseph	Pavlov, Ivan
Carver, G. W.	Fleming, Alexander	Mother Teresa	Rockefeller, John D.
Curie, Marie	Ford, Henry	Nightingale, Florence	Salk, Jonas
Edison, Thomas A.	Freud, Sigmund	Oppenheimer, J. Robert	Wright, Orville

ARTS..........................141

Armstrong, Louis	De Mille, Cecil B.	Gilbert & Sullivan	Picasso, Pablo
Balanchine, George	Disney, Walt	Hemingway, Ernest	Pound, Ezra
Bartok, Bela	Eliot, T.S.	Hitchcock, Alfred	Renoir, Auguste
Berlin, Irving	Ellington, Duke	James, Henry	Rodin, Auguste
Caruso, Enrico	Erte	Joyce, James	Shaw, George Bernard
Cezanne, Paul	Faulkner, William	Man Ray	Solzhenitsyn, Alexander
Chaplin, Charlie	Fitzgerald, Ella	Nabokov, Vladimir	Stravinsky, Igor
Chekhov, Anton	Fitzgerald, F. Scott	Olivier, Laurence	Wells, H.G.
Coward, Noel	Frost, Robert	O'Neill, Eugene	Wright, Frank Lloyd
Dali, Salvador	Garbo, Greta	Orwell, George	Yeats, William Butler

INTRODUCTION

This is a book about the most fascinating, frustrating and inspiring subject in the world: People. More specifically, it is about some of the people who left their mark on the 20th century, and on the course of human history. It is a small tribute to some who made the world a different and usually better place.

Some of the people portrayed here—Albert Einstein and Pablo Picasso are obvious examples—had extraordinary gifts. And used them. But more of these people made their mark because they had extraordinary vision, or ambition, or compassion, or courage. They believed in themselves and in their purpose, whether it was political, artistic, athletic or scientific. Then they put their beliefs into action, betting every fiber of their being that their chosen course was right.

Viewed in the usual sense—the sense of success being the realization of a dream, the attainment of a goal—some of these people succeeded, and others failed. But viewed in a truer sense—the sense of success being a process of devotion and dedication rather than a result of that devotion and dedication—every one of these people succeeded. Even those who never did reach their ultimate object left powerful examples of what can be accomplished by a single human being with a dream. And the courage to pursue it.

Readers should note that this book is not an attempt to name *the* greatest people of the 20th century, for the simple reason that there is no objective way to measure greatness. There is not even an objective way to measure who "belongs" to the 20th century! So the final list of people included was subjective, based on the opinions of the editors and producers of the book and editors of the Associated Press, and was decided upon only after what is called in diplomatic circles "a full and forthright exchange of views". The primary criterion used was a person's impact on the world at large, or on his/her field of endeavor. While some consideration was given to how long into this century a potential subject lived, more weight was given to when their actions were felt. Thus, people like Cecil Rhodes, Florence Nightingale and Auguste Renoir, who all died early in this century, have been included because the impact of their work is still being felt today.

With each subject, we have tried to show, in both words and pictures, the human being as well as the famous figure. We have tried to include the small details, the personal quirks, the little triumphs and disasters that will give you a feeling of these people as flesh and blood, not as statues outside a public building or images on a screen. And for those who would like to use this book as a reference, we have created a separate box for each subject showing given name (many of which you may never have heard), date and place of birth, marriages (or lack thereof), highlights of their careers and, where applicable, date of death. We have also broken the book down, somewhat arbitrarily, into four sections: Government and Politics, Sports, Arts, and Science, Industry and Medicine. Those people who did not obviously fit into one of the four categories were included where it seemed most appropriate.

There is much joy in this book. There is more pain. There is also doubt, and deprivation and vilification. The people in these pages paid a price for their achievements. They paid in Churchillian currency—blood, toil, tears and sweat. Not one of them won a lottery. Yes, luck played a part in some of their stories, for that is the way life is. But luck did not make them great. They made themselves great.

History did not make them. They made history. As can anyone willing to tap the well of greatness within each one of us.

GOVERNMENT AND POLITICS

SUSAN B. ANTHONY

Asked her opinion on marriage, Susan B. Anthony, who spent fifty years fighting for women's right to vote, said "Marriage, to women as to men, must be a luxury, not a necessity; an incident of life, not all of it. I do not even believe in second marriages after one of the parties is dead, so sacred and binding do I consider the marriage relation (ship)."

Born in rural Adams, Mass. in 1820, this American pioneer of women's rights saw the inequities thrust upon women and spent her entire lifetime fighting them. When she was young a man didn't need a wife's consent to apprentice away their child, and her wages legally had to be paid to him.

Anthony fought to right such inequities, and her weapons were the podium, the printing press, the petition and a quick retort to ridicule. And while she was advancing the women's cause, she also waged a war against slavery. She was Quaker-born, a spinster who advocated temperance, an abolitionist, a crusader fighting to gain women the right to hold property and to work for a fair wage. But while she sternly defended the sanctity of marriage she crusaded tirelessly to change the marriage institution and make it fair to women. Often she was criticized as a radical who went too far.

Her outspoken ideas, combined with her stern expression, her tightly combed gray hair, her long, dark dresses and ever-present red shawl exemplified Susan B. Anthony's single-minded determination to advance the cause of suffrage for women in the U.S. The common thread that ran through her life was justice; always the standard which she applied: whether an act would help or hinder the drive for basic rights.

She completed her education in New York and accepted employment as a teacher, but she soon left and became assistant manager of the family farm in upstate New York. During this time she met and was exposed to the views of such men as William Lloyd Garrison, Wendell Phillips and Frederick Douglass and became convinced she, to, could become an advocate of reform.

However, her initial efforts as an agent for the Daughters of Temperance and the American Anti-Slavery Society were disappointing for she encountered discrimination as a woman. She was soon to meet and become friends with Elizabeth Cady Stanton and, influenced by Stanton's vigorous defense of women's rights, helped found the American Equal Rights Association (1866).

In 1872, Anthony became a cause celebré when she was arrested in Rochester, N.Y. as she attempted to cast her vote in the election, claiming that the provisions of the 14th and 15th Amendments applied to all citizens, male and female. She was tried and, although convicted, was not sent to jail, thus thwarting an appeal. This was only one of the many battles against discrimination that she waged during her lifetime.

From 1892 to 1900 Anthony was president of the National American Woman Suffrage Association, which she helped to found, and with Elizabeth Cady Stanton, Matilda Jocelyn Gage and Ida Husted Harper, compiled and edited the first four volumes of *The History of Woman Suffrage*. Her ceaseless work and travel won recognition for women's suffrage in both America and Europe.

After the Civil War, she made enemies of former allies among the abolitionists by insisting that if women did not gain the right to vote, then freed black men should not be enfranchised, either.

On her 50th birthday she said, "I am so glad of it all (the accolades given her) because it will teach the young girls to be true to principle—to live an idea, though an unpopular one—that to live single, without any man's name, may be honorable."

And while women did not yet have the vote, nationwide, by the time Miss Anthony died on March 18, 1905, many things had changed. Women were voting in four states; marriage and property laws were changing and younger women

Suffragette Susan B. Anthony

were there to take the reins. Although it wasn't until 1920, fifteen years after her death, that women finally won the right to vote nationwide, Susan B. Anthony is a true heroine of the women's movement.

Given Name: Susan Brownell Anthony
Born: February 15, 1820, Adams, Massachusetts
Unmarried
Highlights: Leading reformer and suffragist, she led the fight for womens' rights and laid the foundation for the movement that got women the vote.
Died: March 13, 1906

GOVERNMENT AND POLITICS

Given Name: Menachim Begin
Born: August 16, 1913, Brest-Litvosk, Poland
Married: Aliza Arnold, 3 children
Highlights: As Prime Minister of Israel (1977-1983) shared Nobel Peace Prize with Anwar el-Sadat of Egypt for their historic efforts to bring peace to the Middle East.

The Prime Minister of Israel stays relaxed while facing the press.

GOVERNMENT AND POLITICS

Chiang Kai-shek

Translated into English Chiang Kai-shek's name means "firm rock" and it was with stubborn, rock-like conviction that the leader of nationalist China waited on Formosa to reclaim mainland China from the Communists who defeated him in 1949. The odds were always against Chiang's return from the island 100 miles off China's coast where he'd fled with two million Nationalist refugees after Mao Tse-tung's victory. But during the 22 years he had been top man in China, Chiang had survived revolution and rebellion, beating back insurgent communists, the Japanese and rival forces within his own party; so long after the world ceased regarding him as China's true leader, Chiang viewed the Reds who had seized one-quarter of the world population as mere bandits, doomed to destruction: it was his mission to exterminate Mao and liberate his people.

Son of a salt merchant and his concubine, Chiang joined the "Brotherhood Society", an early version of Dr. Sun Yat-sen's "Kuomintang", in 1908, after returning from Japan where he finished his education. The Kuomintang, which would become the Nationalist Party, had been formed to oppose greedy warlords who were chopping up China and unify it into a republic. In 1911 Chiang, who quickly became Sun's close associate, was appointed head of revolutionary forces in Chekiang after a revolt against the Manchu Dynasty. After Sun died in 1925, the now Generalissimo Chiang led an all-out effort to overthrow the Peking-based government. Although Chiang's party and the communists were pursuing the same end, in 1927 the two parties split, and Chiang defeated the Communists in a bloody coup. In 1928 Generalissimo Chiang was elected Chairman of the National Government of the Republic of China. The United States was the first country to recognize Chiang's government at Nanking. Other major powers soon followed suit. Chiang's forces spent the 30's locked in violent conflict with the Communists, who were organizing under Mao in rural China, and with Japan, which in 1931 seized Manchuria. Unable to fight on both fronts Chiang said, "Give me 10 more years to take on Japan." It would be 15 years before he tried, and failed, to regain Manchuria. Meanwhile, he battled the Japanese for 8 years, suffering 3 million casualties, until, with the December, 1941, attack on Pearl Harbor, the United States and its allies entered the effort to defeat Japan. Also joining the fight in an uneasy alliance were the Chinese communists.

During the war Chiang Kai-shek, long a symbol of the embattled hero to Americans, was elevated to world status as a member of the Big Four—the others were President Roosevelt, Prime Minister Churchill and Generalissimo Joseph Stalin. When Japan surrendered he returned triumphantly to Nanking—and a resumption of the struggle with the Communists. As Roosevelt had before him, President Truman tried to mediate between the two sides. Betrayed by the Soviets, whose reneging on a post-war treaty Chiang felt cost him Manchuria, and beaten by the communists, Chiang left the mainland.

During the war Generalissimo Chiang had conceived the "scorched earth" policy of retreat—when pressured by the enemy to withdraw, his troops were under order to leave nothing at all for the Japanese to utilize. But this policy of buying time by relinquishing space would not apply to his vision of recapturing the mainland as he plotted and planned on the 240 mile-long island where Nationalist China was resettled.

Austere and stern, Chiang, though converted to Christianity by his wife, Mayling, the American-educated daughter of the powerful Soong family, lived by the words of Confucius—"If the leader is virtuous, the people will be virtuous." Monk-like in demeanor he was often short-tempered, even cruel. His government was prosperous though plagued with corruption. Security leaks tipped off the Communists to his plans before he embarked upon them. Still, from Taipei, the capitol city, he created on Taiwan (the provincial name for the island of Formosa), with its population of 11 million Taiwanese, a nation far more powerful than its numbers would suggest. While across the China Sea Mao was effecting change by violent Marxist means, Chiang accomplished bloodless land reforms. His military force was formidable for such a small nation. He established an economy so strong that eventually it was the first Asian country to discontinue U.S. aid.

World events kept alive Chiang's dream of returning to the mainland. In 1950 the Korean War placed the U.S. 7th Fleet at Formosa, protecting the island against expected invasions from the Communists. When the war ended, 14,000 Chinese communist prisoners of war elected to settle on Taiwan rather than return to Red China. In America, the powerful "China Lobby", a group of anti-Communist senators active since the '40's in Chiang's behalf, argued that with its crucially located offshore islands of Quemoy and Matsu, Taiwan must continue to receive strong U.S. support and recognition as the true Chinese government.

Still, Chiang waited and bided his time. In 1966, reelected to his fourth term as head of state, he vowed that "the old soldier" was ready to return. Mao had just initiated the bloody cultural revolution which Chiang thought would turn out to be a "Frankenstein" that would topple his foe. Once again, the Generalissimo was disappointed.

Out of traditional Chinese respect for old age, an enfeebled Chiang was elected to yet another 6-year term just before he died in 1972. He tacitly surrendered control of the government to his son, Defense Minister Chiang Ching-kuo. Enormously bitter, he had seen in 1971 the U.N. oust his Taiwan government and seat the People's Republic of China in the General Assembly. He swore that neither he nor his people would ever recognize the validity of the U.N. vote. Although the U.S. had opposed Taiwan's expulsion it supported the admission of mainland China to the U.N. With Henry Kissinger making preparations for President Nixon's visit to the mainland, it would be only a matter of time before the U.S. would finally turn its back on Taiwan as the legitimate government of China. The old soldier's conviction that he would re-conquer what he had lost, that his China would prevail as the true China, would never be realized.

Given Name: Chiang Chung-cheng
Born: October 31, 1887, Ningbo, Zhejiang, China
Married: Miss Mao, 1905, 1 child
Married: Mei-Ling Soong, 1927
Highlights: Led Koumintang revolt against Chinese war lords and headed fight against Japanese in World War II. After losing mainland to Communist forces founded Republic of Taiwan.
Died: April 5, 1975

GOVERNMENT AND POLITICS

The Generalissimo, still in charge at age 75, relaxes at Taipei on the island of Formosa.

GOVERNMENT AND POLITICS

Winston Churchill

In 1940 when Winston Churchill became Prime Minister of England the 65-year-old Member of Parliament told the British he had "nothing to offer but blood, toil, tears and sweat." Taking over at the request of King George VI after Neville Chamberlain's "peace in our time" appeasement policy against Hitler had failed dismally, Churchill did break down and weep later that year when France fell to the Nazis.

Passionate in his hatred of Hitler, he was even more passionate in his determination to save his embattled little island from destruction by "the odious apparatus of Nazi rule." Wherever he went in the dark days of the war—making the halls of Parliament ring with his thunderous tones, visiting the troops in France, going into bomb shelters during the London Blitz in his famous "Blitz suit" coverall—Churchill embodied the indomitable spirit of his people. With his jutting bulldog jaw and hunched shoulders he even looked like John Bull, cartoonists' rendering of the typical Brit. When "Good Old Winnie" appeared, holding up two outstretched fingers in a "V for Victory" sign, crowds cheered.

Where there was war, Churchill seemed to be on the scene. In 1895 he went to Cuba as an observer for the Spanish Army, there to put down an insurrection. (It was there that he first developed a liking for Havana cigars.) He served as correspondent for a London newspaper during the Boer War, making a spectacular escape when he was imprisoned in Pretoria. During World War I he fought in France. Despite his acquaintance with war Churchill believed mankind wanted to live in peace. His pleas that England rearm to discourage Hitler fell on deaf ears in Parliament. In his last years, heaped with honors and prizes bestowed on him as a war hero, he stated that peace was the "last prize" he sought.

Churchill began his 60-year career of public service as a red-haired firebrand serving in Parliament under Queen Victoria. At the age of 80, ailing though eager to campaign for his "heir apparent" Anthony Eden, he resigned as Prime Minister at the urgings of his wife Clementine and members of his party, who wanted a younger leader. "I am now nearing the end of my journey", he told Parliament. Then he rode from the Prime Minister's residence at 10 Downing Street to Buckingham Palace to tender his resignation to Queen Elizabeth. When he emerged, he doffed his familiar top hat and, puffing on his inevitable cigar drove off, flashing a shy smile and his V-for-Victory sign.

During his career Churchill earned a permanent place in world history not just as an architect of victory but as a brilliant orator. His legacy of inspiring speeches is unmatched in modern times. The greater the disaster, the greater the heights to which his grandiloquence rose, bursting with deathless phrases that gave almost spiritual solace to the British people. After the evacuation of Dunkerque, which the Allies viewed as a victory but Churchill labelled a disaster, he nonetheless elevated the pilots of the Royal Air Force to Olympian status—"Never", he said, "has so much been owed by so many to so few." He met Hitler's force with words that were largely bluff, telling the House of Commons as Hitler overran France, "If we can stand up to him ... all Europe may be free ... if the British Commonwealth and England last for 1000 years, men will still say, 'This was their finest hour'". "We will never surrender", he claimed defiantly, his rolling tones sounding a call to battle. "We shall defend our island whatever the cost will be. We shall fight on the beaches, we shall fight on the landing grounds, we shall fight in the fields and in the streets."

Churchill's talent with words was not confined to his flaming speeches. He was a prolific author of 20 books, including biographies of his illustrious forebears, "History of the English Speaking Peoples", which he worked on for 20 years, and his four-volume memoirs of the war period (one was titled "Their Finest Hour") When he received the Nobel Prize for Literature in 1953 it was for his oratory as well as his writing. A member of the prize committee remarked, "The literary prize is intended to cast luster over the author but this time it is the author who gives luster to the prize."

Also in 1953 Churchill was knighted by Queen Elizabeth. Years earlier, in 1945, right after he'd failed to win reelection as Prime Minister, he'd displayed the barbed wit that was the other side of his eloquence when he declined both the knighthood and the Order of the Garter offered him by King George: "Why should I take the Order of the Garter from my sovereign", he said, "when his people have just given me the Order of the Boot?"

The cheers of British crowds for their war leader were still ringing in his ears when Churchill and his Conservative Party lost the 1945 election. To his people Churchill was a symbol of war. They wanted something new and thought they'd get it with Clement Attlee and the Labor Party. Churchill rose to defeat with the same zeal he'd risen to the threat of defeat by Hitler. Relishing his role as leader of "His Majesty's Loyal Opposition" he attacked Attlee as a "sheep in sheep's clothing", decried the decision to quit India as "the clattering down of the British Empire," said creeping socialism was "making the country look like a jackass" and campaigned to get back in office. Driving up and down the English countryside he waved his cigar, made the V sign and pointed to queues longer than the ones during the war. At 77 the rugged old war hero was put back in office with a resounding victory, his primary aim the prevention of World War III.

1945 wasn't Churchill's only defeat. Early in his career, as First Lord of the Admiralty, he was blamed for the tragic loss of British and Empire troops, at Gallipoli, when 250,000 fighting men died trying to open the Dardenelles. "I am finished", declared Churchill at the time, resigning his cabinet post and going off to fight in France. Later he was cleared of responsibility for the debacle. Reactions to some of Churchill's other decisions were often lively. Vegetables were hurled at him once in Parliament by opponents of his position on tariffs. Women suffragists beat him with umbrellas for his opposition to their cause.

Although he didn't champion women's rights Churchill was strongly influenced by the two women in his life. On his 50th wedding anniversary he said of his marriage to Clementine that it was "the most fortunate event that ever happened to me in my whole life." The Churchills' had four sons and one daughter. The other woman was his mother, the former Jennie Jerome of New York. He attributed the roots of his close association with America to her background.

Churchill was as familiar a figure to Americans as their own presidents. He visited the U.S. 14 times, to confer, receive honors and make speeches. One of his most famous postwar speeches was made in Fulton, Mo. in 1946 when he declared that an "Iron Curtain" divided Europe in two. He regarded the British-American relationship as "that great unwritten alliance" which was the surest protector of Western civilization. During the war he met repeatedly with Roosevelt, on battleships at sea, at Casablanca, Cairo and Yalta. They were on a "Winston and Franklin" friendship basis. When Joseph Stalin of Russia joined them to plot the war or chart the peace they were known as the "Big Three." Churchill was the last survivor of the famous trio.

Serving Britain during the depths of its war crisis, through its "finest hour" and into the atomic age, Churchill didn't always approve of his country's or civilization's progress. Cars were one thing he took a strong dislike to, calling the automobile "a poor substitute for the horse, marking a very gloomy milestone in the progress of mankind."

Consoling his people through wartime deprivation and urging them to sacrifice, Churchill personally preferred the Victorian-style "Good Life". He had a passion for the expensive cigars which he continued to smoke, much to his doctors' consternation, even after he'd had two strokes. He loved fine wines and brandy. "If you want to make Winston

GOVERNMENT AND POLITICS

Churchill smiles as he leaves the Prime Minister's residence at 10 Downing Street on his way to address the House of Commons.

GOVERNMENT AND POLITICS

happy", said his wife, "give him a good dinner." The British people applauded his high living as much as they admired him for his appearances in bomb shelters in coveralls, an outfit he adopted the night a chandelier fell on the table in the middle of dinner when a bomb fell next door to the Prime Minister's residence at 10 Downing Street. (He and his cabinet minister guests finished their meal before they descended to an air raid shelter. Twelve people were killed next door.)

Churchill was able to support his life style largely through his writings. When he'd finished his war memoirs the New York *Times* and *Life* paid over a million dollars for serialization rights. Besides writing, he was an amateur painter. In 1958, the same year "History of the English Speaking People" was published, his paintings went on a worldwide tour. Although the Chicago Art Museum refused to exhibit the works of an amateur, huge crowds flocked to see his work at the Metropolitan Museum in New York and the Smithsonian in Washington, D.C. In England the Royal Academy of Art turned over its galleries to an amateur's work for the first time.

Churchill may have been an amateur painter, but as a warrior, statesman and genius with words, his phrases and accomplishments place him at the top of 20th century immortals.

Given Name: Winston Leonard Spencer Churchill

Born: November 30, 1874, Blenheim Castle, England

Married: Clementine Hozier, 1908, 5 children

Highlights: Prime Minister of England, 1940-1945; 1951-1955. Led England through World War II. Also won Nobel Prize for Literature in 1953 for his writings and oratory.

Died: January 24, 1965

"Good Old Winnie", with ever-present hat, cane and cigar, visits English coastal fortifications in August, 1940.

GOVERNMENT AND POLITICS

Georges Clemenceau

His nickname, "The Tiger," and an indomitable "will to victory" characterized the life of statesman Georges Clemenceau, pioneer for democracy and upholder of the French Third Republic.

Born on September 28, 1841, in Mouilleron-en-Parens of western France, he grew up strong willed, impulsive, proud and savagely independent. His father, Benjamin, a Voltarien, positivist and admirer of the Revolution of 1789 introduced young Georges to the men who were plotting to overthrow the emperor Napoleon III.

In 1861, while studying medicine in Paris, Clemenceau, with some friends, founded a journal, *Le Travail*, which set forth views characterizing his future political action. It was seized by the police and Clemenceau was imprisoned for 73 days. Upon his release he started a new paper, *Le Matin*, which was also seized by the authorities. Having completed his studies, Clemenceau left for the United States, arriving in New York at the height of the Civil War and spent from 1865-69 meeting writers and journalists for his own political enrichment.

After marrying one of his pupils, Clemenceau returned to France and set himself up as a doctor in Vendee, but politics soon took him back to Paris. In July 1870 Napoleon declared war on Germany and two months later the French were defeated at Sedan and the empire collapsed. Clemenceau was among the crowd that invaded the Palais-Bourbon on September 4th Soon afterward he was named mayor of the 18th district of Paris (Montmartre) and as a Radical Republican deputy voted in the National Assembly held in Bordeaux, voting against the preliminaries of the harsh peace terms demanded by Germany. Clemenceau left Bordeaux determined to avenge France's "shameful humiliation".

The next years of political activity saw Clemenceau starting another newspaper, *La Justice*, which became the principal organ of the Radicals in Paris and he rapidly built a reputation as a political critic and as a destroyer of ministries. From 1902-09 Clemenceau defended freedom of thought, belief, consience and education and served as Premier. This post ended in 1909 after a violent and unexpected argument with the influential statesman Theophile Delcasse and Clemenceau began to travel abroad.

Clemenceau stood against anything that could undermine France's moral strength and when World War I broke out in July 1914, he called upon every Frenchman to join the fray. President Raymond Poincare again called Clemenceau to the premiership in November 1917, knowing that only Clemenceau could maintain French national unity. In a short time the new Premier raised national morale and sustained it through the March onslaught of a fresh German offensive. The next month Clemenceau obtained unification of the Allied command under Gen. Ferdinand Foch and led the French delegation at the Paris Peace Conference.

He presided with authority over the difficult session of the 1919 Paris Peace Conference as the Treaty of Versailles was prepared, sitting with "head held high, tilted backward, between broad shoulders, bony hands in gray gloves resting on the table before him, dark eyes almost hidden behind bushy eyebrows, yet sparkling brightly when he addressed a delegate."

At last, on November 11, 1918, when the armistice was signed by the defeated Germans, this last survivor of the 1871 protest in Bordeaux found satisfaction. But an old political grievance brought the Tiger down. Clemenceau had denounced some members of the Left as defeatists in 1917; in 1920 they defeated him in the presidential election. He retired from politics and died on November 24, 1929.

Clemenceau is remembered for the powerful contributions he made to the victory of the Allies in World War I and is remembered as the "father of Victory" by the combatants.

Given Name: Georges Clemenceau

Born: September 28, 1841, Moulleron-en Parens, France

Married: Mary Plummer, 1869, 3 children

Highlights: Premier of France from 1906-1909 and again from 1917-1920, he was a leading democratic statesman, helped formulate the Treaty of Versailles, following World War I.

Died: November 24, 1929.

After his retirement, the face of "the Tiger", Georges Clemenceau, showed some of the results of 50 years in politics.

GOVERNMENT AND POLITICS

Charles DeGaulle

When Charles DeGaulle died, French President Georges Pompidou announced, "France is now a widow." DeGaulle's "marriage" to his native France had been a long one—from the battlefields of World War I to the jubilant procession he led through the Arc de Triomphe in liberated Paris in 1944, Through crisis after crisis in Postwar France. DeGaulle was a giant of his time, and the strongest French ruler since Napoleon.

Tall, aloof yet curiously paternal, DeGaulle had the bearing of a man of destiny. As a child, he had listened as his professor father told stories of the age-old glories of the French nation, and Charles DeGaulle had a pre-ordained look, as if he alone had been born to save France and revive and restore it to a place of preeminence in the world. His bearing was autocratic, almost regal. Although his speaking voice was distant and awkward, he could thrill crowds by leading them in "La Marseillaise" when he had finished addressing them.

Wounded three times and imprisoned by the Germans after the bloody battle at Verdun, DeGaulle was a World War I hero. For bravery in battle and his 5 attempts to escape the enemy prison, he was cited for bravery after the war by Marshall Henri Petain, an early admirer. Later, Petain wrote of DeGaulle, "One day a grateful France will call on him." Ironically, Petain himself was the first to be called—when France capitulated to the Nazis the old Marshall came out of retirement to lead his beaten people as head of the puppet Vichy government.

DeGaulle never forgave those of his countrymen who gave in to the Germans, frequently and bitterly referring to them as sheep who had been headed towards slaughter since the end of World War I. As the leader of the "Free French", he had escaped to England during the Occupation. From there he broadcast inspiring messages of hope and encouragement across the Channel to the French, recalling France's eternal glories. He scoffed when the Vichy regime sentenced him to death.

During the war, DeGaulle gained a reputation among allied leaders for being so pro-French as to be unreliable. President Roosevelt said, "He may be a great man but he has a messianic complex." Winston Churchill claimed that of all the crosses he had to bear the Cross of Lorraine (DeGaulle's symbol) was the heaviest. In 1944 the allies planning D-Day looked past the heroic general, already regarded as France's leader, for a more reasonable Frenchman to deal with. DeGaulle never forgot this slight and 20 years later refused to attend commemorative ceremonies at Normandy.

When the war was over, France turned to DeGaulle as the undisputed leader to make the transition from wartime confusion to order and recovery, but after only 16 months DeGaulle, disgusted by political bickering, left government. In

General Charles De Gaulle embarks for a post-war flight to Chicago, Illinois in August, 1945.

1958 when his nation was teetering on the brink of Civil War, the old general was waiting in the wings. He rewrote the constitution, called for a national referendum, his favorite tool of governing, and became the first President-Premier of the Fifth Republic. With his personality and authority firmly established at home, DeGaulle had to immediately solve the Algerian crisis. France's North African colony was seething with unrest. Always a realist, DeGaulle was convinced that the days of colonial empire were over. He evolved a plan for a Free Algeria—an "Algerian Algeria", he called it, rejecting the claims of the one-million Europeans settled there. After a failed coup d'etat by rightwing generals and two assassination attempts, DeGaulle, again using a national referendum, skillfully maneuvered a bloodless separation of Algeria from France.

In his efforts to return France to a position of world prominence far greater than its numbers would indicate, DeGaulle continued to irk France's natural allies in the West. He always cloaked his actions in mystery, claiming that "mystery" was an essential quality of a successful chief of state. Attempting to "go it alone" as a third force between Washington and Moscow, he held France aloof from other European nations. In 1963 he refused to sign the Moscow Treaty outlawing nuclear testing, claiming France had the right to its own "force de frappe." In 1964 his government recognized Red China against fierce U.S. opposition. In 1966 he broke with NATO. Like Napoleon, he had hopes of an alliance with Russia, an "understanding from the Urals to the Atlantic" which would protect their nations from any unwelcome intrusion by "Les Anglo-Saxons." Late in his career he learned from bitter experience that the Russians were unreliable and became a bitter foe of the Soviets and Communism.

Travelling widely as statesman and spokesman for France's interests, DeGaulle persevered in his crusade to make the small nation an independent world force. In 1968 he was in Roumania when reports of student unrest in Paris reached him. At first he reacted with characteristic disdain but when labor unions joined the students in street fighting and riots he returned home to be confronted by the "Events of May". He called new elections and won overwhelming support. But it was obvious that his policies no longer corresponded to the wishes of students and workers, and his conviction that he was the incarnation of France was fatally undermined. In 1969 when a crucial referendum on administrative reforms did not produce the personal mandate he was looking for, the old soldier whose life had been wed to France's destiny retired, shocked and dazed. Refusing to comment on politics or world events, he lived only one year as a private citizen.

Premier De Gaulle reviews French troops in Paris in November, 1970.

Given Name: Charles Andre Joseph Marie de Gaulle
Born: November 22, 1890, Lille, France
Married: Yvonne Vendroux, 1921, 3 children
Highlights: Leader of the Free French forces during World War II and of the French nation afterward. President of France 1958-1969.
Died: November 9, 1970

Dwight D. Eisenhower

Dwight David Eisenhower seemed to have two distinctly different public faces. One was the genial, smiling fellow from Abilene, Kansas everyone called "Ike"—the fellow who, as the 34th President of the United States in the '50's, presided over the most prosperous decade not just in U.S. history but in world history. With a car in every garage and a free college education available to any G.I. who wanted one, the American Dream of material well-being seemed to come true. The Americans sporting "I Like Ike" buttons were beginning to enjoy the Good Life. They swept the popular war hero into office on a record-breaking vote.

The other Eisenhower was the Five Star General who, as Supreme Commander of Allied Forces in Europe, led America and its allies to victory in World War II. It was Eisenhower who snatched North Africa from Marshal Rommell and his "Desert Rats", squeezed Italy out of the war and masterminded the critical D-Day invasion of France in June, 1944, that began the final assault on Hitler. After the war the General was lionized as a genius in London, hailed as a savior when he returned home to the states: even the Germans admitted his brilliance, confessing his attack in North Africa had come as a total surprise. General Eisenhower was not the man with the grin Americans grew familiar with on their new medium, television. He was the fighting man who, the night before he sent the largest military force ever assembled onto the Normandy beaches, told his soldiers, "We will accept nothing less than full victory." After they'd broken through the Siegfried Line onto Reich territory, he ordered them to "Destroy the enemy: on the ground, in the air, destroy." The eyes staring at the German army's Chief of Staff as he signed his country's surrender and pleaded for mercy for his people were hard, steel-blue. The voice demanding that from now on Germany must obey all orders issued by the Allies was cold.

It was not surprising that after the war, when Eisenhower had retired from the army and was serving as president of Columbia University, President Harry Truman appointed him Commander of the NATO forces in Europe which were organized to resist Russian aggression. Nor was it surprising, given his tremendous popularity, that both the Republican and Democratic parties wanted Eisenhower to run for President. The Republicans had asked him to oppose Roosevelt in 1943—"Baloney!" was Eisenhower's response. He declined again in 1948 when both parties approached him, some Democrats wanting to replace Truman. In 1952 he finally accepted the Republican nomination, leading the party to a smashing victory against Adlai Stevenson. Despite a major heart attack suffered during his first term, in 1956 he won reelection in an even greater landslide.

In his first inaugural address Eisenhower, who when elected was the oldest man to become President (he was also the first President to reach 70 while in office) stated that his main goal would be to achieve peace with honor, based on strength and unity in the free world, with no appeasement to the Russians, who, already entrenched in Eastern Europe, were spreading Red imperialism throughout the world. Although he decried what he called "this damnable thing called war" he believed that "a soldier's pack is not so heavy as a prisoner's chains." During the '50's both the U.S. and Russia developed the hydrogen bomb and the arms race between the two became a priority of both nations. Nuclear submarines, intercontinental ballistic missiles and detection systems were produced at an alarming rate. At the same time, Eisenhower and Soviet Premier Nikita Kruschev attempted to create a thaw in the Cold War. Kruschev visited the U.S. but Eisenhower's invitation to visit Moscow was cancelled when the Russians downed a U-2 spy plane, manned by American Francis Gary Powers. This incident caused great embarrassment to the administration, which at first denied any knowledge of the spy plane system.

Still a General in 1951, Eisenhower addressed Congress on the need to rearm Europe.

GOVERNMENT AND POLITICS

Given Name: Dwight David Eisenhower
Born: October 14, 1890, Denison, Texas
Married: Mamie Geneva Doud, 1916, 2 children
Highlights: President of the United States, 1953-1961. Commander-in-Chief of Allied forces in Europe during World War II.
Died: March 24, 1969

Another area of embarrassment to the U.S. was Russia's early triumph in the space race. The launching of Sputnik I, a rocket developed in secret by the Russians that landed on the moon and planted a hammer and sickle emblem there, was of great psychological advantage over the Americans, who claimed successes in weaponry greater than the Russians. Next the Russians sent a dog into space, followed shortly by America's first Jupiter-C satellite launched from Cape Canaveral, Florida. The race was on, with the U.S. choosing its first 7-man team and both countries hurling satellites into space where, it was predicted, the next war would take place.

Back on earth, President Eisenhower continued to pursue the international policies of his predecessor, Truman. The U.S. did not go to the aid of the brave Hungarian insurgents who rose up against the Communists in 1956, for fear of precipitating World War III. In Africa, Latin America and the Middle East, the U.S. watched as Soviet influence spread. Eisenhower's belief in the "domino theory"—if one country went communist others near it would fall—led him to commit the U.S. to the defense of South Vietnam, in Southeast Asia, a decision that began the nation's futile involvement in that area. On the very doorstep of America in Cuba, Fidel Castro, with Russian backing, began a "hate America" campaign which led to the breaking-off of diplomatic relations with the island.

When Richard Nixon, Eisenhower's Vice-President, was challenged by John F. Kennedy in 1960 to deny that U.S. prestige and power had declined under Eisenhower, Eisenhower claimed he was proud to have achieved his greatest goal, that of keeping the peace. He had personally travelled thousands upon thousands of miles, especially after his Secretary of State, John Foster Dulles died, as a good-will ambassador for the nation.

At home, Eisenhower's policies were more conservative and pro-big business than Truman's. The longest steel strike in history occurred during his presidency. He presided over the end of an emotional period in the country's history—Senator Joseph McCarthy's witchhunt for communist-sympathizers. And he used his skills as a military strategist to respond to the beginning of a bloody, violent chapter in America's domestic life: the civil rights movement. After a Supreme Court decision unanimously declared that the segregation of students by race was unconstitutional and Governor Orval Faubus of Little Rock, Arkansas ordered the National Guard to prevent nine black students from entering an all-white high school, Eisenhower sent in 1000 men from the 101st Airborne Division. Wearing helmets, and with bayonets at the ready, they remained at the school for 64 days. During the Eisenhower administration the first Civil Rights legislation since Reconstruction was passed to protect black voting rights.

While in office Eisenhower was viewed as a good-natured old soldier who, as a former general, was good at giving orders to others but would usually rather be playing golf. Although when he left office he was at the peak of his popularity, pictured in golf cap with a silly grin on his face, he was the butt of editorial cartoons. But in 1970 secret files were opened that revealed Eisenhower worked much harder than anyone guessed. Richard Nixon later confirmed that Eisenhower was a complex and devious man under whom America prospered because he was always in charge. That was an ironic comment from a man who was, at the time he made the remark, himself President, about to be brought down by those very qualities—complexity and deviousness—which he attributed to the man under whom he'd studied for the office.

GOVERNMENT AND POLITICS

In 1945, Eisenhower urged the House Military Committee to adopt compulsory peacetime military training.

GOVERNMENT AND POLITICS

Indira Gandhi

In a speech on the eve of her 1984 assassination, Prime Minister Indira Gandhi said, "I don't mind if my life goes in the service of the nation. If I die today, every drop of my blood will invigorate the nation."

Indeed, long before she was sworn in as India's Prime Minister in January, 1966, Mrs. Gandhi had given herself to the cause of India. The only child of her nation's first Prime Minister, Jawaharlal Nehru, she had spent much of her childhood alone, with both of her parents imprisoned by the British. A caller at the Nehru home once asked why it looked deserted. "What else will it be?"replied the 5-year-old Indira, "when all the inmates except me are in prison?" At 12 she organized a children's division of Gandhi's non-violent resistance movement. In 1938 she became a member of the Congress Party and spent 13 months in prison herself. After her mother died the child her father called his "beloved Jewel" became India's "First Daughter", a sari-wrapped, bent and sorrowful figure always following a few steps behind Nehru. She became a member of parliament, living in Nehru's household with her two sons after her husband (a businessman who was no relation to Mahatma Gandhi) died. After her father's death, a group of Nehru's supporters chose the grey-haired, grandmotherly woman, whom they thought they could control, to be his successor.

Although her father's fierce adherence to democratic principles would have scorned such Rajah-type tactics as inherited power, it was as if Mrs. Gandhi had been training to be prime minister all her life. Through crisis and chaos the intense woman known variously as "Madamji", "Madam", "Mrs. G.", "Amma", or simply "She" ruled with a firm and often, some would contend, dictatorial hand. At first she constantly evoked her revered father's name. Soon after her election, travelling to Washington to receive promises of aid to fight back the threat of famine from President Johnson, she stated her intention that India remain committed to her father's policy of non-alignment. Back in India she faced spiraling inflation, foreign exchange deficits, rebellions, bad relations with Pakistan, self-immolations of Sikh leaders, student riots, strikes, and defections from her Congress party. In 1971 her popularity soared when Indian troops defeated the Pakistan Army and the new state of Bangladesh was created. Again drought and famine struck, causing general discontent, and, coupled with charges of corruption in her regime, an opposition movement was formed in 1975. Shocking those who recalled her father's reverence for democratic practices, Mrs. Gandhi declared a national emergency, curtailing civil rights, imprisoning thousands of her enemies and imposing censorship during a period which came to be known as a "reign of terror." Claiming her stiff measures were necessary to prevent total collapse of order, she survived this crisis as she had others. Her governing style and image, however, suffered. As one diplomat said, "Indira is a consummate fighter. But she has been fighting so long she seems to have forgotten what the battle is for."

Throughout her two decades as Prime Minister Indira Gandhi struggled with the warring religious factions that have traditionally divided India. In 1975 she ordered government troops to invade the Sikhs' holiest shrine, the Golden Temple in Punjab, and over 600 were killed. Two Sikh members of her bodyguard were her assassins, making her, like Mahatma Gandhi, another victim of the religious hatred her father had harangued crowds against all his life.

Mourned even by her critics as the force that had held the fractious country together, Mrs. Gandhi was eulogized by her son Rajiv, whose immediate appointment as her successor revived accusations of dynastic ambitions, as "mother not only to me but to the whole nation . . . who worked for a united, peaceful, prosperous India."

Indira Gandhi surrounded by some of her "Seva Dal" volunteer units.

Given Name: Indira Nehru
Born: November 19, 1917, Allahabad, India
Married: Feroze Gandhi, 1942, 2 children
Highlights: Prime Minister of India, 1966–19 Leader of India through drought, famine, conflicts with Pakistan, violent religious differences.
Died: October 31, 1984

GOVERNMENT AND POLITICS

On October 18, 1984, thirteen days before her assassination, Indian Prime Minister Indira Gandhi addressed a political rally at Patna, India.

GOVERNMENT AND POLITICS

Mohandas Gandhi

Mohandas Gandhi's fellow Hindus regarded him as a saint on earth. They called the frail ascetic "Mahatma", or "Great Soul", and for over a quarter of a century their leader preached "soul force" ("Satyagraha"), the use of all types of non-violent resistance, in the struggle to free India from the imperial yoke of Britain.

Educated in London, Gandhi had lived in South Africa for 21 years, successfully practicing law and fighting for the rights of Indian citizens settled there. A bloody massacre in which British troops killed hundreds of Indians convinced him that freedom could not be won by force. His methods of civil disobedience and passive resistance were the tactics later used by an American student of Gandhi's teachings, Martin Luther King, during the Civil Rights Movement in the South.

Gandhi came by his heritage of protest naturally—his father had once been jailed for not apologizing to a British officer. Although supporting the British cause in the Boer War and during World War I, Gandhi viewed British Imperialism as the "Satan" of his time.

In 1929 the Indian National Congress was formed and Gandhi was placed in charge of the campaign to remove India, known as the "jewel" of the Empire, from the British crown. With no title, the small, wily and witty Hindu peered through wire-rimmed glasses and preached love, truth—and freedom. His program of resistance included strikes, refusal to pay taxes, and refusal to obey the court systems. He was repeatedly arrested, spending a total of 12 years in prison, forcing compromises from the British. "I always get the best bargains from behind prison bars", he once said. He went on life-threatening fasts, time after time vowing to continue "unto death" to win a concession. Fearing public reaction to his death during a fast, the British had no choice but to compromise. In 1930 Gandhi led a dramatic 200-mile march to the sea to protest Britain's salt tax. He was joined by his four sons and they were all arrested, bringing Gandhi and the Indian national cause world-wide attention.

Besides his crusade for Indian freedom, Gandhi preached the simple life. He based his philosophy on Christ's Sermon on the Mount, which teaches renunciation as the highest form of religion. He adopted the spinning wheel as the symbol of a spiritual life as well as economic freedom from Britain. He spent many hours at his own spinning-wheel, calling home-spun cloth "sacred" cloth, his simple loin cloth and shawl creating an awe-inspiring effect on his people as well as the disciples who flocked to him.

Throughout India's struggle towards independence the teeming subcontinent was wracked with bloody riots as warring Hindu, Sikh and Moslem factions protested a unified India. Eventually, India would be partitioned and the separate state of Pakistan created. Winston Churchill, who opposed giving India her freedom, predicted that after independence there would be even more blood and misery.

After the last Viceroy, Lord Mountbatten relinquished Britain's control on August 15th, 1947, a bloodbath erupted between the Moslems and Gandhi's Congress Party. Weeping over the killing, the architect of his country's freedom said that he had failed in his most important goal—teaching his people to love their enemies. He told a disciple he had almost lost the will to live. A year later he was assassinated by a Hindu Brahmin who opposed his religious tolerance.

Although all his life Gandhi had tried to renounce the title "Mahatma", saying he was unworthy of it, his protege Jawaharlal Nehru, first Prime Minister of the Dominion of India, praised Gandhi as the Great Soul who guided his people through their dark struggle and had earned another title: the father of modern India.

GOVERNMENT AND POLITICS

Lloyd George

The only Welshman to ever become Prime Minister of England, David Lloyd George is credited with pioneering the National Health Insurance Act, which made provisions for sickness and invalidism. This ground-breaking legislation, in conjunction with his Old Age Pensions Act, is often identified as the foundation of the modern British welfare state.

Born in Manchester, England on January 17, 1863, David was raised by his uncle, a Baptist minister in North Wales. He was determined to be a solicitor and at age 21 passed his bar examinations. He soon took an active part in local politics and was elected to Parliament in 1890. There he attracted much attention for his vigorous attacks on the Conservatives and his championship of Welsh nonconformity and Welsh nationalism.

He was viewed as an unorthodox, independent Liberal, a view which was enhanced by his bitter opposition to England's policy during the Boer War. This brought him rather violently to the public's attention. And it also showed that David Lloyd George was a man ready to decide matters for himself and not merely follow the herd. He won further prominence in English politics by leading the nonconformist opposition to the Conversative government's Education Act of 1902, and as a representative of nonconformist interests, he was appointed president of the Board of Trade to Sir Henry Campbell-Bannerman's Liberal cabinet. Here, Lloyd George was highly successful as a champion of business and a labor negotiator, and in 1908 Prime Minister Herbert Asquith promoted him to Chancellor of the Exchequer.

Lloyd George became an active reformer, horrifying traditionalists by introducing his famous budget that imposed increased taxes on luxuries, incomes and land. His motives for this "people's budget" of 1909 was to make money available for a war on poverty. The budget proposal provoked a clash with the Conservative-dominated House of Lords and ended in curtailment of the House of Lords' power to veto legislature.

Although at first Lloyd George was reluctant to approve Great Britain's entry (August 1914) into World War I, he soon demanded greater vigor and efficiency from the government, advocating a knockout blow against Germany. When the news of a short supply of English munitions reached England, Lloyd George was put in charge of the newly-created Ministry of Munitions. In his prime at age 52, he made a brilliant success of this position, ensured that a steady supply of guns and shells reached the western front, and became a hero to the press. But politically, he made many enemies.

David Lloyd George addresses a Drum Head service in May, 1935.

GOVERNMENT AND POLITICS

Not satisfied with the progress of the war, Lloyd George became a strong supporter of general conscription and put through the conscription act of 1916. Then the fall of Romania increased his discontent. He sent down a proposal to reorganize the war cabinet and effectively maneuvered Prime Minister Asquith's resignation. Lloyd George became Prime Minister (1916-22) and a dominant figure in the new five-member coalition war cabinet.

Lloyd George imposed an effective regime of "war socialism" upon the British people, but he quarreled with his generals and was unable to cut the heavy casualties on the western front. His small war committee, a sort of inner cabinet, proved successful in speeding up decision-making and action. Although he went on to press for unity of military control among the Allies this was not really achieved until 1918. Yet, this unity, combined with the arrival of American troops somewhat earlier than had been expected, did much to bring the war to a successful conclusion and Lloyd George was popularly regarded as the man who won the war.

Before going as peace delegate to the Paris Peace Conference in Versailles, Lloyd George strengthened his position by winning a huge election victory for his coaliton following the 1918 armistice. The last four years of his premiership were anticlimatic. He was the principal British negotiator at Versailles and, on the whole, on the side of generosity and moderation.

At home, the Conservatives were increasingly restless under Lloyd George's leadership. His government's housing program was a disaster; there was mounting unemployment and labor unrest; and a major recession began in 1921. In Ireland he initially adopted a policy of harsh repression against the nationalist rebels, but he finally negotiated a treaty in 1921 that established the Irish Free State. This settlement was his one major postwar success, but it damaged his relations with the Conservatives on whom his government depended. They withdrew their support after the Chanak crisis (1922) which nearly brought Britain into a war with Turkey.

After the coalition fell in October 1922, and the decline of Liberalism, Lloyd George's political fortunes waned. Nevertheless, in the economic depression of the 1930's, Lloyd George was the only political leader to put forward new and constructive ideas for dealing with unemployment. Shortly before his death on March 26, 1945, he was awarded an Earldom and became First Earl of Dwyfor.

Given Name: David Lloyd George
Born: January 17, 1863, Manchester, England
Married: Margaret Owen, 4 children
Married: Frances Louise Stevenson, 1943
Highlights: Prime Minister of England, 1916-1922. Led country through World War I, instituted major social changes.
Died: March 26, 1945

The former Prime Minister looks over his 1941 barley crop on his farm in Surrey.

GOVERNMENT AND POLITICS

Emperor Hirohito

When Emperor Hirohito announced Japan's surrender to the Allied forces over the radio on August 15th, 1945, it was the first time his subjects had heard his voice. "The war situation has developed not necessarily to our advantage", he said in a nervous monotone, his comment a classic of understatement to a population that had just suffered devastation at Hiroshima and Nagasaki.

A shy, retiring man never comfortable as "god-king", Hirohito was isolated from the people he ruled over five decades. According to imperial custom, he was taken from his parents as an infant and trained by household functionaries for one purpose: to be future Emperor. At 20 he went abroad, the first member of the Imperial family to leave Japan. He travelled throughout Europe, developing a taste for bacon and eggs, as well as for Western clothes. All his life, he shunned Japanese food—and a palace official once confided he never even owned a kimono.

Hirohito became emperor in 1926. His reign was designated "Showa", meaning "enlightment and peace." But during the '30's Japan embarked on numerous military actions which finally resulted in full-scale war. Hirohito apparently had little to do with these activities. He was given carefully screened facts, and newspapers were scissored by palace aides so reports would jibe with the information he received from his ministers. After V-J Day, when the question arose as to whether or not Hirohito should be tried as a war criminal, General Douglas MacArthur said, "Don't call the Emperor into court. If you do, he'll probably offer to assume all the blame himself. He's that kind of man."

At MacArthur's insistence Hirohito surrendered his divinity, turned over his vast wealth to the national treasury and was officially designated a "symbol of state." Perhaps more difficult for him, than these losses was his surrender of one of his nation's most deeply guarded beliefs, that it is better to die than to be dishonored. After Nagasaki and Hiroshima he told his officers, "The time has come when we must bear the unbearable."

Princess Nagako was chosen by court guards to be Hirohito's empress. When she produced four daughters in a row, Hirohito, whose father was the son of a royal concubine, was advised to find a concubine to secure a male heir. He refused and eventually the Empress gave birth to Crown Prince Akihito. When Akihito chose to wed a commoner he met on the tennis court in 1959, his parents were delighted. Their union was called a "love match". So many people bought television sets to watch their wedding that domestic television sales were the highest ever.

During the postwar period the emperor, now a mere figurehead, began to venture out among his people, opening sporting events and performing ceremonial duties. With his jerky walk and sometimes unshaven face he was quite a different figure from the splendidly uniformed man riding a white charger in wartime military parades. He became a recognized expert on marine biology, on which he wrote several books.

Still, the emperor's movements were strictly controlled by tradition. When he wanted to retire and place the aging Crown Prince on the throne, the Imperial Household would not hear of it. Twice a year, Hirohito and his family appeared behind bulletproof glass on a palace balcony. Crowds of older Japanese cheered and waved flags, but to the younger Japanese the former "Son of Heaven" was only a curiosity from a bygone era.

Hirohito as a boy in the school uniform at Cakushin, then Peer's school.

Hirohito collects plants while vacationing at the royal villa at Nasu Heights, about 100 miles northeast of Tokyo.

Given Name: Hirohito, Emperor of Japan
Born: April 29, 1901, Tokyo, Japan
Married: Princess Nagako, 1924, 7 children
Highlights: Emperor of Japan since 1926. Led Japan into World War II. After Japan's defeat he relinquished his imperial powers and became a "symbol of the State" as Japan grew into a modern democracy and one of the world's great economic powers.

GOVERNMENT AND POLITICS

Emperor Hirohito of Japan is a recognized amateur biologist.

GOVERNMENT AND POLITICS

Adolf Hitler

The name Adolf Hitler is synonomous with evil in modern times. As leader of the Nazi Party and dictator of the German people, his brutal schemes to systematically exterminate huge numbers of people in order to lead his nation to its destiny as the "Master Race" were so bestial that it is almost impossible to discuss him in human terms.

Hitler capitalized on a fanatical nationalism born out of 19th century ideas of Germany as a race of supermen. He was a fan of composer Richard Wagner's operas, in which gods and heroes acted out ancient German myths. Their spectacular bigger-than-life sets and stage effects would strongly influence the mass rallies Hitler's Third Reich staged in Berlin. Philosopher Frederich Nietzsche's belief that the will to power is man's primary instinct fueled Hitler's satanic vision of a world empire that would emanate from Berlin, the dreamed-of Master Race cities empty, at last, of the Jews whose death by a "Final Solution" in camps across Eastern Europe would be the primary goal of his underlings.

Looking for a scapegoat after their humiliating defeat in World War I, Germans easily lit upon the Jews, who entered post-war Germany in large numbers. Hitler, a social engineer who wanted to change the world completely, believed he could shovel people around like concrete to accomplish his goals. He linked his belief that biology-is-destiny with the growing anti-Semitism around him, placing the "Jewish Problem" at the center of his politics.

Raised in Austria, Hitler never finished high school. Before 1914 he sold postcards he'd painted to make a living, picking up ideas about socialism and anti-Semitism in Vienna. Fighting in the trenches in Flanders in France, he was decorated for bravery. When rumors came that Germany had lost the war he didn't believe them. "Just the whisperings of a few Jewish youths," he scoffed.

In Germany after the war Hitler became the leader of the small National Socialist German Workers', Nazi, Party, attempting and failing, in the "Beer Hall Putsch", to seize the Bavarian government. He was imprisoned for 9 months, during which time, already an eccentric with a growing following, he dressed not in the prison uniform but in lederhosen, and had many visitors. While in prison he wrote "Mein Kampf," a book of his ideas for Germany's destiny, which, besides the elimination of Jews, included expansion by force beyond its present borders. He also described how, through his willpower, he would persuade the German people to forego liberty in exchange for security.

In 1929, Germany, just recovering from a disastrous post-war inflation, was hit by the financial earthquake set off by the Wall Street Crash. Six million people were thrown out of work.

In 1930, benefiting from economic turmoil, Hitler's Nazi Party received Six million votes to beome the second largest party in the Reichstag, Germany's parliament. This victory assured his march to power. Ironically, six million would be the number of people eliminated in the death camps. In 1933 an aging President Hindenberg appointed Hitler chancellor. Three months later Hitler's Cabinet was voted into office.

Hitler's first goal was to rearm Germany and commence expansion Eastward. He politicized the military in order to ready them for carrying out his plans. He appealed to the people at huge rallies, with costumes, lighting and architectural backdrops inspired by the Wagnerian opera festival at Bayreuth. His own style, with its exaggerated oratorical gestures, was borrowed from a Munich beer hall comedian and practiced in front of a mirror. Foreigners who met with him, familiar with his "mad orator" act from newsreels, were surprised that he could speak in a reasonable manner.

By 1938 Hitler had ceased attempting to woo his people or persuade them to believe in going to war. He dropped any political content in his speeches, simply appearing before them as a symbol while, behind the scenes, he became a militarist making secret gangster-pacts with foreign leaders, getting his way at home by force and terror. He occupied Austria and Czechoslovakia in 1938 and atacked Poland in 1939, proving British Prime Minister Neville Chamberlain's "peace in our time" appeasement disastrous. The Germans occupied Belgium and France. Britain, aware of Hitler's plans to cross the English Channel, declared war. In 1941, Hitler invaded Russia, with whom he had signed a non-aggression pact, and was met with fierce resistance by the mighty Red Army. That same year the U.S. entered the war, assuring Germany's defeat.

A week before the war in Europe ended, Hitler died by his own hand in a bunker beneath Berlin, the city he had envisioned as the center of an empire. Dying with him were his long-time mistress Eva Braun, whom he had just married, and his dog. A doctor who saw him described him as "a living corpse, a dead soul. Gone were the powers to charm, to fascinate, to bend others to his steel will." Another described him as "a human wreck, gobbling creamcakes, babbling regrets." Three days before he killed himself, he said, "Afterwards, you rue the fact that you've been so kind."

The man who regretted having been so "kind" had, at the time of his death, largely achieved his central goal.

In camps like Auschwitz, called "the greatest institution for human annihilation of all time", mass gassings had, since 1942, been disposing of up to 2,000 human lives every 12 hours. The SS officers he politicized had assisted Hitler in committing the greatest crime in human history. Under cover of war, with every nation distracted, Hitler had nearly rid Europe of the Jews. His legacy has little to do with a race of supermen. His memorial is written in names like Auschwitz, Dachau, and Buchenwald.

Given Name: Adolf Hitler
Born: April 20, 1889, Braunau, Austria-Hungary
Married: Eva Braun, 1945
Highlights: "Der Fuhrer" of Nazi Germany, 1933-1945. Led Germany into World War II, established concentration camps in which over 6 million Jews and other "undesirables" were exterminated.
Died: April 30, 1945

GOVERNMENT AND POLITICS

Hitler points out the progress of his army on the Eastern Front to Turkish General Ali Fued Erden in October, 1941.

"Der Fuhrer" and his wire-haired terrier relax in East Prussia in the early days of World War II.

GOVERNMENT AND POLITICS

Ho Chi Minh

Ho Chi Minh changed his name several times during his life, but he never changed his vision. He dreamed of an independent Viet Nam, free of foreign domination and holding sway over the neighboring countries of Laos, Cambodia, and Thailand. That was the only way, he felt, that his country could maintain its separate identity in the shadow of Red China.

He persisted with his vision and his efforts for over five decades, but never saw his dream realized. Although the fall of Saigon in 1973 essentially brought to fruition his dream of a unified Viet Nam dominating the Southeast Asian peninsula, Ho did not live to see it. He had died in 1969.

Ho was born in 1890 in Thanhoa, Viet Nam. His father was a scholarly colonial employee of the Mandarin class who was fired by the ruling French for his anti-French attitude. After studies in Hue and Saigon, Ho, whose real name was Nguyen That Tan, headed for Europe in 1912 as a cabin boy on a French steamer. He eventually settled in Paris, and it was there that he adopted Communism, which he saw as a means to achieve his patriotic ends. One of his friends in Paris was a Chinese student named Chou En-lai, who was destined to become Premier of Communist China.

In 1923, Ho, known by then as Nguyen Ai-Quoc, went to Moscow to study at the University of the Toilers of the East. There he began a close friendship with Stalin. He then moved on to China, where he formed small communist units among exiles for infiltration into Viet Nam. After Chiang Kai-Shek turned on the communists and drove them underground, Ho spent the next 13 years traveling between Moscow and China, and was jailed several times.

When the Japanese invaded Viet Nam (then called French Indo-China) in World War II, Ho returned and organized the Viet Minh underground to fight them. To get help from the Chinese Nationalists and the United States, he swore he was not a communist. About the same time he adopted the name Ho Chi Minh, variously translated as "the enlightened one", "he who shines" and "he who sheds light". But to his countrymen, he was "Uncle Ho".

Two days after the Japanese surrender, Ho proclaimed the independent Republic of Viet Nam, in which his Viet Minh organization was in the minority, but held key posts. Ho convinced the French to oust the Chinese Nationalists, and got them to recognize Viet Nam as a free state within the French union. The peaceful accord lasted only nine months. Then a Viet Minh attack on French troops started an eight year war that was finally decided by a decisive Viet Minh victory at Dien Bien Phu in 1954. The Geneva conference that followed split Viet Nam in two, North and South, with the United States pledging it would help keep South Viet Nam from falling prey to its Communist neighbors.

Ho's response was to form the National Front for Liberation of South Viet Nam, the political arm of the Viet Cong guerillas who fought in the south. When Americans entered the war, Ho was not dismayed. "We held off the French for eight years," he said. "We can hold off the Americans for at least as long. Americans don't like long, inconclusive wars. This is going to be a long, inconclusive war."

The frail looking man with the gray hair and wispy gray beard was right. The war lasted until 1973 when the Americans, weary of the fighting and the divisions it caused at home, withdrew the last of their troops. Saigon was then renamed Ho Chi Minh City.

Ho Chi Minh addressing an international audience in August, 1946.

GOVERNMENT AND POLITICS

President Rajendra Prasad (left) and Prime Minister Jawaharlal Nehru flank Ho Chi Minh on his 1958 state visit to New Delhi.

Given Name: Nguyen That Tan
Born: May 19, 1890, Thanhoa, Viet Nam
Unmarried
Highlights: Led the Viet Minh organization that ousted the French from Indo China, then led North Viet Nam in defeating the United States and unifying Viet Nam under the Communists.
Died: September 3, 1969

GOVERNMENT AND POLITICS

John Maynard Keynes

Not since Karl Marx wrote "Das Kapital" have one man's theories and writings so influenced governmental activity in the economic sphere. His ideas, considered by many in his time to be radical, were the basis for many new policies in Franklin Roosevelts "New Deal", as well as many new directions in his native England.

Keynes had a generally gloomy view of the world, and felt that government action could, and should, counteract the "boom and bust" cycle of capitalism. He advocated governmental "pump priming" expenditures during times of recession or depression, and "forced savings" to pay for war, prevent wartime inflation, and provide a pool of purchasing power to carry the economy through the predicted postwar "slump".

Lord Keynes, who was made a baron in 1942, edited the Economic Journal for 34 years, from 1911 until 1945, when he had to resign because of the pressure of other work. The periodical had a relatively small but highly influential readership and was an excellent vehicle for Keynes to use in espousing his theories.

During the depression, Keynes was quoted as saying that "banks and bankers are by nature blind", and also that "bankers are the most romantic and least realistic of men". His views on the gold standard, and those of the Bank of England, were long in sharp contrast. So when Keynes was elected a director in 1941, a friend asked if he had finally become orthodox "On the contrary," Keynes replied. "Orthodoxy has at last caught up with me."

Keynes was the author of several major books on economics, but his most important work was the "General Theory of Employment, Interest and Money", first published in 1936. It espoused government intervention in the free market and deficit spending during the low periods of the business cycle. One story has it that when asked if his policies might cause problems in the long run, Keynes responded by saying "In the long run, we are all dead."

A successful private investor as well as economic theoretician, Keynes did very well in the lush 1920's, and was able to preserve much of his wealth because he accurately foresaw the crash of 1929. In later years, he used some of his personal wealth to support the arts and Cambridge University, from whose King's College he had graduated in 1905 after earlier years at Eton.

Economists and politicians can, and do, still argue heatedly over the validity of his theories. But none will deny the impact made by the founder of "Keynesian economics".

Lord Balfour, British Minister to the United States, (left) and Lord Keynes pause on White House steps in 1945, after negotiating a $4.4 billion loan.

GOVERNMENT AND POLITICS

Lord Keynes and his wife as seen just a month before his death in April, 1946.

Given Name: John Maynard Keynes
Born: June 15, 1883, Cambridge, England
Married: Lydia Lopokova, 1925
Highlights: Economist and theorist, his ideas helped shape the economic policies of the western world from the 1930's on.
Died: April 21, 1946

Lenin

Vladimir Ilyich Lenin, founder of Russia's Communist party and first leader of the Soviet state, is known among Moscow sculptors as "The Breadwinner." They know they can sell any statues they make of Lenin. Hundreds thousands of statues of him adorn the sidewalks and squares of Russian cities where he is worshipped with an almost religious fervor. Huge portraits of his head—almost bald, his jutting jaw and fierce gaze pointing the way to a socialist future—are plastered on billboards and buildings. Every day hundreds of Soviets line up to view his embalmed body at the mausoleum in Red Square in Moscow. By the 50th anniversary of his death in 1984, over 100 million Soviets had visited the mausoleum, where newlyweds are encouraged to leave bouquets. In 1984 signs proclaimed Lenin "Our Banner and Weapon." "Lenin is always with us", stated a front-page Pravda article. "Leninism is irrevocable law."

"Comrade" Lenin, Russia's greatest hero, became a professional revolutionary after his brother was hanged in a plot against Tsar Nicholas. He and other young rebels studied the works of German philosopher Karl Marx—"Das Kapital", "The Communist Manifesto"—which urged the overthrow of capitalism. Exiled to Siberia for three years, Lenin then went into voluntary exile in Switzerland where he founded the Bolshevik Party, edited "The Spark", a revolutionary newspaper distributed internationally, and in 1905 held the first Bolshevik Party Congress.

Lenin believed any disaster, including the Great War, must be exploited to hasten the destruction of Imperial Russia so the new Russia could be built. Still in Switzerland in 1917, he concluded that Russia, weakened by the war, was ripe for revolution. With Germany's help he was smuggled into his country in a sealed car to lead, with the help of Leon Trotsky, the uprising that established the Soviet government. Among the dramatic events he presided over were the bloodless storming of the Tsar's Winter Palace, the October Revolution and the murder of the Tsar and his family.

Lenin in his study reading Pravda *in October 1918, after he and the Bolsheviks had assumed power.*

GOVERNMENT AND POLITICS

As modern Russia's first leader Lenin founded the secret police—the Cheka—to suppress any opposition to his plans for peace and land redistribution, the two major issues confronting him during his regime, until a stroke forced him to retire in 1924. His plan for land reform was protested by the peasants, who planted fewer crops and caused a famine, resulting in the quasi-liberal New Economic Policy of 1921. Joseph Stalin, who won out over Trotsky to succeed Lenin, imposed collectivized farming soon after he took over the government. Lenin gave up everything for the revolution, which he believed would inevitably unite all the workers of the world under international communism. Until he died he expected the apocalyptic worldwide uprising that would make this happen. His ideas for social change were purely scientific, worked out with his intellectual friends with no concern for the masses as composed of individual human beings. Even the comrades he plotted with were not really friends but receptacles for his theories. Once when some of them wanted to collect funds for famine victims, Lenin dissuaded them. "Hunger", he said, "performs a progressive function." It would "cause the peasants to reflect on the fundamental fact of capitalist society."

A ruthless dictator, Lenin hated religion, viewing it as communism's most powerful enemy. He hated saints. In him the religious impulse was replaced by the same fierce will to power that motivated Adolf Hitler. A contemporary of his once said that his idea of a Marxist society was like the French King Louis XIV's idea of the state—"Moi."

After Lenin's death, Petrograd (originally St. Petersburg), the center of the revolution, was renamed Leningrad and the capitol of Russia moved to the Kremlin in Moscow.

Given Name: Vladimir Ilich Ulyanov
Born: April 22, 1870, Simbirsk, Russia
Married: Nadezhda Konstantinova Krupskaya, 1898
Highlights: Leader of the Bolshevik Revolution against Czar Nicholas II, founder of Communist Russia and its first Premier, 1917-1924.
Died: January 21, 1924

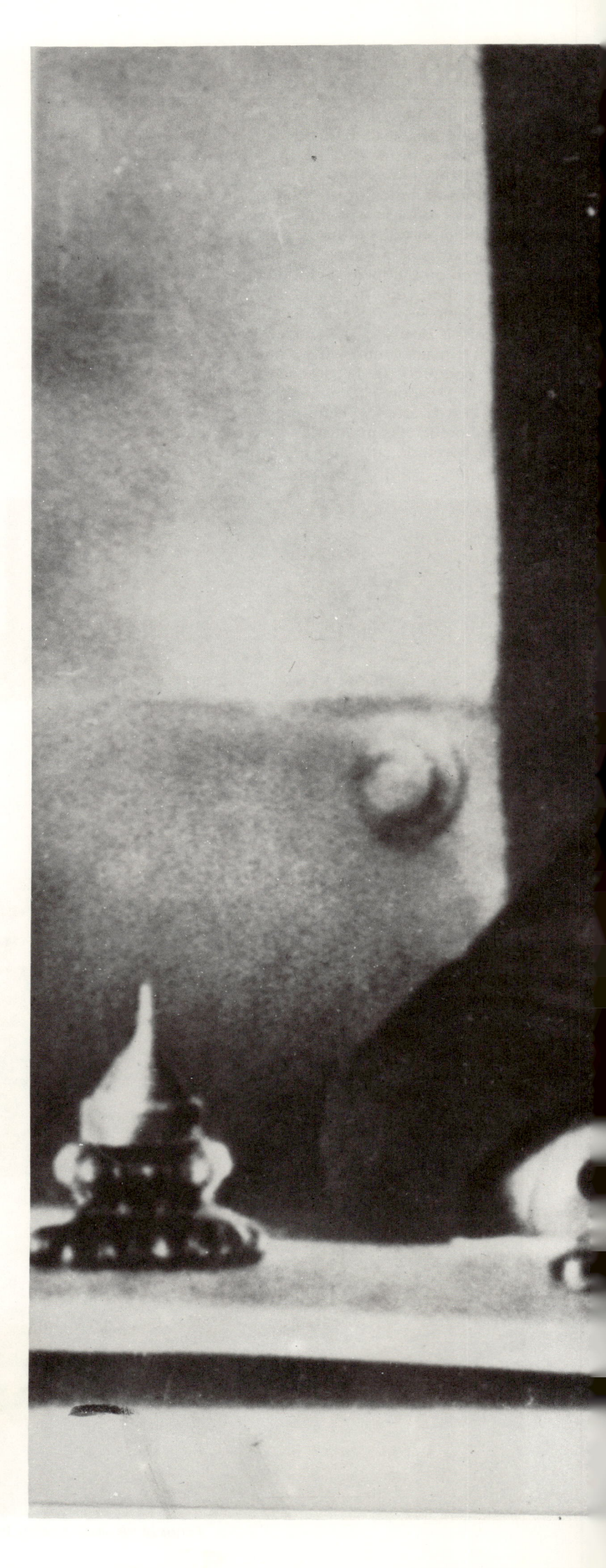

A 1918 portrait of Lenin.

Charles Lindbergh

When Charles Lindbergh landed his "Spirit of St. Louis" at Le Bourget Airport north of Paris, the "Lone Eagle" who had flown the first non-stop trans-Atlantic flight became an instant international hero. Cheering Frenchmen tore pieces off the cloth plane for souvenirs and mobbed the shy, boyish American. But in later years the hero's image would be darkened by personal tragedy and clouded by controversy.

"Lucky" Lindbergh—he earned his nickname after several bail-outs on the airmail route he flew between St. Louis and Chicago—was showered with medals and honors in France and Britain. When he returned home President Calvin Coolidge presented him with the first Distinguished Flying Cross and New Yorkers welcomed him with a tumultuous tickertape parade. Uneasy in the limelight, Lindbergh became secretive in a way that would make the public suspicious of him in the future.

As America's Air Age Pioneer Hero, Lindbergh began a tour as a goodwill ambassador for the U.S., travelling to, among other countries, Mexico, where he met the daughter of the American ambassador, Anne Morrow. After a much-publicized romance, they were married. Lindbergh trained his wife to be his co-pilot, navigator, photographer and wireless operator, and the two made trail-blazing flights to the Yucatan, discovering lost Mayan cities, as well as to China and other farflung locations.

Always hiding from publicity, the Lindberghs built a home in a secluded part of New Jersey, and it was there that tragedy struck America's Golden Couple. Their first-born child, 20-month-old Charles, Jr., was kidnapped and murdered. Before the body was found a $50,000 ransom had been paid. After a sensational trial carpenter Bruno Hauptman was executed as the abductor-killer. The Lindberghs fled to Europe, where they lived for several years.

Alarmed at growing signs of conflict between Germany and France and England, and aware of the potential for destruction in the use of aircraft in war, Lindbergh developed an isolationist policy. The Lindberghs returned home and as a leader in the America First Committee, Lindbergh spoke out coast to coast against America's entering a war he felt she could not win. He was accused of being pro-Nazi, reviled by President Roosevelt and called "the fuehrer of the United States" by a U.S. Senator.

Insisting that what he wanted was a negotiated peace, Lindbergh resigned his commission in the Army Air Corps Reserve. Nonetheless, he spent the war years as a citizen-consultant to fliers, performing many raids himself. He also gave U.S. Intelligence invaluable information he'd gained while in Europe in the '30's about Hitler's air force, the Luftwaffe. After the war ended many felt Lindbergh wasn't given credit for often heroic wartime efforts because of his earlier activities but in 1954 he was made a Brigadier General in the Air Force Reserve.

Lindbergh published three books. "We" was about himself and his one-seater plane, which resides in the Smithsonian Institute. "Life and Flight" is a philosophical discussion about scientific materialism and moral forces. "The Spirit of St. Louis", which took him 14 years to write, is an account of his thoughts, emotions and doubts during the historic flight to Paris. It became a popular movie and won him a Pulitzer Prize. Towards the end of his life, he became interested in conservation, and although he hoped to write a book containing his views of the subject he never did.

In his later years, Lindbergh continued his interest in aviation, acting as a consultant to the Defense Department as well as to Pan American World Airways. He had persistent doubts about scientific discoveries contributing to human progress. "If we are finally to be successful", he once said, "We must measure scientific accomplishments by their effects on man himself."

> **Given Name:** Charles Augustus Lindbergh
> **Born:** February 4, 1902, Detroit, Michigan
> **Married:** Anne Spencer Morrow, 1929, 2 children
> **Highlights:** A pioneer aviator, first man to fly the Atlantic solo non-stop in 1927. A leader in the development of aviation for military and peaceful purposes. Winner of worldwide honors for his contributions to aviation.
> **Died:** August 24, 1974.

Officers of the Missouri National Guard and the 35th Division Air Corps surround Lindbergh in February, 1928.

GOVERNMENT AND POLITICS

In 1926, Lindbergh was Chief Pilot for Robertson Aircraft Corporation which made mail planes he and other pioneers flew.

Colonel Lindbergh (left) and Harry Guggenheim after a 1928 flight to Washington for the International Civil Aeronautics Conference.

General Douglas MacArthur

In 1952, after 52 years of military service, General Douglas MacArthur began a new career in private industry as chairman of Sperry-Rand Corp. "It is peculiarly agreeable", he commented, "That on this late day of my life" (he was seventy-two) "I can pass from a profession of destruction to one of construction—to build rather than destroy. I think it is a gift of God that permits an Old Soldier to end that way."

But the "old soldier" didn't choose to end his military career as he did. In the spring of 1951, objecting to MacArthur's strong opposition to the way the Korean War was being waged, President Harry Truman took an action that caused worldwide shockwaves—he ousted MacArthur from his posts as Supreme Allied Occupation Commander in Japan; U.N. Commander-in-Chief in Korea; U.S. Commander-in-Chief for the Far East; and Commanding General of the U.S. Army in the Far East.

The tall, craggy old soldier was a hero around the world, a symbol, with his long-stemmed pipe, inevitable dark glasses and squareset jaw, of American resistance in the face of overwhelming odds. As Field Marshall of the Philippine Islands, he had been forced in 1942 to give up the hopeless defense of those islands. Vowing to return to liberate them, he fled with his wife and small son in a PT boat under the very eyes of the invading Japanese. In 1944, fighting his way back by his strategy of "island-hopping", he returned triumphantly at the head of an armada of warships. Places like Corregidor and Bataan, where captured Americans had been led on a "March of Death" by the Japanese, lost and regained under MacArthur's leadership, became symbols of resistance, resilience and the victory of American grit. After the war ended MacArthur was credited with being the principal architect of victory not just in the Philippines, but in the entire Pacific theater of war.

Earlier in his career, MacArthur, who came from a military family, had headed the valiant Rainbow Division in World War I. Gassed and wounded in trench fighting he was decorated for bravery (often decorated, he never wore his medals) and in 1925, made a full general, the youngest to achieve that rank. He retired from the army, but in 1937 was called to serve in the Philippines. In 1944 MacArthur was made a full general. After Japan surrendered, he was placed in charge of converting the defeated nation into a democracy, a cause he took up as passionately as he had the recapture of the Philippines. Ruling Japan as a benevolent dictator for five years, he was revered as almost a "living god" by the Japanese, including Emperor Hirohito, whom MacArthur had saved from standing trial as a war criminal.

When Russian-trained North Korean troops invaded the Western-supported Republic of South Korea, MacArthur was the choice to lead the free world's campaign to stem Red aggression. He did not hide his opinions that the U.S. should bomb Manchuria and China and join with Chiang Kai-shek's Nationalist troops to invade the mainland and get rid of the communists once and for all. Truman, on the other hand, was committed to the "limited war" strategy backed by the U.N. Fearing that MacArthur's plans risked starting World War III, an unthinkable risk now that the atomic bomb had come into use, Truman dismissed the General on the grounds that he was "unable to give his whole-hearted support to the policies of the administration and the U.N." MacArthur's dismissal caused an uproar not only in Congress and the U.S. but around the world.

In his farewell speech, delivered to Congress and broadcast on radio and television, MacArthur recalled the words of a barracks song popular when he was at West Point—"Old soldiers never die", he quoted, "They just fade away. And like the old soldier of that ballad I now close my military career and just fade away, an old soldier who tried to do his duty as God gave him the light to see that duty."

When MacArthur left Japan, one-million people jammed the streets to catch a last glimpse of the five-star general. Returning home for the first time in 14 years the Old Soldier received tumultuous welcomes at every stop—Honolulu, San Francisco, Washington and finally, in New York, a ticker tape parade with a crowd of 7½ million and, according to the Sanitation Department, 3249 tons of paper. As he had been twice before, in 1944 and 1948, he was asked to run for President. "I do not intend to run for any political office", he stated flatly. "The only politics I have is contained in the simple phrase known well by all of you—God Bless America."

Given Name: Douglas MacArthur
Born: January 26, 1880, Little Rock, Arkansas
Married: Louise Brooks, 1922 (divorced 1934)
Married: Jean Faircloth, 1937, 1 son.
Highlights: General of the Army. Directed Allied victory over the Japanese in World War II, then directed Japan's conversion to a modern democracy.
Died: April 5, 1964

GOVERNMENT AND POLITICS

A laughing General MacArthur chats with Lt. Gen. George Kenney at Tacloban Airfield on Leyte island.

GOVERNMENT AND POLITICS

Major General William Hoge talks to MacArthur at a command post near Chingyong, Korea in March, 1945.

General MacArthur, Commander in Chief of the Southwest Pacific, makes a visit to the forward area on his birthday in 1944.

GOVERNMENT AND POLITICS

Mao discusses the "peaceful liberation" of Tibet in May, 1951.

Benito Mussolini

His philosophy was "live dangerously". He did.

During his twenty years as head of the Italian government, at least six attempts were made on his life. One bullet fired at him cut both nostrils. Another cut his sash. On another occasion, a bomb exploded near his car.

That Mussolini generated such extreme reactions in his opposition was not surprising. He was a man of great passion in a nation of passionate people. A gifted orator, Mussolini would play the Italian crowds as a master violinist would play a Stradivarius. Smashing his fist downward, he would bring the crowd to a crescendo with promises of restoring the glories of the Roman Empire.

But instead of leading Italy to glory, Mussolini led it to abject defeat.

He had assumed power on October 31, 1922, when King Vittorio Emmanuele asked him to form a government. That request followed Mussolini's ultimatum, in which he said "give us power peacefully, or we shall take it by force," and a well-organized march on Rome by thousands of black-shirted Fascists. Their party enjoyed great popular support in an Italy that had been in a constant state of strife and disorder since the end of World War I. (Mussolini had founded the Fascist Party in 1919 after his break with the Socialists, on whose ideas he had been raised as a poor boy in Dovia.)

Within a month of becoming head of government, Mussolini assumed dictatorial powers and became "Il Duce" (the leader). He immediately started molding Italy in his own arrogant image, and took steps to stamp out every vestige of opposition to his Fascist regime. He destroyed opposition newspapers, instituted press censorship, and even had laws passed making it a criminal offense to insult him.

Mussolini was a cunning, pompous opportunist who picked his international targets carefully. Early in his tenure, on the pretext of Greek responsibility for the murder of five Italian members of a commission in Greece, he invaded the island of Corfu and did not withdraw until his demand for a 50,000,000 lira indemnity was met. In 1935, Mussolini sent the Italian military to overrun a near-defenseless Ethiopia over the objections of Great Britain and 51 other nations who imposed futile economic sanctions against Italy.

Throughout the early 1930's, Mussolini maintained Italy's position with the Allies and against Germany. He even called the Stresa conference, at which Great Britain, France and Italy denounced German rearmament and pledged themselves to maintaining peace. But after Hitler helped supply Italy when it was blockaded by the League of Nations in retaliation for the Ethiopian invasion, Mussolini threw in with the Nazis. The German-Italian Axis had early, easy successes in Albania and Africa, but then things began to go awry for them. . . . especially for Italy.

Native and British armies retook many of the African lands conquered by the Fascists, and the British navy had crippled or bottled up the Italian fleet. When bombs began to fall on Italian cities, the people became less and less enamored of "Il Duce", and Allied forces invading Sicily were greeted by cheering crowds.

On July 25, 1943, the Fascist Grand Council overwhelmingly passed a resolution asking Mussolini to turn command of the Italian armed forces over to the King. Mussolini did this the next day, and was arrested after his meeting with the King. He was held prisoner in an isolated hotel on an Apennine peak until his rescue by German paratroopers. After a visit to Germany, he returned to set up a "shadow" government, since the King had made peace with the Allies and the defense of Italy was totally in German hands.

Mussolini died at the hands of Italian partisans, who captured him from a German troop column in which he rode disguised as an enlisted man. His dead body, along with that of his long-time mistress, Clara Petacci, was hung upside down in the square of Milan, where it was stoned and beaten by angry crowds. The man whose motto had been "Better to live a day as a lion than 100 years a sheep" had been slaughtered like a lamb.

German officers follow Mussolini (light uniform) and Hitler on a stroll during their August, 1941 meeting somewhere behind the German-Russian front.

"Il Duce" reviews his motorized divisions following the fall of France in 1940.

Given Name: Benito Mussolini
Born: July 29, 1883, Dovia, Italy
Married: Rachele Guidi, 5 children
Highlights: Premier of Italy, 1922-1943. Conquered an almost defenseless Ethiopia. Allied Italy with Germany in World War II and led his country to defeat.
Died: April 28, 1945

Dr. Walter Funk (left), German Minister of Economics, confers with Mussolini on a 1941 visit.

Jawaharlal Nehru

In 1920 young Jawaharlal Nehru paid a visit to an Indian village that changed his life. There the privileged only son of a wealthy Brahmin, the upper crust of India's caste system, saw conditions that filled him with shame and sorrow, over his own easy life and the poverty and degradation in which India's multitudes barely survived. He later wrote that this visit led him to join Mohandas Gandhi's campaign of civil disobedience to work towards independence from Britain and improvement of India's impoverished plight.

Educated in England at the Harrow School, Nehru was the quintessential Colonial Indian, a "queer mix of East and West." But there was no conflict of cultures once he dedicated himself to freeing India from the Crown. As president of the All-India National Congress he travelled tirelessly throughout the vast country, inspiring even those in the multi-lingual land who couldn't understand Hindi or English, his two languages, with his passionate oratory. He became a thorn in the side of British authority. Repeatedly arrested, he spent a total of 13 years in prison. His last jail term was served from 1942 to 1945, when he and Gandhi initiated the "Quit India" movement at a time when India was seriously threatened by Japan. Nehru enlisted his entire family in the fight for freedom. His father contributed much of his fortune to the cause, his mother was beaten in a disturbance, his wife, sisters and daughter were all imprisoned at one time or another.

While in prison Nehru developed his "Mixed Economy" theory to combat India's bottomless poverty, a plan by which the state assumes management of key industries (banks, insurance companies) while leaving plenty of scope for free enterprise. His proposals ran counter to Gandhi's dream of returning India to a traditional handcraft system but did not undermine the two leaders' friendship or their goal for Indian freedom.

In 1947 when Britain finally departed from an India divided by the partition of Pakistan, Nehru was the indisputable choice for first Prime Minister of the new Dominion. His first task was to quell the bloody riots among Hindus, Sikhs and Moslems which resulted from a dispute over the border province of Punjab. This was followed by Gandhi's assassination and a time of national crisis from which Nehru emerged unchallenged as the father of modern India.

Lovingly known by hordes of Indians as "Panditji" or "Chacha" ("Uncle"), Nehru gave his entire life in service to India. His legacy was a sense of national identity and purpose, a parliamentary system of government, and an international position as leader of Third World countries. Wooed by the U.S., Russia and China, he refused to side with any superpower. "The only camp we should like to be in is the camp of peace and good will", he once said. He was an enigma in world affairs, a "running dog of imperialism" to Joseph Stalin, an ingrate to the U.S., who poured millions in indispensable aid into the troubled subcontinent, money Nehru downplayed so it would not seem as if India had exchanged dependence on Britain for dependence on the U.S. Although an early defender of Red China's desire for peace, he later threatened to fight when Communist troops claimed Indian border territories as their own.

Throughout the Cold War, India remained a model of non-alignment for the emerging countries of Asia and Africa. "I am not against communism", Nehru once said. "I am not against capitalism. I am for India and nobody else. I am for the Indian people."

Although almost all his 17 years as Prime Minister were overshadowed by a dispute over Kashmir, Nehru never ceased his vigorous exhortations that the divided Indian people make peace with each other. Adoring throngs, who loved him the more for his personal sacrifices in the name of India, were forever clamoring to greet him, draping wreaths of flowers over his shoulders. Always close behind Nehru during those years was his only child Indira, the daughter who during her childhood knew him only through his letters from prison and would one day follow in his footsteps and become Prime Minister herself.

Prime Minister Nehru (right) jokes with British High Commissioner Malcolm Mac Donald (center) and Canadian High Commissioner Escott Reid (left).

GOVERNMENT AND POLITICS

Before the 1958 Asian-African Conference, Nehru posed with Major Saleh Salem (left) of Egypt and Abdul Khaled Hassouna (center), Secretary-General of the Arab League.

Nehru releases a white pigeon, symbol of peace, at a mass rally celebrating his birthday in 1956.

Given Name: Jawarahl Nehru
Born: November 14, 1889, Allahabad, India
Married: Kamala, widowed 1936, 1 child
Highlights: Prime Minister of India 1947-1964. "Founding Father of modern India." Responsible for keeping India non-aligned with either Communist or Western block.
Died: May 27, 1964

GOVERNMENT AND POLITICS

Pope John XXIII

Pope John XXIII, the man chosen to succeed Pius XII as head of the Roman Catholic church, could not have been more different from his predecessor. Pius was from an aristocratic Roman family; John was the son of a poor laborer who worked the land. Pius was tall and lean, with an ascetic air and patrician manner. John was like the peasants in Northern Italy where he came from—plump and jolly, with the manner of a country curate: they called him "The Smiling Pope."

Raised in the shadow of the Alps, John (Angelo Roncalli) was the 4th born of 12 children, a devout child who at 11, when other boys left school to work their father's farms, asked to attend the Seminary at nearby Bergamo. After he was ordained a priest, he performed administrative and teaching duties in Bergamo until 1914, when he served as a chaplain in the Italian Medical Corps. When the war ended he coordinated worldwide missionary activities for the church and then began a 25-year career in the Vatican's diplomatic service in Bulgaria, Turkey, Greece and other countries. In 1944, when he received notice that he'd been chosen as the Pope's representative in newly-liberated Paris, he rushed to Rome. "Are you mad?" he asked, wary of the assignment made difficult by the Vatican's ties with the French Vichy government during the Nazi occupation. However, the by-now seasoned diplomat mended fences so effectively that when he became Pope the French acted as if one of their own had been chosen.

After eight years in Paris Father Roncalli was made Cardinal Roncalli by the Pope, and sent to Venice, where he assumed the ancient role of Patriarch of the city. His ten years there began with him riding in an elaborate procession of gondolas up the Grand Canal. He talked charity and social rights with his Venetian flock, establishing himself as a man of the people—he would become known as "the people's Pope" after he went to Rome. He also made clear stern moral views on such diverse matters as birth control, which he vociferously opposed, and tourists' dress habits, which he regarded as improperly scanty. "Even on the Equator," he said, "lions wear their coats."

When John became Pope at the age of 76, he was regarded as too old to accomplish anything, a mere "filler" until a more "fit" Pope could be located. But from the moment he was installed he established himself as a "public" Pope and the people's Pope. His was the first coronation to be covered by television, the glittering medieval ceremony at St. Peter's in Rome viewed by millions around the world. He broke the tradition of the papal self-imposed imprisonment, leaving the Vatican to be with his flock in Rome. He visited a Rome prison, the first Pope of modern times to do so, speaking to the convicts as if they were wayward children.

At a time of mounting world-wide racial tension—in Africa, nations were demanding self-determination, in the U.S. the civil rights movement was exploding in city streets—John (who chose his papal name in honor of his father Giovan Battista Roncalli), reached out to promote the brotherhood of man. He created the first black African cardinal, and the first Japanese and Filipino cardinals. On Maundy Thursday, the night before Good Friday, 1960, he washed the feet of black Americans, Japanese, Polynesians and other minorities to commemorate Jesus' washing his disciples feet at the Last Supper and make a statement against racial discrimination.

John's greatest "public" triumph was Vatican II, the Ecumenical Council held in Rome in 1962 attended by 3000 bishops and other church officials from around the world. Besides opening a dialogue with "non-believers" behind the Iron Curtain and strengthening ties between Roman Catholics and other Christian sects, Vatican II assigned to the Catholic Church the role of "Church of the Poor", with a commitment to assist the underprivileged nations of the world. Even so, the Pope remained adamantly opposed to birth control. Though in 1959 it had been predicted that the world population would double in the next 40 years, the Pope felt a redistribution of goods, with the rich feeding the poor, was the way to deal with population problems. He believed that people should be allowed, even encouraged, to have as many children as they wanted to.

Given Name: Angelo Giuseppe Roncalli
Born: November 25, 1881, Sotto il Monte, Italy
Unmarried
Highlights: In 1958, became Pope John XXIII, the 261st Supreme Pontiff of the Roman Catholic Church. Convened the Second Vatican Council which generated a worldwide ecumenical movement to foster harmony among the members of major religions.
Died: June 3, 1963

GOVERNMENT AND POLITICS

At the closing of the first phase of the Ecumenical Council, December 8, 1962, Pope John XXIII imparts his Apostolic Blessing on all present.

GOVERNMENT AND POLITICS

CECIL RHODES

Cecil John Rhodes, the diamond mining magnate who bequeathed most of his fortune to establish scholarships at Oxford, is a name which is now linked with the best, and the worst, of 19th century British imperialism.

When he was born in Hertfordshire, England, July 5, 1853, central Africa was virgin territory and it was still possible to make a fortune and acquire power by what Rhodes called "philanthropy plus five percent" and to dream of conquest.

Poor health prevented him from a professional career as a barrister or a clergyman and instead of attending university he went to South Africa in 1870 to work on a cotton farm with his brother. The cotton farm failed a year later, at about the same time Cecil and Herbert succumbed to 'diamond fever' and they moved to Kimberley, the center of mining. Herbert was restless and stayed only until 1873, but Cecil's characteristic determination kept him at Kimberley off and on for years, until at last his luck turned.

Rhodes was early seen as a man apart. He kept to himself and dreamed his dreams. Unlike other adventurers seeking their fortunes, he admired the pastoral Boers—the descendants of the Dutch settlers in South Africa—and respected their love of the land. A severe illness in 1872 led him to make a journey of convalescence to the north, from which he returned with a fresh view of the potentialities for British expansion in Africa. Another illness in 1874 isolated him still more, as did his habit of intellectual study and he returned to England in 1873 to study at Oxford. For eight years he divided his life between the mines in Kimberley and the academic halls of Oxford until he tok a belated degree in 1881.

Gradually, he advanced from being a speculative digger to a man of substance with ambitious ideas on the future of the diamond industry. His first partnerships were with young men as impoverished as himself, such as C.D. Rudd, with whom he formed the De Beers Mining Company. Success brought him a new and valued friend, Alfred Beit, a German who knew the diamond market intimately. With Beit's help, Rhodes expanded his claims until all the De Beers mines were under his control and in a furious competition he bought up other shares in De Beers and began acquiring lesser mines until by 1891 his company, De Beers Consolidated Mines, owned 90 percent of the world's production of diamonds.

He also acquired a large stake in the Transvaal gold mines and formed the Gold Fields of South Africa Company in 1887. Both Rhodes's major companies had terms in their articles of association allowing them to finance schemes of northward expansion.

With the coffers filling from diamonds and gold, Rhodes went on to pursue his extravagant dreams of acquiring the continent of Africa for the British Empire; building a railway from the Cape to Cairo; reconciling the Boers to the British flag; and even recovering the American colonies for the British Empire. With these ideas in mind he went into politics in 1881 and was elected to the parliament of the Cape Colony, a position he held for the rest of his life.

His determination to keep a road open to the north involved him in many disputes. Other imperial powers—the Germans, Belgians and Portuguese—were competing for the uncharted interior of Africa, as were the Transvaal Boers. Mineral wealth, communications and, eventually, white settlement were his objectives in acquiring Bechuanaland, Mashonaland and Matabeleland. "If we get Mashonaland," he would say, "we shall get the balance of Africa."

Through this period powerful allies joined Rhodes; such as Lord Rothschild; and influential journalists, empire builders and politicians. But Rhodes also attracted suspicion and hostility. In 1889 the British Empire granted him a charter setting up the British South Africa Company, a commercial concern with vast administrative powers. Then in 1890, as Prime Minister of Cape Colony, Rhodes resolved to work for an understanding between British and Afrikaners and for a policy guaranteeing them both equality under the British flag. The company occupied Mashonaland in 1890 and by the end of the century Rhodes's company controlled a huge area, including Southern Rhodesia (now Zimbabwe) and Northern Rhodesia (now Zambia) which were named for him.

In 1896 Rhodes's premiership was brought to an end by the Jameson Raid, which unsuccessfully sought to topple the Afrikaner government of Paul Kruger in the Transvaal. But before the ensuing Boer War ended Rhodes died. In July 1880, the nine-foot statue of Cecil John Rhodes was pulled from its pedestal and cheers of jubilant blacks seeking to remove a symbol of the past oppression of white rule and British colonization.

Rhodes' favorite photo of himself.

Cecil John Rhodes, circa 1895

Given Name: Cecil John Rhodes
Born: July 5, 1853, Hertfordshire, England
Highlights: British imperialist, industrialist and statesman, he was the founder of the De Beers Mining Company and Prime Minister of Cape Colony (South Africa). Established Rhodes Scholarships at Oxford.
Died: March 26, 1902

Rt. Hon Cecil John Rhodes photographed for "Harper's Weekly" on the veranda of his residence, Groote Schnur, at Rondelos, near Cape Town.

GOVERNMENT AND POLITICS

Eleanor Roosevelt

When Eleanor Roosevelt died President John Kennedy eulogized her as one of the great ladies in the history of our country. Senator Jacob Javits said, "Her personal goodness affected the entire climate of her age." Many have called her the most important public woman of the 20th century. For 12 years, while her husband was President, she was the most admired woman in the world.

Long before the Women's Movement, Mrs. Roosevelt was the symbol of the new woman in the postwar world. Running political meetings, going down into coal mines and up in airplanes, visiting wounded GI's in battlefield hospitals and orphans in wartorn London, she went public with women's inherent qualities of compassion and nurturing in her efforts to assist the poor, the sick and the disenfranchised.

Eleanor grew up a child of financial privilege and emotional deprivation. Her mother, who died when Eleanor was 8, was a noted beauty who called her "plain, almost ugly" little girl "Granny." I was "a solemn child without beauty. I seemed like a little old woman", said Mrs. Roosevelt. Her father was the love of her childhood, a big game hunter who called her his "Little Nell." He was unstable, undependable, and he died when she was 10.

At 15 Eleanor went to England for her first formal education, attending a school run by a French woman with liberal ideas and a strong personality whose influence would shape the young woman's life. She referred to these school years as her happiest, and went back to New York to make the debut expected of a girl of her social standing . . . and work in social causes in New York. She also met her distant cousin, Franklin. His liveliness attracted her. He thought her discipline would curb his tendency towards excesses. They married and lived in New York, where he went to law school and she had their five children. Franklin's mother Sara, a domineering woman with whom Eleanor didn't get along, lived with them. Sara reigned, telling the Roosevelt children "Your mother only bore you."

Eleanor continued her social work and Franklin went into politics. He was stricken by polio, and besides helping him regain his vigor Eleanor became his political representative. She became active in women's causes—the League of Women Voters, Women's Trade Unions. She taught school, and ran a non-profit furniture factory that employed disabled men. By 1928, when her husband became Governor of New York State, she was a political leader in her own right, heading up the women's campaign for the Democratic Party.

While Eleanor remained serious and devoted to causes, Franklin, through his illness and successes, always loved a good time. His wife didn't enjoy going to parties with him. She said she felt like a spoilsport, or a policeman. In 1918 she found out he was involved with her social secretary, Lucy Mercer. She offered to divorce him but her husband turned her offer down. When the President died at Warm Springs, Georgia, in 1945, Lucy Mercer Rutherford was at his side.

Given Name: Anna Eleanor Roosevelt
Born: October 11, 1884, New York City
Married: Franklin Delano Roosevelt, 1905, 5 children
Highlights: Activist for womens' and childrens' rights, womens' participation in politics. Author and columnist. United States representative to the United Nations
Died: November 7, 1962

Mrs. Eleanor Roosevelt at a 1960 press conference in her home.

Opposite left: Mrs. Roosevelt seen leaving her teaching post at the Todhunter School for Girls in 1935.

Opposite center: Mrs. Roosevelt models the crepe satin gown to be worn at the President's 1934 Birthday Ball.

GOVERNMENT AND POLITICS

Eleanor's knowledge of her husband's infidelity wounded her as her father's undependability had done when she was a child. It also reenforced her determination to be independent. For the rest of her life she surrounded herself with supportive friends—a woman with whom she lived in a cottage on the grounds of the Roosevelt estate at Hyde Park; Harry Hopkins of the WPA, after Roosevelt was elected president in 1932; a state trooper; and Louis Howe, the President's closest advisor.

As the First Lady, Mrs. Roosevelt developed an unparalleled partnership with her husband with which they served the country during the Depression and World War II. She would come into the oval office and say, "Franklin, I think you should . . .", offering her opinion on some vital issue. She was referred to as "a cabinet minister without portfolio."

Passionate and opinionated, Mrs. Roosevelt's ideas weren't always acceptable to her husband or to other people. Active in the liberal and reform wings of the Democratic Party until the end of her life, she was accused of meddling in politics. She supported Americans' rights to join the Communist Party until she proved to herself the Communists couldn't be reasoned with. She stood up to Senator Joseph McCarthy in his Red witchhunt. Brought up in a household where strong anti-Semitic and anti-Negro prejudices were instilled, she was a staunch supporter of Jewish refugees attempting to escape Hitler's Europe and later, as Truman's appointment to the U.N. General Assembly, of the State of Israel. Accused of stirring up racial prejudice, she was an early civil rights advocate in the White House. In 1939 she quit the DAR, an exclusive organization for descendents of colonial settlers, when they refused to let black contralto Marian Anderson sing in their Washington hall. Miss Anderson sang instead to 75,000 at the Lincoln Memorial. As war drew near in the late 30's, she argued to eliminate racial discrimination in the armed services.

In 1936 Mrs. Roosevelt began to publish in papers across the country her syndicated column, "My Day." At first it concentrated on women's issues but later the focus of her columns shifted to issues of national interest. Readers combed her columns for clues as to where the administration stood on various issues.

Mrs. Roosevelt's ceaseless activities, perpetual travels and boundless energy brought on numberless "Eleanor" jokes in the '30's and '40's. In the end, though, derision turned to universal admiration. Although she received countless honors and degrees and was met with respect and adulation all over the world, she seemed to ask for little. The day of Franklin Roosevelt's death in April, 1945, when Vice-President Harry Truman rushed to the White House to offer condolences and ask what he could do for her, she responded in a characteristically generous manner—"No, Mr. Vice-President," she said, "now it's *you* we have to worry about."

Actress Lauren Bacall, Mrs. Eleanor Roosevelt, singer Marian Anderson, circa 1960.

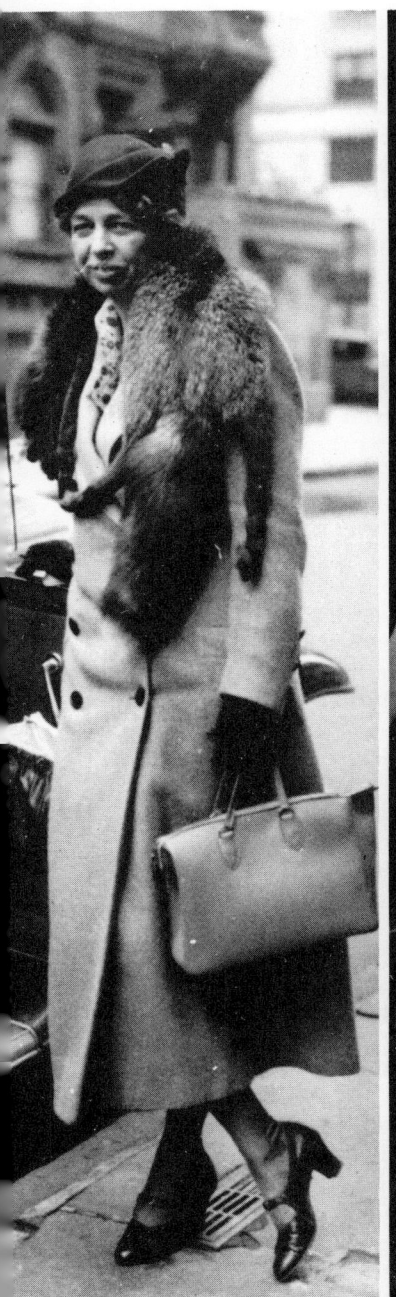

Mrs. Claire Booth Luce is greeted by Mrs. Roosevelt at Waldorf Astoria dinner.

Franklin Delano Roosevelt

When Franklin Delano Roosevelt first ran for President on the Democratic ticket in 1932 there were many who regarded him as a lightweight, especially when they compared him to his tough fifth cousin, President Teddy Roosevelt. Franklin, tutored by governesses until the age of 14, educated at the "Gold Coast" schools of Groton and Harvard, hardly seemed the man to lead the poor of the nation out of the gloom of the Great Depression. "The Laughing Boy of Hyde Park" was what one publication called him, referring to his family estate on the Hudson River and to his affable style. Yet Roosevelt's smiling face beamed into national politics at just the right time.

His style and his campaign theme song—"Happy Days Are Here Again"—were in sharp contrast to the dour manner of President Herbert Hoover, whose laissez-faire policies towards a nation gone broke seemed stuck in the mood of the plaintive "Brother, Can You Spare a Dime". Roosevelt, a tremendous figure of a man despite legs left withered and useless from infantile paralysis, became the nation's 32nd president, won huge electoral victories when he ran for a 2nd term, an unprecedented 3rd term, and, by public demand, a 4th term. During 12 years of national and international turmoil he won, too the adulation of millions of Americans as saviour of the poor and dozens of nations as the man who led them to victory over the Axis powers. Claiming sweeping powers from Congress to accomplish a social revolution at home and a massive armed effort abroad, he was also bitterly accused of demagoguery, dictatorship, and by those who like him had been raised in privilege, he was reviled as a "traitor to his class."

Coming to the White House off a career as New York State Senator, Assistant Secretary of the Navy during World War I, and, for two terms, Governor of New York State, Roosevelt faced a nation sinking under economic depression, with 12 million workers unemployed. Never matched for his use of politics as show business, he immediately charmed the American public by using the new medium, radio, to broadcast weekly "fireside chats." In his inauguration speech he had told America it had "nothing to fear but fear itself", and vowed to work for a "new deal" for the forgotten man, the victim of the depression. His sweeping program for recovery was known as the New Deal. During his first hundred days in office he and his advisors—a group of college professors labelled the "brain trust"—asked Congress for powers never before entrusted to a peacetime President, initiating programs that were the basis of American social programs for decades. "Alphabet agencies" were formed in dazzling profusion to speed economic recovery—the NRA (National Industrial Recovery); AAA (Agricultural Adjustment Administration); CCC (Civilian Conservation Corps) the Social Security Act, which guaranteed wages for the jobless, aged, and others. Many of the programs for which Roosevelt found support easily in the "100 days" were later disputed. He was accused by Republicans and some within his own party of trying to "pack" the Supreme Court with appointees sympathetic to his more controversial pet projects. He was under fire for the staggering pricetag for public relief and public works, a pricetag paid for by taxes businesses and the rich resented paying, or left unpaid, resulting in unbalanced budgets and an unprecedented public debt. Roosevelt contended these were inevitable in his administration's efforts to keep America's head above the inundating waters of the world depression. Progressives, intellectuals, and the young, not to mention millions rescued from despair, elected him in 1936 in a landslide against Republican Alf Landon, with a mandate to continue the New Deal.

Active in promoting the President's New Deal was his wife Eleanor, a distant cousin, the favorite niece of her "Uncle Teddy". Mrs. Roosevelt set a precedent as a "working" president's wife, not only with her activities in charitable causes but as a syndicated newspaper columnist. Her column "My Day" championed the status of women. The Roosevelts had five children, a daughter and four sons, all of whom served in the Armed Services during World War II.

As he grappled with the economy at home, Roosevelt saw the war clouds gathering over Europe and in the Pacific. For his repeated warnings to Congress that they prepare for an emergency, he was accused of being a warmonger. In his campaign for a 3rd term (he defeated Wendell Wilkie) he promised American parents that "your boys are not going to be sent to foreign wars." However, as Hitler marched across Europe he took steps to beef up the defense of Great Britain, upon whose strength he felt American security depended. Before his third term began, the president had overseen the passage of a draft law, put industry on a wartime production basis, and declared a state of "unlimited national emergency." Then, while Japanese emissaries were in Washington talking peace, came December 7th, 1941, the day the President said would "live in infamy." The Japanese attacked Pearl Harbor and America went to war.

Despite his increasing disability, (the two canes he'd used to support himself eventually were exchanged for a wheelchair) Roosevelt was a tireless leader of the nation's war effort. Besides proposing bigger and bigger military budgets, struggling with wartime inflation, asking the American people to sacrifice through harder work and rationing of products such as sugar and gasoline, he made frequent swings around the nation to check on war plant production and the national mood. Abroad, he planned with other leaders strategies for winning the war, himself being the titan linking the prodigious war efforts in Europe and the Pacific. He met frequently with Winston Churchill, with whom he developed a close personal friendship. With Joseph Stalin of Russia, he and Churchill were known as the "Big Three." They met in Cairo and Tehran to plan such strategies as the "Second Front", an invasion of North Africa designed to siphon off German troops who were battering Russia in full force. With the including of Chiang Kai-shek of China the Big Three became the "Big Four", plotting the war in the Pacific.

Just before the war ended, Roosevelt met with Churchill and Stalin at Yalta in the Crimea to work on "blueprints for peace" so the United Nations could avoid the sort of hasty mistakes of the Versailles Treaty, which after the first World War had left Europe vulnerable to Hitler's invasions and another world war.

In 1944 Roosevelt, exhausted from bouts with influenza and bronchitis, was sent off for a month's rest, after which his doctor declared him perfectly fit for a man of 62. Although he said he would prefer to retire, he acceded to the will of his "commander-in-chief—the sovereign people of the United States" who wanted him to see the war through to the end, and ran for a 4th term, defeating another Governor of New York, Thomas E. Dewey. A year later, a month before Allied Victory in Europe, Roosevelt was dead, and Vice-president Harry S. Truman directed the end of the war.

Having made history at home with his New Deal program for the Great Depression, and around the globe as leader of the 30 United Nations who defeated Hitler and the Japanese, Roosevelt died as two momentous chapters of history were just beginning to unfold: the concessions made at Yalta to Stalin had set the stage for the Cold War between East and West, and the Atomic Age began, with the bombing of Hiroshima and Nagasaki. Roosevelt was aware of both developments. Churchill convinced him before his death that they'd been duped by Stalin. And in 1944, Churchill and Roosevelt had signed an agreement that when the Manhattan Project bomb finally became available, "it might, perhaps, after mature consideration, be used against the Japanese."

GOVERNMENT AND POLITICS

Given Name: Franklin Delano Roosevelt
Born: January 30, 1882, Hyde Park, N.Y.
Married: Anna Eleanor, March 17, 1905, 5 children
Highlights: President of the United States 1933-1945.
Only U.S. president to be elected four times 1932, 1936, 1940, 1944.
Led U.S. in World War II.
Instituted many new and controversial government programs to end economic "Great Depression" of the 1930s.
Died: April 12, 1945

President Roosevelt and his secretary, Margaret Le Hand, during a 1935 visit to his home in Hyde Park, New York.

GOVERNMENT AND POLITICS

Chief Elk, a Sioux Indian, shakes hands with President Roosevelt after his nomination for re-election.

On August 14, 1935, surrounded by members of Congress, Roosevelt signed the Social Security Bill into law.

Anwar Sadat

Anwar Sadat, who won the Nobel Peace Prize in 1978, was assassinated in Cairo while watching a military parade celebrating Egypt's 1973 victory over Israel in the Mideast war.

Before he ordered his country's troops across the Suez Canal in what became known as the Yom Kippur War, Sadat, who for three years had served as President of the United Arab Republic (Egypt's official name), had seemed like a lack-lustre replacement for the charismatic Gamal Abdel Nasser. With his flashy grin, fancy British-tailored suits and empty threats of war against Israel, Sadat had been the butt of frequent jokes. 1973's "glorious crossing" gained him his people's confidence.

Sadat was a creation of war. He was one of the original "Free Officers" in the army who during the late '30s plotted to overthrow the Egyptian monarchy. During World War II, regarding Britain as Egypt's prime enemy, he took part in an unsuccessful effort against the British army. He spent two years in a British prison on false charges for a different crime, escaping by going on a hunger strike. After the war, he was part of a group formed to get the British out of Egypt and was once more imprisoned, this time for two and a half years, as a suspect in the murder of an Egyptian collaborator with the British.

In 1952 Sadat aided his old friend Nasser in the surprise attack that deposed King Farouk and established Nasser's government. His task was to seize the Cairo radio station and, precisely at 6:00 AM, announce the coup. Officers around the country waited to begin their actions as soon as Sadat's announcement was broadcast.

But six o'clock passed. The daily reading from the Koran began. Finally, half an hour late, Sadat came on the air, and the revolution was on. Sadat, a pious Moslem, who bore at the center of his forehead a dark callous from years of praying with his head to the ground, had not been able to bring himself to interrupt the morning prayer and had waited respectfully until it was finished before his announcement.

Like many Arabs, Sadat was a bitter foe of Israel. He had opposed President Nasser's 1970 agreement to a cease-fire in the "war of attrition" Egypt had embarked on to reclaim every inch of territory gained by Israel in the 1967 "6-Day" war. Despite doubts that he would continue the constantly-extended cease-fire when he became president, he did so.

Egyptian Vice-President Hoshi Mubarak, Sadat and War Minister General Mohamed Abdel Ghani El Gamassy take salutes at a military parade.

A devout Moslem, President Anwar Sadat prays at a new mosque in Seppium, Egypt in December 1977.

GOVERNMENT AND POLITICS

Impatience and unrest grew in Egypt as students protested a war economy without a war. The 1973 war renewed Egypt's sense of national purpose, as well as solidifying Sadat's support.

Although Sadat came to power and prestige through war, he wanted to be remembered for his efforts towards peace. One of the volumes of his memoirs is entitled "Sadat: A Man of Peace." In it he describes thoughts he had while in solitary confinement in a Cairo jail. "He who cannot change the very fabric of his thought", he concluded, "will never be able to change reality and will never, therefore, make any progress." In 1977, Sadat made a dramatic visit to Israel on a mission of peace. There he met with Prime Minister Menachem Begin. Together the historically bitter enemies repeated public pledges of no more war. Like Sadat, Begin was known as a man of war. Israel and the world feared he could be a "war" prime minister when he was elected in 1977. But also like Sadat, Begin had the qualities of courage and flexibility which allowed him to soften the traditional emnity between Jews and Arabs.

Sadat's epochal journey to Jerusalem was followed by the two men meeting together with President Carter at Camp David in the U.S. in 1978. There they worked out a fragile framework for peace in the Mideast. In signing the agreement, Sadat paraphrased the biblical prophet Isaiah—"Let us work together until they beat their swords into ploughshares and their spears into pruning hooks." It was for their work at Camp David that Begin and Sadat shared the Nobel Prize that same year.

Many Arabs hated Sadat for his peace-keeping efforts. They objected that there was no timetable for self-determination for the Arabs on the West Bank in Palestine. When Sadat died, the president of Lebanon said it was the trip to Camp David that had killed him. Yasir Arafat, head of the PLO (Palestine Liberation Army) was gleeful at Sadat's death.

Sadat himself, who had recently cracked down hard on seething unrest in Egypt by reviving his secret police, said before he died that Egypt was suffering from too much democracy. With uncharacteristic gloom he predicted that peace would end with his death. Gunned down by Moslem fanatics—whom he defiantly stood up to confront even as they aimed at his open car—Sadat did manage to leave as his legacy an uneasy peace in the Middle East.

Given Name: Muhammad Anwar el-Sadat
Born: December 25, 1918, Talah Minufiya, Egypt
Married: Jehan, 1949, 4 children (3 children by earlier marriage.)
Highlights: President of Arab Republic of Egypt, 1970-1981. Shared 1978 Nobel Peace Prize with Menachem Begin of Israel for their efforts to bring peace to the Middle East.
Died: October 6, 1981

Yasir Arafat (left) leader of the Palestine Liberation Organization, is greeted by Sadat in 1977.

GOVERNMENT AND POLITICS

Joseph Stalin

When Joseph Vissarionovich Djugashvili became a revolutionary agitator he took the surname Stalin—"man of steel"—to protect him from the Czar's police. The name turned out to be appropriate for the complex, ruthless man who, for over 20 years, ruled Russia with an iron hand, transforming it from a backward country whose farmers worked the land with wooden plows into a modern superpower equipped with atomic reactors. Patriarch of communism, father of victory in World War II, Stalin ruled with the cruelty a harsh parent might use on illiterate children, employing tactics that taint history's view of his formidable achievements.

Born in a little Georgian village to a shoemaker father and his uneducated serf wife, Stalin was prepared by his devout mother for a career in the Georgian Orthodox church. But at 15 he was expelled from the seminary for espousing the doctrines of Karl Marx whose writings would lay the foundation of the Bolshevist and, later, communist government. As a political agitator Stalin carried the idea of Bolshevism to the masses.

He directed the publication of the first issue of Pravda, still today the Communist party newspaper. Sent to jail 8 times and into exile 7 times for his anti-czarist activities, Stalin was in a camp in Siberia in 1917 when Czar Nicholas Alexander was overthrown. After Nicolai Lenin led the Bolsheviks to victory in the "October Revolution" that same year, Stalin embarked on a power struggle with his arch rival, Lenin's first lieutenant Leon Trotsky, a struggle in which he prevailed, becoming party secretary under Lenin. When Lenin died in 1922, Stalin became head of the 12-member Politburo and chairman of the Communist party. He introduced a quasi-liberal constitution to serve the people's needs, but soon began a merciless campaign to convert Russia to a socialist republic by violent means. When the kulaks, Russia's well-off peasant class, resisted his program of collectivization of farming land, Stalin stated, "The kulak is the enemy of the government. He is to be liquidated as a class." The kulaks' grain crop was seized, and over a million of them starved to death. Initiating a series of "five-year plans" to speed up Russia's industrialization, Stalin set out to eliminate all opponents of Bolshevism and his ideas. Sweeping and bloody purge trials in the '30's attempted to get rid of "the unprincipled and idealless band of professional wreckers, diversionists, spies and murderers". Stalin ordered them destroyed, "exterminated mercilessly as enemies of the working class and enemies of our country." Ordered shot as well were supporters of Trotsky (who himself had fled into exile and was killed in Mexico in 1940), and blunderers and officials who slowed down production. Trotsky once said of Stalin's methods, "Stalin cannot stop. He resembles a man who drinks a salt solution to quench his thirst."

In 1939 Stalin signed a non-aggression pact with Hitler, whose armies were marching Eastward across Europe, and in 1940 joined with the German army in the cruel rape of Poland. But when Hitler broke the "friendship" treaty and invaded Russia, Stalin countered with an army he had been quietly modernizing. Calling up images of Mother Russia and the 1812 victory over Napoleon, he asked every man, woman and child to consider himself a soldier in the cause to defeat Hitler. Stalin personally directed the mighty Red Army, which eventually lost 2 million men. The epic battle of Stalingrad in 1943 (the city was named for Stalin in 1917 when his Bolshevist forces had defeated the Czar's White Russian army there) was the turning point for the Reds. So many Nazis died that their troops who fought there were called the "Army of the Dead." Stalingrad, although razed to the ground, became a symbol that the Russians would beat back the Germans.

During the war, Stalin was one of the "Big Three" Allied leaders, meeting with President Roosevelt and Prime Minister Churchill at Tehran in Iran, and at Yalta in the Crimea to discuss the war and its aftermath. An adroit bargainer, he gained predominance for Russia in Eastern and Central Europe where, when the war was over, he staged bloody show trials to get rid of the enemies of communism. The period of Russian occupation was called "Peace by Terror." Roosevelt, who had been fooled by Stalin's politeness, said after Yalta, banging his fist on his wheelchair, "We can't do business with Stalin. He has broken every promise he made."

The end of the war was the climax of Stalin's career. Although at Yalta he'd said the war couldn't have been won without American aid, he told the Soviet people Russia was the main force in the allied victory. A barrier of secrecy went up between Russia and the West, called by Churchill an "Iron Curtain." Stalin controlled information coming out of and into Russia, creating an abyss of fear and suspicion between East and West. The Cold War replaced fighting wars as Russia attempted to retain communist control over Eastern Europe and seize control in other countries viewed as ready for communist takeover.

In postwar Russia Stalin began another series of five-year plans. With great sacrifices extracted from the Soviet people, production of steel, coal, iron, oil and electricity quickly surpassed pre-war standards. Russia developed its own atomic warhead and began producing weapons that started the arms race. But in the country, life was hard, with the agricultural output down below 1928 levels.

In 1946 Stalin started a witchhunt against intellectuals, attempting to change attitudes of the Russian people by using naked police force. His program was a forerunner of the mid-60's Cultural Revolution in Mao Tse-tung's Red China. Secret police went after famed artists like composer Dmitri Shostakovitch. When they attacked his 9th Symphony, he wrote an ode to Stalin's forestry plan. Many intellectuals were sent to forced labor camps and replaced by frauds and cranks, such as the doctor whom Stalin promoted for a time who thought old age could be postponed by the use of bicarbonate of salt enemas.

Stalin's last years were dominated by his eccentricities and a "personality cult" in which he stage-managed himself to be the embodiment of all human wisdom. In 1949, on his 70th birthday, Pravda extolled him as the "inspirer of Creation." His anti-Westernism intensified into anti-semitism. He sent many Jews to the camps and painted the enemy-U.S. as ruled by "Wall Street Jews." One of his last varieties of persecution centered on wives of Jews, whom he sent into exile in the camps. He revived the bloody purges of the 30's, going after friends and party officials he suspected of being disloyal. Ironically, his state of mind at the end was not unlike Hitler's. Living in self-imposed isolation, he completely lost touch with normal life. His food was tested in a laboratory before he would touch it. He had his last crony, his butler, arrested as a spy, and his doctor, whom he accused of spying for the British, was kept imprisoned and in chains. Fittingly, his death was followed by hundreds of random killings by his secret police.

At the 1956 Communist Party Congress, the tyrannical rule of Joseph Stalin was denounced by Soviet Premier Nikita Kruschev.

Given Name: Joseph Vissarionovich Djugashvili
Born: December 21, 1879, Gori, Georgia (USSR)
Married: Widowed 1917, 1 child
Married: Nadajda Allilvieva, 1919, 2 children
Highlights: Premier of Soviet Union 1924-1953.
Directed heroic defense of the USSR against Nazis in World War II.
Responsible for murder, execution, starvation or imprisonment of over a million political opponents.
Instituted Cold War.
Died: March 5, 1953.

GOVERNMENT AND POLITICS

Official Soviet photo of Joseph Stalin, 1949.

An undated portrait of Sun Yat-Sen as a young man in Western clothes, perhaps taken during, or just after, his years at a Christian school in Hawaii.

Harry S. Truman

Meeting with reporters the day after President Franklin Roosevelt's death made him the 33rd president of the United States, Harry S. Truman said, "I don't know if any of you fellows ever had a load of hay or a bull fall on you, but last night the whole weight of the moon and stars and all the planets fell on me . . . please pray for me, I mean that."

Truman, a self-described "homegrown all-American product from Missouri", had been vice-president only 3 months when he was suddenly charged with overseeing the end of World War II. Convinced that to do so would save countless American military lives, he ordered the atomic bomb dropped on Hiroshima and Nagasaki, a decision that not only ended the war but ushered in the Atomic Age and with it a redefinition of both war and peace.

Tough as that decision was, Truman later said his toughest decision was ordering American troops into Korea in 1951, a calculated risk he took to stop Communist aggression. During that war, he made another tough decision—he stripped General Douglas MacArthur, who had served heroically as liberator of the Philippines and overseer of Japan's recovery, of all his posts in the Far East. MacArthur wanted to escalate the Korean War into outright attack on Red China, an action Truman feared further risked starting World War III.

The Korean conflict was the only "hot" war during Truman's 8 years as President. Most of his foreign policy centered on waging the Cold War with Russia and her allies. The Marshall Plan and the Truman Doctrine were set up to pump massive aid into battered Europe and military assistance into Greece and Turkey. NATO (the North Atlantic Treaty Organization) was established as a peacetime military alliance between the U.S. and her European allies. Truman appointed another war hero who in 1952 would follow him into the White House, General Dwight D. Eisenhower, Supreme Allied Commander. The UN was launched as a diplomatic body where peaceful negotiations could settle international disputes.

Probably the most dramatic of Truman's Cold War challenges was the Berlin Blockade. In 1948 the Russians tried to squeeze the Western occupying forces out of Berlin, setting up a blockade around the French, American and British zones. For 327 days the allies airlifted supplies into the beleaguered city until Russia backed down, suffering a severe diplomatic defeat. In 1953, as he prepared to vacate the presidency, Truman pointed with pride to a big globe in the oval office—"During these eight years we've kept that old globe out of disaster," he said, summing up his foreign policy record.

Truman admitted he was more at home on Main Street, U.S.A., than on Pennsylvania Avenue. Raised on a farm, his father's business reversals prevented his going to college. He fought in some of the heaviest action in France during World War I, returning a Major to Kansas City to open a haberdashery with an army buddy. The 20's deflation ruined his business and he later said the thing he was proudest of in his life was paying back the $20,000 he owed to creditors. Entering politics, Truman was a machine Democrat who eventually went to Washington becoming part of the "Silent Senators" who rubber-stamped Roosevelt's New Deal programs. He was an outspoken critic of the Republican party which he accused of hating the poor and catering to special interest groups and rich bankers.

When World War II broke out, Truman, who was too old to fight, did the next best thing: he fought overspending in the war effort. His success as a watchdog of spending later found its way into a motto prominently displayed on the President's desk: "The Buck Stops Here." His reputation in this area put him in line as a choice for vice-president when Roosevelt was looking for a running mate in 1944.

Beset by international turmoil on a suddenly shrunken planet, Truman also underwent heavy criticism and tough sledding at home. His domestic programs—civil rights, immigration laws, the rights of workers—were extensions of Roosevelt's New Deal, called under Truman the Fair Deal. His vetoes of bills, proposed by Republican and Southern Democrat opposition, were often overridden. He fought for programs later Presidents would see realized, his style dogged and scrappy, his delivery plain and direct. He battled demagogue Sen. Joseph McCarthy in the early '50's when the Senator conducted a witchhunt for communists in government and other areas of influence. Although his actions weren't always consistent, Truman was consistently a man of action. Though pro-labor, he seized the steel companies in 1952 to avert a strike. When the Supreme Court ruled he had acted unconstitutionally, he released them back to the owners, setting off a crippling strike.

Truman's lack of pretension endeared him to the American public, his folksy, hometown philosophy suited the country's mood. "If you can't stand the heat, get out of the kitchen", he advised those who complained of the vicissitudes of politics. He called Joseph Stalin "Uncle Joe" behind his back. When in 1948 it looked as if the urbane, confident Governor of New York, Thomas E. Dewey, would defeat him for his second, and only elected, term, Truman vowed to "Give 'em hell." With the new nickname "Give 'Em Hell Harry", he took off on a whistlestop, handshaking person-to-person campaign that resulted in a history-making personal victory.

Truman's "family man" image also appealed to the public. A favorite cameo of the President had him wearing a wild sports shirt, relaxing at the piano playing "The Missouri Waltz". He checked out everything with his wife Bess, whom he'd met in Sunday School when they were children and referred to as "The Boss." The Trumans had one child, Margaret. When her singing debut in Washington received a less-than-rave review from a music critic, the President responded in his typical scrappy manner, sending off a letter threatening to punch the critic in the nose.

He was also devoted to his mother, whom he frequently left Washington to visit. Of all the tributes ever paid him, he said, hers was the one that meant the most: "That boy", she said, "Could plow the straightest row of corn in the County. He was a farmer who could do everything there was to do just a little better than anyone else."

When Truman had served the two terms Congress voted to limit the Presidency to, he returned to Missouri, rejecting job offers that would have paid large salaries. He said he didn't intend to capitalize on "the world's most honorable office." He wrote his memoirs and oversaw the construction of a library named for him where his papers would be housed. He gave the library all the gifts he received while President, saying they belonged to the people. When he was in his 70's his daughter Margaret, interviewing him on TV, asked how he wanted to be remembered. "I hope to be remembered as the People's President", replied the man from Missouri.

GOVERNMENT AND POLITICS

On his 67th birthday, in 1951, President Harry S. Truman grinned when presented with a birthday cake having only 21 candles.

GOVERNMENT AND POLITICS

Given Name: Harry S. Truman
Born: May 8, 1884, Lamar, Missouri
Married: Bess Wallace, 1919, 1 child
Highlights: President of the United States, 1945-1952. Made decision to drop atomic bomb on Japan. Committed United States troops to defense of South Korea.
Died: December 26, 1972

Truman posed on the steps leading to the Presidential plane as he left to make a foreign policy speech in Detroit.

GOVERNMENT AND POLITICS

Woodrow Wilson

In 1916 when Woodrow Wilson, America's 28th president, was campaigning for a second term, World War I was raging overseas. Wilson, an ardent pacifist who had fought growing anti-German sentiment to keep his nation neutral during his first term in office, ran under the slogan, "He kept us out of war."

The former president of Princeton University and governor of New Jersey admitted before he came to Washington he didn't know much about foreign affairs. A Democrat, he thought Republicans were better at that sort of thing. On the eve of his inauguration in 1913, he told a friend, "It would be an irony of fate if my administration was to deal chiefly with foreign affairs." During his first term he concentrated on tariff reform, instituted the Federal Reserve System and the Federal Trade Commission and, though he sent troops into Latin American countries to protect American interests, managed to avoid involvement in Europe. But in 1917, declaring America had a mission to "keep the world safe for democracy", Wilson led the country into the conflict against the Germans. Assuming wide powers, he successfully converted the nation to a wartime footing, with a fighting force of four million men.

Just before the end of the war, Wilson issued his "Fourteen Points" as a basis for a peace treaty. The last one provided for the League of Nations in which nations would resolve their differences by peaceful discussion. He also listed "Five Particulars" he wanted included in negotiations with the Germans, one of which promised justice for the enemy. Intending to use his enormous prestige to press for acceptance of his peace plan, Wilson sailed for Europe to attend the peace conference at Versailles in France.

With the formidable U.S. in the war and the promise of clemency in Wilson's proposals, Germany surrendered in November, 1918. But the leaders gathered at Versailles were bitterly divided on terms for peace with the Germans. France demanded massive reparations, and in the terms eventually hammered out, the losers were punished and the victors rewarded. What was regarded by the Germans as a "dictated peace" made them take the entire blame for the war and, since it would make economic recovery difficult, already contained seeds of another world conflict.

While Wilson was in Europe he suffered a stroke, which was concealed from the public. Back home he suffered another, also hidden, and then a third, which left him virtually incapacitated. His Vice-President, a man remembered for little else except his remark that "what this country needs is a good 5-cent cigar", did not assume presidential powers. Instead, Edith Wilson, the president's second wife, took over for the last 17 months of Wilson's term. A woman with only two years of schooling, she signed bills with a childish scrawl and forged the President's signature on bills. "We have petticoat government!" declared one of Wilson's congressional critics. "Mrs. Wilson is President!"

Meanwhile, Wilson, though sick and senile, continued to lobby with a religious zeal for approval of the Versailles Treaty. Insisting there be no compromises, he wrote letters from his sickbed pleading with Senators and Congressmen to go along with the Treaty. The letters met with a growing tide of isolationism; their effect was to harden the opposition, and in the end the U.S. was the only nation which did not sign. Wilson's idea for a League of Nations was dead.

Wilson's over-zealous and uncompromising idealism in proposing and pushing for his "Fourteen Points" are blamed as the reasons for their defeat in Congress where in 1918 Republicans held the majority, thus undermining his political support. The Germans viewed the Treaty of Versailles as a betrayal of Wilsonian principles, which had promised a League and self-determination for nations. In 1919 Wilson won the Nobel Prize for Peace. The creation of the United Nations after World War II grew out of principles laid out in Wilson's "Fourteen Points."

In 1913, President Wilson and Joseph Tummulty posed at the White House.

President Wilson marching in a Liberty Loan parade on New York's 5th Avenue.

GOVERNMENT AND POLITICS

Given Name: Thomas Woodrow Wilson
Born: December 28, 1856, Staunton, Virginia
Married: Ellen Louise Axson, 1885
Married: Edith Bolling Galt, 1915
Highlights: President of the United States, 1913-1921. Led nation in World War I, proposed League of Nations in his "14 Points". Won Nobel Peace Prize in 1919.
Died: February 3, 1924

Woodrow Wilson, seated, and Joseph P. Tummulty, his secretary.

GOVERNMENT AND POLITICS

SPORTS

Muhammad Ali

He had fast hands, fast feet, and a fast mouth. He was as quick with a joke as a jab, and a master at creating controversy, press coverage, and giant gates.

Almost single-handedly, Ali revived the dying sport of boxing, which was suffering from a severe lack of colorful champions. But Ali transcended boxing. He was in many ways a living embodiment of his turbulent times—times that included the explosive Civil Rights movement and the Viet Nam war. He aroused passions in many who never saw him fight or, for that matter, never even saw a boxing match, and almost every American had a position strongly for or strongly against Ali. Few people were neutral about the brash black man who made rash statements, often predicting victories with insulting rhyme, and then backed them up with gifted, and often courageous, performances . . . both in the ring and out of it.

Ali's first fame came when, as Cassius Clay, he won the light heavyweight gold medal at the 1960 Rome Olympics. Then in 1964 he stunned the boxing world, most of whose "experts" gave him no chance, by defeating heavyweight champion Sonny Liston to win the title for the first of his record three times. Following his victory, the new champion announced that he was a member of the Nation of Islam, known as the Black Muslims, and that henceforth his name would be Muhammad Ali. Cassius Clay was his slave name, he said.

Now a major, and controversial, figure, rather than simply the upstart "Louisville Lip", Ali won the rematch with Liston in 1965 with a first-round knockout that came after what some said was a perfect right hand, and others called a phantom punch. He then successfully defended his title seven times in the next two years before boxing groups stripped him of his title.

The reason they gave was his refusal to be inducted into the Army and subsequent conviction for draft evasion, which carried a $10,000 fine and 5 year prison sentence. Ali, who had said, "I ain't got nothin' against the Viet Congs", appealed the conviction, which was eventually reversed by an 8-0 decision of the Supreme Court in 1971. For more than three years, while his appeal was working its way through the courts, Ali had been deprived of the chance to make a living by fighting, and was out of action for what might have been his prime boxing years.

He lost a split decision to then-champion Joe Frazier on his first try to regain the title that had been taken from him out of the ring. That was his first loss in a career that ended with a 56-4 record, during which he won the heavyweight title two more times: from George Forman in 1974 and from Leon Spinks in 1978, after Spinks had won the title from him earlier that same year.

Ali had made 10 title defenses before his loss to Spinks, among them the "Thrilla in Manila" against Joe Frazier. That savage fight, in which both fighters used every ounce of their skill and courage, ended when a blinded Frazier could not come out for the 15th round.

After his retirements (he announced his retirement in 1979, but came back for two more fights) Ali tried his hand at acting, but was unsuccessful. The man who could "float like a butterfly, sting like a bee" was never as good at playing fictional characters as he was at playing the role of "The Greatest".

Given Name: Cassius Marcellus Clay
Born: January 17, 1942, Louisville, Kentucky
Married: Sonji (divorced 1966)
Married: Belinda Boyd, 1967 (divorced 1977)
Married: Veronica Porsche, 1977, 5 children
Highlights: Only man ever to win the world heavyweight boxing championship 3 times.

Ali at his Deer Lake, Pennsylvania training camp in 1980.

In 1979, Ali combed his hair after each round of two show fights staged in West Berlin.

Roger Bannister

On May 6th, 1954, a tall, boyish 25-year-old medical student named Roger Bannister achieved the goal track fanatics had dreamed of for years—he broke the four-minute barrier in the mile run. Supremely confident that day at Oxford, England, Bannister ran with the gliding, loping motion he had developed through years of theory and practice, finishing in 3 minutes, 59.4 seconds.

His fellow Britons, just emerging from the postwar doldrums, went wild. They had recently crowned a queen, and were looking for new, upbeat heroes to block out the devastating memory of war. Bannister filled the bill as a peacetime victor in the Battle for Britain. Chunks of the Iffley Road track were sold as souvenirs. In America, Bannister was lionized with an excitement hardly matched 15 years later when the U.S. put a man on the moon.

Afterwards, Chris Chataway, one of the pace setter's that day, reminisced about the hysteria that made Bannister an instant sports hero. Many people will go faster, he said. But nobody will ever again do the mile in four minutes for the first time.

Running was never Bannister's prime ambition. It was a pastime he stuck with, thinking it might get him a trip abroad. As a student at Oxford he was advised against running as sport—he was told he didn't have the style for it. But his scientific mind was fascinated with theories of motion and weather and he persevered. Eventually he won a major team meet, discovering on the track that source of nervous energy that puts the body in overdrive—the "last lap sprints" he became noted for—and surged ahead of the pack to victory. Sent to the Helsinki Olympics in 1952 as Britain's bright running hope, he never even got into contention, flopping miserably as England's most illustrious sports' fan, the Duke of Edinburgh, looked on. Bannister knew only a "supreme performance" could blot out that humiliation. During a particularly bad spell of weather he trained rigorously under a program described by an observer as "wet, rough and full of punishment", his eye on the Inter-University run at Iffley Road. The rest is sports history.

Over the years Bannister, frequently asked to speculate on the enormous attention his victory received, has often described the almost magical appeal of running the mile. He calls the mile itself "a mathematical accident which nonetheless offers a kind of perfection which only happens in sport." The reasons it took so long to break the four-minute barrier, he says, were not physical but psychological. Since Iffley Road his record has been beaten regularly, partly because present-day runners train more and better.

SPORTS

Roger Bannister views New York from the Empire State Building just a week after breaking the 4-minute mile at Oxford, England on May 6, 1954.

Bannister, who was later knighted for encouraging young athletes, ran with two youngsters on the grounds of the United Nations Headquarters during his 1954 New York visit.

Given Name: Roger Gilbert Bannister
Born: March 23, 1929, Harrow, England
Married: Moyra Elver Jacobson, 1955, 4 children
Highlights: First man to break 4-minute mile on May 6, 1954 at Oxford, England. Knighted in January 1975.

SPORTS

Nadia Comaneci

"You have to change all the time if you want to be first. You have to make things more difficult for yourself every day." This is the challenge by which Nadia Comaneci lives.

In 1976 at Montreal an elfin, 14-year-old Nadia exploded into the consciousness of the sports world by turning in a series of perfect 10s in her gymnastic specialties and carting off seven Olympic gold medals to her home in Romania.

Nadia Comaneci was born in November 12, 1961 in the little town of Gheorghe Gheorghiu-Dej in Bacau County, Romania. The daughter of a machinist and working mother, she has one sibling, a brother.

Nadia worked hard under the watchful and careful tutelage of her coach, Bela Karoli, the man who discovered her on a playground at the age of six. She was only seven when she entered her first gymnastics class and showed so much promise she was picked for special instruction, practicing three to four hours a day.

Described by sports reporters as "the queen of the uneven bars and balance beam", she displaced the defending titleholder, USSR gymnast Ludmila Tourischeva, on July 22, 1976 at the Olympics held in Montreal and became ladies' individual all-round champion.

She was only 14 and a mere 86 pounds when Nadia scored the historic first 10-point Olympic performance on the uneven bars and her popularity was such that she was elected Female Athlete of the Year by the Associated Press. By the time she was 15, Nadia was awarded one of Romania's highest honors, the title of "Hero of Socialist Labor" and the golden "Sickle and Hammer" medal in a ceremony staged at the Sports and Culture Palace and broadcast by national radio and television networks. The following year she was named "Female Athlete of 1976" by the Associated Press and given the Babe Didrickson Zaharias trophy. She was the second gymnast to be so honored. Ogla Korbut was the first in 1972.

Comaneci also completed at the 1980 Olympics in Moscow where she won two more gold medals (balance beam, floor exercises) and a silver (all-round). In 1981, at age 19, Nadia was described by newspapers as "an aging superstar . . . growing old gracefully." She was living with her parents in Bucharest and in her first year at the university, studying physical education and language and performing gymnastics on tours. But she will be best remembered as the heroine of the 1976 Olympic Games in Montreal.

Romania's Nadia Comaneci and America's Bart Conner hold up their trophies after winning international competition at New York's Madison Square Garden, in 1976.

SPORTS

Given Name: Nadia Comaneci
Born: November 12, 1961, Onesti, Romania
Highlights: First gymnast to score a perfect 10 in Olympic competition. Heroine of 1976 games at Montreal where she won 3 gold medals, a silver and a bronze.

Comaneci strikes a perfect pose on way to a perfect 10 and gold medals at the 1976 Olympics in Montreal.

SPORTS

Wayne Gretzky

From the time he first entered the National Hockey League with the Edmonton Oilers in 1979 at age 19, hockey player Wayne Gretzky drew the attention, and admiration, of the sports world. In his first year he became the youngest winner of the Hart Memorial Trophy as most valuable player and also tied for the league scoring title with Marcel Dionne.

Then he set to work on the record book. In 1980-81 he had 184 points and 109 assists, both records. The following year he soared to new heights, scoring 92 goals, 120 assists and 212 points.

Named, "The Great Gretzky" by enthusiastic sports writers, Gretzky has had a greater impact on the way hockey is played than any player in history, with the exception of Bobby Orr. By age 23, Wayne Gretzky held 37 National Hockey League records and had become the 18th player in NHL history to accumulate 1000 regular-season points. And he did it at a younger age and at a far quicker pace than anyone before him.

"Wayne is the greatest hockey player in the world," said Glen Sather, Oilers' coach, "but he's a better person than he is a hockey player. The great athlete possesses the will and the way to have a good time while performing."

Former star Bobby Hull said Gretzky came along when hockey needed a change. And "he accepted the challenge. He has a fantastic style and is about four steps ahead of everybody."

Pat Quinn, coach for the Los Angeles Kings, said of Gretzky, "When he comes out on his first shift and pops one, you know he'll probably have it most of the night...."

Born in Brantford, Ontario on January 26, 1961, Wayne "The Kid" Gretzky, quickly became one of the best players the NHL ever had. Playing center for the Edmonton team, Gretzky won the league MVP award in each of his first six seasons. He broke his own assist record with 125 in 1983 and 135 in 1985. In 1984 and 1985 Gretzky lead the Oilers to the Stanley Cup, and has set by far the fastest scoring pace in NHL history.

Former NHL scoring champion Phil Esposito said, "He'll be the first player, if he plays long enough and doesn't get hurt, to get 2,000 points. If he plays as long as I did, 18 years, he'll score 1,000 goals."

Given Name: Wayne Gretsky

Born: January 26, 1961, Brantford, Ontario, Canada

Unmarried

Highlights: Most prolific young scorer ever to enter the National Hockey League. Holds single-season records for goals, assists and points, and will easily break all-time record if he continues at established pace.

SPORTS

"The Great Gretzky" brought his hockey stick to a 1983 charity golf event at the Westchester Country Club near New York City.

SPORTS

Sir Edmund Hillary

Sir Edmund Hillary, first man to scale Mount Everest, was described as "a quiet-spoken, shy perfectionist". The New Zealand mountaineer and explorer became interested in mountain climbing while a fourteen-year-old schoolboy. As he grew older he acquired more experience and spent two seasons a year in the Southern Alps of his country, New Zealand, perfecting his rock-climbing technique and learning ice work.

Hillary went into the beekeeping business with his father in 1936. During World War II he served in the Royal New Zealand Air Force as a navigator with a Catalina patrol squadron in the South Pacific. After the end of the war, although he had been seriously wounded, the six-foot three-inch tall veteran resumed mountain climbing. In 1951 he went on the New Zealand Gashwal expedition. Then, because of his skillful ice technique, Hillary was named by the New Zealand Alpine Club to accompany Eric Shipton on a reconnaissance of Everest by taking a southern route through Nepal. The next year he was a member of a British expedition to Cho Oyn, west of Everest in the Himalayas.

Then in October of 1952 Eric Shipton, who was destined to head the 1953 assault on Mt. Everest, withdrew, and Colonel John Hunt assumed leadership of the group of British climbers. Hunt organized his expedition with the comprehensiveness and care for detail of a commander plotting the strategy of a major military operation.

Mt. Everest, the highest mountain in the world, is 29,028 feet, and called by Tibetans, "Chomolungma—'Goddess Mother of the World.'" It was not until 1920 that the Dalai Lama of Tibet granted permission to the Royal Geographical Society to ascend the mountain. Between 1921 and 1952 eleven assaults were made and at least fifteen lives were lost.

For several months Colonel Hunt trained his mountaineers on the steep tors of Scotland and in the Alps of Europe. By the time the party was ready to climb it included 362 Nepalese porters, 36 Sherpa guides and 10,000 pounds of baggage, which included new lightweight oxygen equipment.

The expedition reached its base camp about April 12, 1953 and within less than a month the entire party was at Camp IV, at a level of 21,200. In all, nine camps were established; the last one was 1,100 feet from the peak. Hunt sent ahead two teams of two men each to attempt the summit. The first team failed ultimate success, but prepared the way and brought back valuable advice for the second team, Edmund Hillary and his Sherpa guide, Tenzing Norkey.

These two set out from Camp IX on the South Col at 6:30 AM and reached the South Peak about 9:00 AM. Hillary stated, "The final ridge was of high Alpine standard and we finally got to the top at 11:30 AM ... I felt ... good at the top. It was a beautiful day with a moderate wind. As we got there, my companion threw his arms around me and embraced me." The beekeeper and the guide remained on the peak about 20 minutes before they descended. An editorial in the *New York Times* said, "Hillary, the New Zealander, along with Tenzing, the Sherpa, 'Tiger of the Snows,' will take his place with Sir Walter Raleigh and Sir Francis Drake." A short time later Queen Elizabeth II knighted Hillary for his achievement.

Sir Edmund Hillary undertook a trans-Antarctic expedition and reached the South Pole by tractor on January 4, 1958. On other trips, to Alaska and Nepal, he did high-altitude research and encouraged the building of schools, bridges and airstrips. He has also written several books. In March, of 1985, at age 63, the Auckland bee farmer, philanthropist, lecturer and writer, was appointed as New Zealand's new ambassador to India and Nepal.

Sir Edmund Hillary in 1963 before a climbing expedition in Nepal.

Given Name: Edmund Percival Hillary
Born: July 20, 1919, Auckland, New Zealand
Married: Louise Rose, 1953, 3 children
Highlights: First man to climb Mt. Everest, 1953. Also led several other major mountaineering expeditions and explorations in Antartica. Knighted for his achievements by Queen Elizabeth.

SPORTS

Hillary tries on new outfit before a 1958 expedition to the South Pole.

A happy Hillary ten weeks after his victorious assault on Mt. Everest on April 12, 1953.

Hillary surveying the debris from the 1975 air crash that killed his wife and daughter.

Rod Laver

Nicknamed "Rocket" in his playing days, Rod Laver was the first professional tennis player to gross $1 million from the game. He was also the first man to win tennis' "Grand Slam" twice, first as an amateur in 1962, then as a professional seven years later. Until the early 1980's, the Grand Slam meant winning all four major tournaments—Wimbledon, the U.S. and French Opens and the Australian Championships—within the same calendar year.

Laver was raised on a farm in Queensland, Australia and was destined for tennis from the very beginning. His mother and father were both tournament players. At 13, he was selected to attend a tennis course sponsored by a Brisbane newspaper and there he caught the eye of Aussie Davis Cup coach, Harry Hopman. At 18, Laver was named to the Australian Davis Cup team and five years later he won everything in sight, including the Grand Slam, a feat no one had accomplished since Donald Budge in 1938. Laver turned pro the following year and soon established himself as the world's number one professional player.

During 1969, the left-handed Laver participated in six open tournaments and his steely wrist and devastating backhand took him past everybody. He won Wimbledon by defeating Tony Roche in the final round without once losing his service. He won the Pacific Southwest with a victory over Ken Rosewall, who had beaten him twice in the finals of the Bournemouth and French Opens. All in all, Laver's coolness under fire was one of the factors that enabled him to win 10 tournaments in 1968.

Laver himself said, "I found that getting upset usually made me play worse and I tried to analyze why I was getting beaten. I'm all for color and conversation, but no matter how much money is involved . . . there is no call for bad behavior."

At the height of his career, critics around the world called Laver the greatest player of all time. Besides being the only player in tennis history to win the Grand Slam twice, he won four Wimbledon singles titles, two U.S. Open singles championships, and three Australian and two French singles titles. He had a superb Davis Cup record, winning 10 of 12 Challenge Round matches.

Although he lacked an imposing physique, Laver was a spectacular shotmaker with an extremely effective topspin backhand generated by his massive forearm. His speed, delicately disguised shots, aggression and concentration brought him 21 titles at the world's Big Four tournaments, including 11 singles crowns.

After 1976 Laver had virtually retired from tournament play and was devoting the major portion of his time to his business commitments.

Laver and his bride walk under an arch of tennis racquets after their 1966 wedding in San Rafael, California.

Given Name: Rodney George Laver
Born: August 9, 1938, Rockhampton, Queensland, Australia
Married: Mary Benson, 1966, 1 child
Highlights: One of the all time great tennis players. Only one ever to win Two Grand Slams, (Australian, French, British, and U.S. singles championships) in 1962 and 1969.

Billie Jean King and Laver dance at the Lawn Tennis Association Ball in 1968 following their Wimbledon singles victories.

SPORTS

Joe Louis

He was one of the most popular heavyweight boxing champions ever to hold the title, and he reigned longer than any champion before or since—just four months short of 12 years. But his ability to destroy opponents in the ring was matched by a tendency to self-destruction out of it.

Louis made millions in the ring, but was left with very little to show for it when he finally retired. He was a self-admitted "high liver", generous in the extreme, and naive in financial management. He had many lengthy and expensive disputes with the Internal Revenue Service, and was forced to come out of retirement in 1949 to earn the money to pay his debts.

At 6'2" and 200 pounds, Louis had the size and the power to put opponents away with one punch, which he did frequently, and quickly. Most of his victories came with early-round knockouts, and his career record of 68 wins against only 3 losses with 54 knockouts, is one of the best in the history of boxing. In the ring, Louis showed none of the anger, hatred or emotion that some fighters bring with them inside the ropes. He simply saw boxing as his trade, and went about laying out his opponents with the same workmanlike attitude that a bricklayer might bring to his task. With the grace and confidence of a stalking panther, he would move in on his prey, perhaps exchanging a few harmless punches. Then a powerful left or right would get through his opponent's guard, and be followed instantly by a dazzling combination of short, jolting punches that would almost inevitably leave the other fighter on the canvas. Louis would turn, walk indifferently to a neutral corner, and wait impassively for the referee to finish the count that would bring him another knockout victory.

Louis first won the heavyweight title on June 22, 1937 when he knocked out James J. Braddock in the eighth round. Before that fight, Louis had established an amateur record of 50-4, with 43 knockouts, and a professional record of 35-1, with 31 knockouts. His one professional loss had come at the hands of Germany's Max Schmeling, who had knocked Louis out in the 12th round of their 1937 bout. In 1938, public emotion ran high for the Louis-Schmeling rematch, especially since the Nazi propaganda machine had said that Schmeling would "prove" the "superiority" of the Aryan race. Louis, much against his will, was cast as the flag carrier for both his race and his country. And he carried both flags high. Seething with anger and injured pride, Louis gave the German such a terrible beating in the first round that Schmeling was in the hospital for a week.

By the time Louis entered the Army in 1942, he had defeated every challenger in sight. After 3 years in the service, during which he put on 96 exhibitions for over 2,000,000 soldiers, he came back to again knock out Billy Conn, the last fighter to give him a tough match before the war. Then, in 1948, following his second defeat of Jersey Joe Walcott, Louis retired, undefeated and champion.

He came out of retirement in 1950 and won 8 of 10 bouts in the next two years, but retired for good after being KO'd by a young Rocky Marciano. Louis, at age 37, simply no longer had the skills and power that had made him one of the greatest heavyweights of all time.

A young, serious Louis shooting pool at his New Jersey training site before his 1935 bout with Max Baer.

In 1940, the heavyweight champion tried a little skiing while in training for a bout with Johnny Paycheck.

In 1937, the Brown Bomber sang the blues over not being allowed to play softball while in training.

Given Name: Joseph Louis Barrow
Born: May 13, 1914, Lafayette, Alabama
Married: Marva Trotter, 1945, 2 children (divorced 1949)
Married: Rose Morgan, 1955 (annulled)
Married: Martha Malone Jefferson
Highlights: World heavyweight boxing champion, 1937-1949. Won 68 of 71 professional bouts, including 54 by knockout.
Died: April 12, 1981

Martina Navratilova

In 1986 when Martina Navratilova won the women's singles tennis championship at Wimbledon, England for the seventh time she continued a winning streak she's been on, with only a few losses interrupting it, since she asked for political asylum in the U.S. in 1975.

The streak puts her well on her way to being the greatest female tennis player of all time. Only one other player, Suzanne Lenglen, has won five Wimbledon titles in succession, a feat Martina bested with her last win. Margaret Court is the only female with more titles. Chris Evert Lloyd, who ruled tennis for nearly a decade, has a longevity edge on Martina. But Martina is fast smashing ahead of friend and frequent doubles partner Lloyd with the pounding drive of her famous and decidedly un-feminine volley. The lefthander has won so many tournaments with her strong serve and all-over-the-court game that sometimes when she enters the women's locker room her tour-mates simply bow.

The world's ranking woman player, Martina makes a habit of "firsts": the first player to win three grand slam events (Wimbledon, France, Australia); the first athlete, male or female, to top 10 million dollars in earnings.

When the then 18-year-old Martina defected it had nothing to do with politics. On tour with the Czech team she got a telegram from her government demanding that she return home. "They put a lot of time and money into training me", she said. "The more I won, the less they could control me. When I got to the top, they got nervous. The trouble started at Wimbledon when I started socializing with Chris, and Billy Jean King, and Rosie Casals. The government thought I was getting too Americanized. They wanted to restrict my career—and keep the money I was making."

Martina says it was easy to be Americanized. In her book *Being Myself*, published in 1985, she says one of the first things she did with her money was buy a Mercedes-Benz. She says she used to say she'd quit tennis when she was 30, but when she got to be 30 she found herself at the top, and decided to stick around for a while. She created quite a stir in her book by describing her sexual preference for women.

In 1986 Martina received a visa to return for the first time since her defection to Czechoslovakia where, as a member of the American team, she competed for the Federation Cup. When she won, it was the first time the Cup had been won by the same player playing for two different countries. While there she was able to see her family, whom she misses—her mother, who used to accompany her on tours, her stepfather, who trained her, her younger sister. Down deep, of course, says the star who seems to be enjoying every minute of life in the United States, I'll always be a Czech.

Navratilova holds up the winners' check from the 1980 Lion's Ladies Cup played in Tokyo.

Given Name: Martina Navratilova
Born: October 18, 1956, Prague, Czechoslovakia
Unmarried
Highlights: World's leading female tennis player, perhaps of all time. Has won 7 Wimbledon singles championships, more than any player in history.

Navratilova reacts to a shot at the 1985 United States Open—she won the match easily, as usual, 6-0, 6-1.

SPORTS

Jack Nicklaus

By the time he turned 26, Jack Nicklaus was recognized as one of golf's greatest champions of all time. The strong man from Columbus, Ohio was not only the most prodigious hitter of all, but he mastered the mental side of the game. He transformed himself from a 15-year-old boy who found it difficult to control his temper when he played poorly to a mature and calm individual who ranked among the biggest gallery favorites.

When Jack Nicklaus turned professional in November. 1961, he left behind perhaps the greatest amateur golf career since the fabulous Bobby Jones. Then he went on to win 20 major championships and more than $4.6 million in 25 seasons, both career records for the sport.

A standout in baseball, basketball and golf while in high school, Nicklaus was 16 when he won the Ohio Open. While still a student at Ohio State University he won the National Amateur title in 1960. In 1959, as a member of the 9-man Walker Cup team, he won both of his matches as the Americans defeated the British at Muirfield, Scotland.

He was U.S. Amateur Champion twice, 1959 and 1961; won the Masters six times (1963, 1966, 1972, 1975, 1986); the Professional Golfer's Association (PGA) five times (1963, 1971, 1973, 1980); the U.S. open four times (1962, 1967, 1972, 1980); and the British Open three times (1966, 1970, 1978).

When he was voted the 1967 PGA Player of the Year, Jack broke all money records and became the only golfer ever to win more than $100,000 in more than five years. And when a poll of professional golfers was made as to who among them played each of the club categories the best, most of them elected Jack the expert with the long-irons.

Born in Columbus, Ohio, on January 21, 1940, Jack Nicklaus was introduced to golf by his father and Scioto Country Club pro, Jack Grout. By the time he was 13, Nicklaus was playing in national tournaments and the year 1961 saw him become the youngest man ever to win the U.S. Open when he upset none other than Arnold Palmer.

As a young man Jack Nicklaus rocketed into prominence as he displayed his great ability by going straight and long off the tees, his average drive being around 280 yards. His booming drives together with the extraordinary length of his iron game placed him among the longest hitters the game has known. Meticulous study of the course, including the charting of distances, combined with an incredible power of concentration, propelled Jack into the limelight of modern golf.

In 1985 Jack Nicklaus continued on the golf circuits, pressing to win his 20th major tournament. At that time he said, "I'm a believer that one doesn't lose his skills through age in the mid-40's. Hogan and Snead played their best golf in their 40's. One (only) loses his skills through lack of work and lack of discipline."

A year later, the 46-year-old Nicklaus who was referring to "the December of my career", won the Masters with a brilliant final round. That win gave him his 20th "major," and made hiim the oldest Masters champion ever. (He had also been the youngest champion ever when he won his first title in 1963.) He had been playing competitive tournament golf for 25 years and had won 18 major professional championships. Although Nicklaus continues to play on the PGA Tour, he has begun to curtail his playing schedule in order to devote more time to skiing, tennis, sport fishing and active management of his far-flung business empire. In 1979 a poll of U.S. sportswriters and broadcasters chose Nicklaus as the Athlete of the Decade, testifying to the fact that he is considered the greatest golfer in the history of the game.

Nicklaus takes an ice cream break during a practice round for the 1980 United States Open.

Jack Nicklaus and family in 1978.

Given Name: Jack William Nicklaus
Born: January 21, 1940, Columbus, Ohio
Married: Barbara Bash, July 1960, 4 children
Highlights: Generally considered the greatest golfer ever. Winner of more major championships than any player in history. Also active in golf course design and real estate development.

Pele

"As far as I can remember, Edson always wanted to become an idol, to prove himself to the world," said Celeste Nascimento, mother of the man known as the king of professional soccer.

What drove the fabulous Edson Arantes do Nascimento, better known as Pele, to become the world's greatest soccer player? Doctor Athayde Ribeiro, the Brazilian soccer player's former psychologist has this opinion: "Ever since he was a child Pele was always seeking perfection, was over-demanding with himself, and always unhappy when he did not find himself at the top."

For decades, soccer has been an international obsession. Its legions of fans are known for a fervor so fierce that soccer riots have become frequent occurrences after important games. But the sport never fared very well in the United States. It was hoped that Pele's charisma would attract fans to the game when he came out of retirement to sign a multi-million dollar contract with the New York Cosmos of the North American Soccer League in June 1975.

Pele, called by fans, "The Black Pearl", was a fine runner and jumper in a non-stop sport that demands these qualities. Sports writers praised him lavishly for being able to "kick and corral a soccer ball with tireless deftness and agility." By October 1974, when Pele announced his retirement from pro soccer after a remarkable 18-year career he had scored 1,216 goals in 1,253 games, the largest number by a single player. He also held the record for most goals scored by a pro player in a single match: eight goals in 1964. He was the only player in history to play on three World Cup winning teams, leading Brazil to titles in 1958, 1962 and 1970. Also, in 1970, after winning the World Cup, Pele was chosen the most valuable player by fans and foreign critics.

Pele was born in 1941 in a poor Brazilian village, Tres Corascos. As a child the unschooled Pele worked as a cobbler's assistant and polished shoes in the backward interior of Brazil. He was reported as having turned to sports to overcome the serious problems of poverty, no education and racism.

He was married in 1966 to a schoolteacher from Santos. He and his wife have two children. In May 1984 the Brazilian superstar of soccer told the press "my athletic phase definitely is over." At 43, Pele had retired from soccer twice, once in 1974 and again in 1977, after his three-year contract with the New York Cosmos had expired.

During the next seven years Pele worked at his various business interests while his sports image continued in U.S. commercials and movies. Then he again appeared in the public eye when he publicly joined the campaign to direct elections for the next president of Brazil, openly opposing the ruling military regime. At that time he said, "When I defend the right to vote I'm not getting involved in politics. I'm defending a right every citizen has."

Although the former sports star claimed to be apolitical, he said, "What really hurts me is to see a country like Brazil, which has no problem with foreign wars or internal guerrillas, faced with so much injustice." Along with speaking out against Brazil's rightist military-run government, Pele was making a new movie based on a play by a Brazilian writer.

Pele (Edson Arantes do Nascimento) besieged by British children. He was in England for the 1966 World Cup matches.

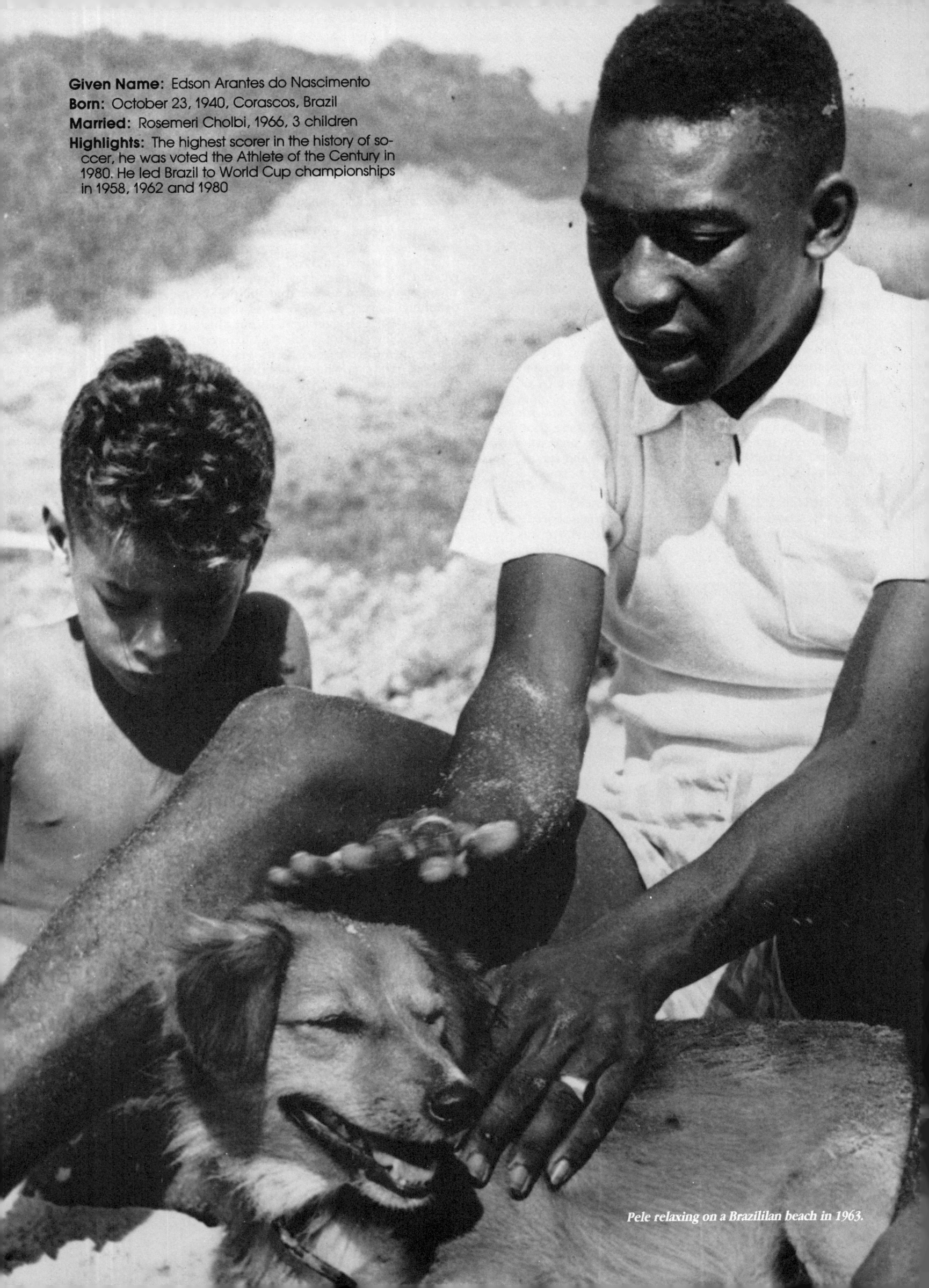

Given Name: Edson Arantes do Nascimento
Born: October 23, 1940, Corascos, Brazil
Married: Rosemeri Cholbi, 1966, 3 children
Highlights: The highest scorer in the history of soccer, he was voted the Athlete of the Century in 1980. He led Brazil to World Cup championships in 1958, 1962 and 1980

Pele relaxing on a Brazililan beach in 1963.

Jesse Owens

"Perhaps no athlete better symbolized the human struggle against tyranny, poverty and racial bigotry. His personal triumphs as a world-class athlete and record-holder were the prelude to a career devoted to helping others." That is what President Jimmy Carter said in his tribute to Jesse Owens.

Although he wasn't invited to the White House in the year of his great Olympic performance, Jesse Owens was honored 40 years later when, on August 6, 1976, President Gerald R. Ford presented him with the Presidential Medal of Freedom at the White House. And in February 1979, he received the Living Legends Award from President Carter.

At a meet in Ann Arbor, Michigan on May 25, 1935, the black American track star broke three world's records and tied a fourth in a little more than an hour. He equaled the 100-yd dash at 9.4 sec; then he set a new long-jump record of 26 ft. 8.25 in. He also set records in the 220 yd dash and 220 yd low hurdles with times of 10.3 sec and 22.6 sec respectively.

And in 1936 he went further. At the Olympic games held in Berlin, Germany, Owens won gold medals in the 100 and 200 meter races and the long jump and was on the winning 4 x 100 meter relay team. His wins also carried political overtones by graphically disproving Adolph Hitler's claim of Aryan supremacy.

Once the Berlin Olympics were over it was back to business as usual for Jesse Owens. He received a hero's welcome and a tickertape parade on Broadway, but it was soon apparent the athlete had returned to a United States not yet ready to accept blacks. To meet the economic needs of his wife and three children, Owens worked in an automobile plant for a while, then he became something of a side-show attraction. He toured with the Harlem Globetrotters, running exhibition races at halftime. Another time he earned money racing against a racehorse in Cuba.

Jesse Owens said, "When I came back after all the stories about Hitler and his snub, I came back to my native country and I couldn't ride in the front of the bus. I had to go to the back door. I couldn't live where I wanted . . . I wasn't invited to shake hands with Hitler, but I wasn't invited to the White House to shake hands with the President, either."

Years later his wife, Ruth Owens, said of that time, "After Berlin he came home as a temporary hero. But that died. They made him a lot of promises; movies, endorsements, things like that. The promises were never kept. They said the climate wasn't right for a black man to get so much attention."

But as time passed and blacks began erasing racial barriers Owens was drawn into the fold. Eventually he became a successful businessman, running his own public relations and marketing firm in Chicago, and later in Phoenix.

The man who, at the beginning of his running career was called, "The Buckeye Bullet", launched youth programs, became a national spokesman for the U.S. Olympic movement and America's "Ambassador to Sports."

He was born James Cleveland Owens on September 12, 1913 in Oakville, Alabama and by the time he was seven he was in the fields picking cotton. The son of a share-cropper, Owens began running when he was nine and he achieved record-setting track performances in high school. Defying bias and humiliation he earned a scholarship which gained him a college education at Ohio State University. He and fighter Joe Louis did more than any others—perhaps even baseball's Jackie Robinson—to break the bonds of racial discrimination.

When accused by some of the more militant of his race of being an "Uncle Tom," Owens replied, "My job here is not to complain. It is to try to make this a better world." Wherever he appeared, kids, black and white, gravitated to him. He had a rare gift of speech and his message was always one of moderation; love your country, love your neighbor, judge a man by his deeds not his race, religion or creed.

The track and field records Owens set in 1935 secured his place of fame for 40 years, until in 1975 the last of his records was broken. Jesse Owens died March 31, 1980 in Phoenix, Arizona at age 66. He had achieved the finest one-day showing in track history.

After his return from the 1936 Olympics in Germany, Owens toured the country as a song and dance man. He is shown here rehearsing in 1937.

Given Name: James Cleveland Owens
Born: September 12, 1913, Danville, Alabama
Married: Ruth Solomon, 1931, 3 children
Highlights: Won 4 gold medals at 1936 Olympics in Munich, Germany. In winning the long jump, he set a record that stood for over 30 years
Died: March 31, 1980

Before leaving for Munich, Jesse Owens treated photographers to some saxophone solos.

SPORTS

Jackie Robinson

"They'll taunt you and goad you," Branch Rickey said to 28-year-old Jackie Robinson in August 1947. "They'll do anything to make you react. They'll try to provoke a race riot in the ball park. Robinson, I'm looking for a ballplayer with guts enough not to react."

And Jackie was that ballplayer, because he was an extraordinary man. Although a dazzling all-around athlete, Robinson will be remembered as the man who exploded the major leagues' racial barrier with the old Brooklyn Dodgers. At the end of Robinson's life baseball commissioner Bowie Kuhn said, "His entire life was courage. Courage as the black pioneer of the game. Courage as a player. Courage in the way he fought for what he believed."

Robinson was born in Cairo, Georgia on January 31, 1919, the youngest of five children. His father deserted the struggling family a year later and his mother moved her offspring to Pasadena, California. Even on the southern California sandlots, Jackie demonstrated such superior skill that other kids would buy him sandwiches and drinks just so they could be on Robinson's team. Later, Robinson would chuckle, "You might say that I turned pro at a very early age."

Robinson's skill carried him to athletic fame at Pasadena Junior College and then as a football-basketball-track hero at UCLA at the end of World War II. He had played semi-pro football for the old Los Angeles Bulldogs in 1941, then went to war as a cavalry lieutenant. A chipped ankle-bone injury kept him from overseas duty and Jackie was discharged in 1944. Jackie was an All-American runner, averaging 12 yards a carry one year for the Bruin football team. He set a Pacific Coast Conference broad jump record and lead the league in basketball scoring. But baseball was to be his ultimate game.

The Kansas City Monarchs, members of a Negro baseball league, signed Robinson in 1945 as a $400 a month shortstop. He was there when Branch Rickey, boss of the Brooklyn Dodgers, said he wanted a black ballplayer who had the guts not to fight back when the tough times came.

Robinson accepted the challenge to play with the 'white boys' at Montreal, then the Dodgers' Triple A farm club. Jackie lead the International League with a blazing .349 average in 24 games and was obviously ready, athletically, for the shot at the major leagues. During the season with Montreal, Robinson's appearance caused new problems for an old game. Spring training games were cancelled in Florida cities not willing to stand for a black kid playing baseball with whites.

But things became easier, if not totally pleasant, during the Fifties. Robinson soon had fellow blacks around the major leagues and by the time he quit in 1956 the National League was already becoming dominated by Negro sensations. As a tough and challenging batter, Robinson crowded the plate and was often hit by pitched balls. He was a daring, menacing baserunner who frayed the nerves of pitchers and catchers.

Robinson was brought to Brooklyn in 1947, where he hit .297, scored 125 runs and led the league in stolen bases (29) as the Dodgers won their first pennant since 1941, and he was named Rookie of the Year. By 1949 he was named the league's Most Valuable Player, leading the league in batting (.342) and stolen bases (37) in addition to scoring 122 runs and batting in 124 runs while reaching a career high of 203 hits. He was an outstanding fielder as well, leading the league in fielding average three times at his position. He was selected five times an all-star infielder. Primarily a second baseman, he also played at third and first base and in the outfield. He played 10 seasons, batting .311. In 1962, his first year of eligibility, he was the first black to be enshrined in baseball's Hall of Fame.

Ranked among the greats in sports, Jackie Robinson is revered for his quiet courage, standing up to the open hostility and resentment he received for being the first man to break the color line in baseball. He retired into a successful business career and became an eloquent spokesman for the cause of civil rights and human dignity.

Jackie Robinson died on October 24, 1972. In a tribute to this pioneer in human relations, Allan Barron, publisher of Black Sports Magazine, said that Robinson "will stand out as a symbol of majestic, black, human dignity."

Given Name: Jack Roosevelt Robinson
Born: January 31, 1919, Cairo, Georgia
Married: Rachel Isum, 1946, 3 children
Highlights: First black man to play Major League baseball. Elected to baseball Hall of Fame in 1962.
Died: October 24, 1972

Jackie Robinson in 1970, happily retired from baseball after becoming the first black to play in the major leagues.

"Babe" Ruth

Ruth stamped an indelible mark on the American game, and changed baseball forever. But more importantly, he was a living legend, and a living embodiment of his time. The era known as "The Roaring Twenties" and "The Golden Age of Sport" belonged to him as no era ever belonged to an athlete.

Ruth played hard, both on and off the field, and his every move was eagerly followed by press and public. Crowds surrounded him wherever he went. Children loved him, and adult fans followed suit. In an age of excess, his vast appetite for food, and other temporal pleasures, drew more approbation than opprobrium. And when, in 1925, a "stomach ache" put him in the hospital and out of the line-up for 50 days, all America waited eagerly for his return.

The object of a nation's affection hardly looked like a sculptor's vision of a hero. Ruth was six-feet-two and 200 pounds, but looked "like a beer keg on short stilts". His top-heavy body was crowned with a large head, big ears, and a broad, flat nose that spread halfway across his face, as if it had stopped a few fastballs. On most men, it would have been a face only a mother could love. On Ruth, it was a face everyone loved.

His popularity was due as much to his attitudes as his baseball exploits. In an era when players were almost powerless in their negotiations with owners, Ruth was directly responsible for a major increase in players' salaries. When it was announced the Ruth would make the then amazing sum of $80,000 in 1930, a reporter asked him how he justified making $5,000 a year more than the President of the United States. Ruth's response was simple and to the point. "I had a better year than Mr. Hoover," he said.

Even though the game of baseball had not spread much beyond America's shores in his time, Ruth's fame did. During World War II, Japanese troops attacking U.S. Marine positions used his name in a strange battle cry. "To hell with Babe Ruth", they shouted as they charged American guns.

The man whom a nation loved did not get off to an auspicious start in life. He was born George Herman Gerhardt, but was orphaned at an early age, and had his name changed to Ruth while living in St. Mary's Industrial School in Baltimore, Maryland. Brother Gilbert, one of the school's faculty, recognized Ruth's prodigious baseball talents, and invited a scout for the Baltimore Orioles to see him play. After watching Ruth in just one game, the scout signed him to a contract as a pitcher for $600 a year. The rest is history that's become legend.

During his 22 year baseball career (1914–1935) Ruth held 76 major league records—so many that the statisticians gave him an entire section to himself in the record books. Although he started as a pitcher, and was one of the best at that position, he was switched to the outfield so his powerful bat could be in the line-up every day. Then his home-run hitting changed the game of baseball from a pitcher's stronghold to a batter's paradise.

In response to fan reaction to Ruth's homers, the ball was changed to put more "rabbit" in it. New York's Yankee Stadium, erected in 1925, became known as "the house that Ruth built". Almost singlehandedly, the big happy-go-lucky "Bambino" brought back the fans who had been driven away by the game-fixing "Black Sox" scandal of 1919 and the dull, pitcher-dominated games of the pre-Ruth era.

Ruth hit more home runs in a season (60) and a career (714) than any man ever had. He also struck out more times (1330). And in those contradictory records, perhaps, lie the secret of the man. Because whatever Ruth did, he did on a grand scale. Moderation was simply not in his nature.

In an age of immoderation, that made him probably the most-loved man in America.

Ruth rehearsing for a 1936 movie short, "Home Run on the Keys"

Given Name: George Herman Gerhard
Born: February 6, 1984, Baltimore, Maryland
Married: Helen Woodford, 1914, 1 child
Married: Claire Hodgson, 1929
Highlights: The most popular, productive and charismatic baseball player of all time. He s[et] dozens of records, including 60 home runs in a season, 714 in a career.
Died: August 16, 1948

Babe Ruth in 1947, practicing chip shots on his lawn in Miami.

Babe Didrikson Zaharias

Even in a state that is famous for doing everything on a larger-than-life scale, Babe Didrikson Zaharias stood head and shoulders above all the other female athletes . . . and most of the men. In fact, her talents and accomplishments were so many that they might sound to some like Texas fiction. But they were real.

She may well have been the most gifted and versatile female athlete to ever compete at the national and international levels. Speed, strength, agility, vision, coordination were all hers in abundance. She also had courage, confidence, and a fierce competitive spirit that helped propel her to one record after another, in one sport after another.

At the 1932 Olympics, at age 19, she won the javelin throw and the 80-meter hurdles by setting world records. She also tied for the high-jump gold medal, but was disqualified for diving over the bar head first. And, had a three-event limit not kept her out of the sprints and broad jump, she might well have won several other medals. A year earlier, at the AAU national championships, she had won the 100-yard, dash, 200 yard dash, discus, and broad jump, in addition to her "best" events.

"Babe"—her given middle name, not a nickname—was also a two-time All America basketball player, an outstanding baseball and softball player, and an exhibition-caliber billiards artist. Her best game, though, was golf.

In one stretch, in 1946 and 1947, she won 17 straight tournaments, a feat that will probably never be duplicated, or even approached. She won the World's Championship three years running (1949-51), and a total of 82 tournaments from the time her golfing career began in 1935 until it was ended by illness in 1953. Although her list of titles included just about every major women's event (she had planned to enter the 1947 U.S. Men's Open, but was ruled ineligible), her greatest victory came at the Serbin Women's Invitational late in 1953, following cancer surgery.

"I guess I'll have to call this the biggest thrill of my life," she said after winning the tournament. "I didn't think I would ever win another one."

Her entry into golf was purely accidental. While shopping for a party dress, she passed a sporting goods store and was attracted by a set of clubs in the window. Intrigued, she bought the clubs and took up the game, which she found easy from the start. She shot 95 on her first round, and not long afterward won medalist honors with a 77 in the first tournament she ever entered. From then on, the outspoken and confident Texan, whose 5'6" frame seemed far too small for her giant feats, set record after record. She also set an example of competitive desire and true courage for all the athletes, and particularly the women, who followed her into competitive sports.

Zaharias after winning the 1950 All-American Women's Open Golf Tourney at Tam O'Shanter country club near Chicago.

Given Name: Mildred Babe Didrikson
Born: June 26, 1912, Port Arthur, Texas
Married: George Zaharias, 1938
Highlights: "The Greatest Woman Athlete of the 20th Century" according to an Associated Press poll in 1949. After winning Olympic gold medals in track and field, she became the leading female professional golfer.
Died: September 27, 1956

Zaharias in Guillane, Scotland after the second day of the British Women's Amateur Championship, 1947. She won it.

SPORTS

SCIENCE, INDUSTRY AND MEDICINE

Alexander Graham Bell

He was described by his father as "hot-headed, but warm-hearted" and "ambitious, to a fault, and apt to let enthusiasm run away with judgment". He was troubled all his life by the universal human need to communicate. He brought his own individual genius to technology and threw the weight of his ability against barriers that held millions apart from their fellow men. This is the story of Alexander Graham Bell and his conquest of solitude for both the deaf and the hearing.

Best known as inventor of the telephone, the Scottish genius, Alexander Graham Bell was also co-inventor of the graphophone, an early type of sound recording, a teacher of Helen Keller, and president of the National Geographic Society.

Along with his insatiable curiosity and life-long desire to help the deaf, versatility and the ability to get things done were the hallmarks of this great man's life. Born March 3, 1847, young Alexander Bell followed the path already pioneered by his father, Alexander Melville Bell and was the second generation to become recognized as a leading authority in elocution and speech correction. A teacher-scientist, Alexander Graham's early achievements on behalf of the deaf and his invention of the telephone before his 30th birthday bear testimony to the thoroughness of his early training.

During his lifetime, the range of his inventiveness is represented in part by the 18 patents granted in his name alone and the 12 he shared with collaborators. These include 14 for the telephone and telegraph, four for the photophone, one for the phonograph, five for aerial vehicles, four for hydroairplanes and two for a selenium cell.

Although his personal life was marked by periodic bouts with ill health, Alexander continued his experiments with sound. In 1872 he trained teachers for the deaf in a school he opened in Boston and a year later he became professor of vocal physiology at Boston University. As Bell taught the deaf to speak during the day at his full time teaching job, he continued his scientific pursuits at night with a young repair mechanic and model maker, Thomas Watson. And on April 6, 1875, Alexander Graham Bell ws granted the patent for his multiple telegraph.

This was a beginning. Two basic principles had been discovered many years before; electromagnetism and induction (using sound to vary a current). Working along the lines that the human ear was the most perfect instrument in all nature for detecting and recording sound, Bell envisioned a membrane receiver that could be modeled closely after the ear and wondered, was it possible that sounds sent over a steel wire could register in the form of speech in a receiver so designed? And further, could a human voice generate strong enough electrical impulses all by itself to be sent over a steel wire, creating, in effect, a magneto telephone?

It could, and it did. While he recuperated from exhaustion at his parents' home in Canada, Bell began to write the specifications for the telephone. And on March 7, 1876, the United States Patent Office granted him Patent Number 174,465 and stated, "the method of, and apparatus for, transmitting vocal or other sound telegraphically . . . by causing electrical undulations, similar in form to the vibrations of the air accopmpanying the said vocal or other sounds,"—and the invention of the telephone was officially recognized.

Within a year the commercial application followed and, a few months later, the first of hundreds of legal suits, which eventually were won as Bell's claims were upheld as being the first to conceive and apply the undulatory current. In 1877, Bell married Mable Hubbard, a deaf student to whom he had given lessons in speech. From there he went on to continued experiments, and achievements in communication which culminated in the invention of the photophone—transmission of sound on a beam of light; in medical research; and in techniques for teaching speech to the deaf.

His lifelong struggle for, and association with the cause of the deaf brought him world-wide attention and in 1880 France honored Bell with the Volta Prize and the award money financed the Volta Laboratory—today an international information center relating to the oral education of the deaf.

Using a chord of steel. Alexander Graham Bell bound the world together and ushered in a new era for communication between people never before known.

In 1906, Bell posed for this photo with the men who had strung a telephone line from his home in Brantford, Ontario to his father's home in Paris, Ontario. It was the world's first long distance telephone line.

Given Name: Alexander Graham Bell
Born: March 3, 1847, Edinburgh, Scotland
Married: Mable Gardiner, 1877
Highlights: Inventor of the telephone, and of many devices and systems for educating the deaf.
Died: August 2, 1922

George Washington Carver

In a lecture to his students, George Washington Carver prophetically observed, "The great Creator gave us three kingdoms, the animal, the vegetable and the mineral. Now He has added a fourth—the kingdom of synthetics."

And indeed, the man who has been called 'the slave who freed the South', was one of the first chemist-scientists to lay a foundation for the new science of chemurgy; the creation of wealth from the dormant power of the soil and air and sun.

Although the exact date of his birth (1859?) is shrouded in mystery, a boy who was born a slave near Diamond Grove, Mo., grew up to become a master at extracting secrets from plants. George Washington Carver revolutionized the agriculture of the South by developing more than 300 products from peanuts, 118 products from sweet potatoes and 75 products from pecans.

As a child Carver was known as "the plant doctor", and as an adult his keen interest in studying plants and their growth habits enabled him to later create synthetic marble from peanut hulls and wood waste; dyes from clay; and starch, gum and wallboard from cotton stalks. And substituting cellulose for steel, automobile-makers would soon be building 350 pounds of agricultural products into every car.

Although Carver's ambition was to be an artist—he studied art at Simpson College in Indianola, Iowa and earned his way by cooking, taking in laundry and working as a janitor, he decided to study horticulture, and in 1896 graduated with a master's degree from Iowa State Agricultural College. Accepting an appointment there as an assistant botanist, Carver took charge of the greenhouse he started, and of the fungus collection that later grew to about 20,000 species which brought him professional fame.

That same year Carver was invited by Booker T. Washington, the noted American Negro Educator, to join the staff of Tuskegee Institute in Alabama and today the Institute houses a museum of Carver's discoveries, collections and paintings.

He spent the rest of his life at Tuskegee, slowly creating a laboratory, rebuilding the exhausted land around the Institute and pursuing research. Much of the South's farming land had been depleted as a result of intensive cultivation of cotton and tobacco and as Carver experimented with nitrogen-producing legumes he found that peanuts and sweet potatoes both improved the soil and grew abundantly there. It was his work in finding new uses for these crops that led him to develop an encyclopedic array of agricultural by-products.

His fame as a scientist and educator grew throughout the world and Carver was honored as few Americans have been. In 1916 he became a Fellow in the Royal Society of Arts in London, and won the Spingarn medal for distinguished service in agricultural chemistry in 1923. In 1935 he became collaborator in the Bureau of Plant Industry of the U.S. Department of Agriculture and received the Roosevelt medal in 1939 for his valuable contributions to science. By the time of his death on January 5, 1943, George Washington Carver had become one of American's most honored scientists.

Dr. George Washington Carver in 1939.

It had been a long hard road. For her doctoral thesis, Mme. Marie Curie had decided to study the mysterious radiation discovered in 1896 by Henri Becquerel. While checking the strength of radiation emitted from uranium compounds she made the unexpected discovery that uranium pitchblende and the mineral chalcolite emitted about four times as much radiation as could be expected from their uranium content. In 1898 she drew the revolutionary conclusion that pitchblende contained a small amount of an unknown radiating element.

Pierre Curie immediately understood the importance of this hypothesis and joined his wife's work. Up until that time no one had "seen" radium. Nobody knew the atomic weight of radium and they began the tedious and monumental task of isolating the elements so their chemical properties could be determined; demonstrating to an incredulous world that radium had measurable atomic weight and did exist. M. and Mme Curie labored four years, battling against lack of money with which to buy pitchblende, the costly ore in which polonium and radium were hidden.

Born Manya Sklodowska in Warsaw, Poland, on November 7, 1867, she was the daughter of an impoverished and patriotic professor in a Poland still in the iron clutch of Russia. After many impoverished years as a teacher and governess, she joined her sister Bronia in Paris and there earned degrees in mathematics and physics at the Sorbonne. In the spring of 1895 she met the physicist Pierre Curie, married him a year later and combining their efforts, the couple went on to score their first achievements in science, still largely ignored by the world.

Pierre Curie headed the laboratory at the Ecole de Physique et de Chimie Industrielle in Paris and had already distinguished himself, along with his brother Jacques, in the study of the properties of crystals.

In 1903, Marie Curie obtained her doctorate for a thesis on radioactive substances, and with her husband and Henri Becquerel, she won the Nobel Prize for physics for the joint discovery of radioactivity. The following year Pierre was killed in a street accident and Marie overcame this blow only by putting all her energy into the scientific work that they had begun together.

She became the first female lecturer at the Sorbonne, and in 1908 she was appointed professor. In 1911, Marie Curie received a second Nobel Prize for chemistry for the isolation of pure radium. By 1918 she was dedicated entirely to the development of X rays in medicine and was the director of the scientific department of the Radium Institute, which she had planned with her husband.

Madame Marie Curie, discoverer of radium, twice winner of the Nobel Prize, the greatest of all women scientists, whose work gave medicine a powerful new weapon died on July 4, 1934.

Pierre Curie

Thomas Edison

Not every one of the inventions of Thomas Alva Edison, America's most prolific inventor, was a success. Out of the 1093 patents granted him by the U.S. Patent Office—the most ever granted a single person—there were bound to be some flops. One was the perpetual cigar, a stogie with a hollow tube and spring-loaded plunger that pushed a wad of tobacco toward a flame near the mouthpiece. Another was the substitution of goldenrod for rubber. A third was cement furniture. Some, though, changed the course of history—his system of electric lighting, the phonograph and a moving picture camera flooded the end of the 19th century with light, music and motion pictures and ushered in modern times.

Edison was a demon for work. When he got an idea, he couldn't stop. He'd work for 60 hours straight with only a few cat naps. He was an inspiration to the teams of scientists at Menlo Park, New Jersey, where he ran the first research center in America. Team efforts and findings from experiments that failed as well as from those that succeeded produced the inventions that made Edison a folk hero often called "The Genius of Menlo Park."

His early inventions were related to telegraphy, which he'd studied when he was 16—his formal education till then consisted of three months in elementary school in Ohio, where he grew up. In his late teens he travelled the Midwest as a telegraph operator. His first invention was a "diplex." useful for transmitting two messages at once in the same direction. In 1877 he became a celebrity after his cylindrical phonograph, which emitted crude sounds stored on tinfoil tape, proved to be the first successful attempt to record sound.

Edison's notebooks are so crammed with ideas that they've been compared to those of Leonardo Da Vinci, the artist-inventor of the Italian Renaissance. But Edison was not an artist—he was a technician.

Before Edison, famous at 35, pulled the switch that gave the world its first incandescent light system, he and his researchers had applied for over 200 patents for components of the system, from dynamos to household sockets. He had experimented with over 6000 materials before he found that common sewing thread, which he carbonized, made the best filament for the light bulb.

He wasn't the first or the only inventor who'd come up with the incandescent lightbulb but he was the first to produce a long-lasting bulb that could be used commercially.

In the summer of 1881, 1500 men began digging up the streets of lower Manhattan to lay cables for Edison's light system, which was backed by tycoon J.P. Morgan. In 1882 Edison turned on the lights for Edison Lighting Company's 59 original customers. Today Sweet's Restaurant on Fulton Street is the only one still on its original site.

The electrical revolution set off on Pearl Street spawned the elevators, electric motor cars and subways that would shape the modern 20th Century city, its glamour and vitality symbolized by, and sparkling under, electric light.

Given Name: Thomas Alva Edison
Born: February 11, 1847, Milan, Ohio
Married: Mary G. Stillwell 1873, 2 children
Highlights: Inventor of incandescent electric bulb, telegraph and phonograph motion pictures, alkaline battery.
Died: October 18, 1931.

Thomas A. Edison examines film in his laboratory in 1889.

Albert Einstein

To one British scholar, he was "the Newton of the 20th Century, a man who has called forth a greater revolution of thought than even Copernicus, Galileo or Newton himself." To the man on the street, he was the living embodiment of the word "genius", and the man whose ideas led to the development of atomic energy.

Albert Einstein achieved world renown in 1905, at age 26, when he expounded his Special Theory of Relativity. That theory postulated the existence of atomic energy. It also held that there was a gravitational bending of light from the stars as the rays passed the sun, and Einstein himself said that observations of the next eclipse of the sun would prove him right. When the eclipse came, in 1919, British scientific expeditions took photographs from remote locations in Brazil and off Africa. Their observations did prove the validity of Einstein's theory, and one British scientist said that Einstein's calculation was "one of the greatest—perhaps the greatest—of achievements in the history of human thought." In 1921, he received the Nobel Prize in physics.

In many ways, Einstein perfectly fit the classic picture of the "absent-minded professor". He was a theoretical physicist who could ferret out the secrets of the universe using only a pen and a pad of paper, yet, by his own admission, needed the help of an expert to fill out his income tax form. Money meant little to him, and he regularly rejected the large sums that were offered to him for articles and testimonials. His work kept him so busy that he turned over complete responsibility for his financial affairs to his wife

Albert Einstein in his Princeton, New Jersey home about 1950.

On an Adirondack vacation in 1936.

SCIENCE, INDUSTRY AND MEDICINE

and then, after her death, to his secretary.

Einstein was born in Ulm, Germany, then grew up in Munich until the family moved to Milan, Italy after his father's business failed when Einstein was 15. Earlier, starting at age 11, he had taught himself geometry, algebra, analytical geometry, integral and differential calculus ... none of which were taught in school. After being turned down once for his deficiencies in languages and the natural sciences, he was admitted to the Polytechnic Academy in Zurich and graduated in 1900. He had a difficult time for two years, and nearly starved until a former classmate helped him get a job as a patent examiner in Bern. That position gave him time to pursue his calculations during working hours, since he was able to do in only an hour what it took others a whole day to complete. In 1905, eight years after he had started it while at school, his Special Theory of Relativity was completed.

In 1933, following Nazi reprisals for his outspoken protests against the treatment of the Jews, Einstein emigrated to America. He joined the Institute for Advanced Studies at Princeton, New Jersey as a professor of theoretical physics. He had asked for a salary of just $5000 a year, but the board had prevailed upon him to accept $15,000, explaining that they had to keep up standards. He joined with a group of other leading physicists in 1939 to urge President Roosevelt to support research in nuclear fission. Roosevelt responded to their requests. Although Einstein never had any direct connection with the work of "The Manhattan Project", his theories were the foundation for the awful reality of the atomic bomb.

Einstein and his step-daughter taking the oath of American citizenship on October 1, 1940.

Einstein plays accompaniment to his wife, Elsa, at the Imperial Hotel, Tokyo, November 1922.

Mme. Irene Toliot-Curie visits Einstein in his study in 1948.

SCIENCE, INDUSTRY AND MEDICINE

Einstein continued to work and teach at the Institute, and in 1950, after 30 years of work, proposed his General Theory of Gravitation. It was an attempt to describe, in one law, everything that goes on everywhere from the inside of one tiny atom to the limits of the universe.

He loved to work in baggy, comfortable, almost shapeless clothes, pen in hand, pipe in mouth. When his wife once commented on his dress, he simply quoted Spinoza: "It would be a sad situation if the bag was better than the meat wrapped in it." Despite his worldwide fame, he remained forever modest, and seemed genuinely embarrassed by the acclaim given him. One fellow Nobel laureate said that Einstein was great "because he has shown us our world in truer perspective and has helped us to understand a little more clearly how we are related to the universe around us."

Someone else described him as "a mystic masquerading as a mathematician". But Einstein himself probably preferred the words of a fellow scientist who said "The biggest element in Einstein's greatness is his humility".

His concepts and calculations ushered in the atomic age. But Einstein was a pacifist who warned against the arms race, saying that it was "a disastrous illusion" and that "the annihilation of any life on earth was within the range of technical possibilities." If he were alive today, the short, humble, rumpled genius would probably take wry satisfaction in seeing his image printed on so many wrinkled sweatshirts.

The teaching Einstein, undated.

Elsa and Albert Einstein in the 1920's.

Given Name: Albert Einstein
Born: March 4, 1879, Ulm, Germany
Married: Mileva Marec, 1901, 2 children
Married: Elsa Einstein, 1917
Highlights: Conceived the theories that led to the development of atomic energy and changed the course of history. Won Nobel Prize in physics in 1922.
Died: April 18, 1955

Sir Alexander Fleming

A mold growing on a culture plate left out by chance in an English professor's lab in 1928 started a medical revolution some regard as just as important in the outcome of World War II as the atom bomb. Alexander Fleming named the green mold, which he noticed had dissolved yellow bacteria surrounding it, "penicillin". Ten years later, a project as urgent as the Manhattan Project would produce the "Wonder Drug" penicillin that would save thousands of wounded men's lives.

As a captain in the British Medical Corps serving in France in the first World War, Fleming had observed that antiseptics used on the wounded often appeared to harm healthy flesh even more than they helped combat infection. Fleming, who had experimented unsuccessfully at St. Mary's Hospital in London with his own tears and those of lab technician volunteers, was looking for a better substance with which to treat the germs of Meningitis, strep throat, childbirth disease, and other illnesses. After his 1928 discovery he published a paper on his findings. They attracted little attention, however, until ten years later when Australian-born researcher Howard Florey and German refugee chemist Ernst Chain teamed up at Oxford to make a thorough investigation of every anti-bacterial substance and came across Fleming's report on penicillin in a journal. This lucky meeting of researchers combined with the gathering warclouds over Europe to eventually produce the miracle of medicine for which, in 1945, all three scientists received the Nobel Prize.

Working with mice, Florey and Chain proved the effectiveness of penicillin in fighting infection. When Britain entered the war in 1940 Fleming stated, "It would seem Providence has been kind in letting us have this most powerful agent against septic infections just when it was most wanted—when against our will we are plunged into a bloody war." Work to develop the drug for human use took on the aspects of cloak-and-dagger. Fearing a surprise invasion by the Germans, scientists at the Oxford lab once smeared spores of the fungus on the insides of their coats to hide their specimens from the enemy. After the bombing of London in 1941 Florey and others fled to the United States where, under the wings of the U.S. Department of Agriculture, they continued their work. With the bombing of Pearl Harbor the production of penicillin became a wartime priority for the U.S. Finally proven effective once and for all in treatment of a dying woman in New Haven, Connecticut, in 1942, the drug went into production. It was used exclusively to treat war casualties, but the ban on civilian use was lifted once, after the tragic Coconut Grove fire in Boston, where its effects on burns of survivors were dramatic and well-publicized. By the beginning of 1943 production of the drug, long slowed by the necessity of growing the mold in flat plates, began to take place under a new system in highly automated bottling plants. By D-Day 1944, enough penicillin had been produced to treat every one of the 40,000 allied soldiers wounded at Normandy.

In later years, it was discovered that penicillin not occurring in nature could attack microorganisms resistant to the natural drug. In 1960 semi-synthetic penicillin, which has a far wider therapeutic use than the natural substance, began to be developed.

In 1944 Fleming, who never received any financial remuneration for his discovery, was knighted by the British crown. When he received the Nobel Prize with Florey and Chain in 1945, he reported that the original culture plate where he'd spotted the miraculous green mold was still in his lab at St. Mary's. Today that same plate, badly decomposed now, is at the British Library where observers can also see on a replica what caught his attention and heralded the Age of Anti-Biotics.

Given Name: Alexander Fleming
Born: August 6, 1881, Lochfield, Ayrshire, Scotland
Married: Sarah Marion McElroy, 1915, 1 child
Married: Dr. Amelia Coutsouris-Voureka, 1953
Highlights: Discovered penicillin. Won Nobel Prize in Medicine in 1945.
Died: March 11, 1955

Dr. Salmen Waksman left, discusses his experiments with visiting Nobel laureate Sir Alexander Fleming in 1951.

SCIENCE, INDUSTRY AND MEDICINE

Henry Ford

Henry Ford might be considered an apt symbol of the transition from an agricultural to an industrial America, for few men did more to change the landscape, character and experience of 20th century America.

"I will build a motor car for the great multitude", Ford proclaimed when announcing the birth of the Model T in 1908. In the next nineteen years he sold 15.5 million of the cars in the United States, a million more in Canada and a quarter of a million in England—half the auto output of the world. The horse disappeared so rapidly that the transfer of acreage from hay to other crops caused an agricultural revolution. The automobile became the main prop of the American economy, a stimulant to urbanization—cities spread outward, creating suburbs and housing developments—and to the building of the finest highway system in the world. And the motor age arrived, owing mostly to Henry Ford's vision of the car as the poor man's utility rather than as the rich man's luxury.

Henry Ford was born on July 30, 1863 on a farm near Dearborn, Michigan, and went to the one-room Scotch Settlement School at age seven. However, as a young boy Henry thought farm life much too hard and monotonous. He was interested in mechanical things and his father taught him how to repair the McCormick reaper, and other farm machinery. At thirteen he repaired his first watch with a hand-sharpened shingle nail. Already he seemed to have a knack for taking things apart and putting them together again without any parts left over.

It was 1876 when Henry first saw a machine that moved under its own power. As he and his father were driving to Detroit on their farm wagon, they came across a portable engine and boiler mounted on wheels, with a water tank and coal cart trailing behind. Henry had seen steam engines used for thrashing and sawing wood, but those had been drawn from job to job by horses. This portable boiler, though, was able to move from place to place under its own power and the possibility of a self-propelled vehicle was implanted in young Henry's mind.

In the fall of 1879, sixteen-year-old Henry worked for the Michigan Car Company for only six days, but it was time enough for him to study its rather primitive assembly line for the manufacture of railroad cars. Then, in 1880, he took a job at Detroit Drydock, a shipbuilding firm, and for the first time came in contact with the internal-combustion engine. Henry loved the steam engine, but he knew instinctively that to build a machine that ran on the road he had to learn how to increase power without increasing weight. So he began to think about electricity and gasoline, reading all the catalogs and technical magazines he could find. A short time later he was hired by Westinghouse to service its versatile steam engines in southeastern Michigan and during his spare time Henry worked in his homemade shop and managed to build a small "farm locomotive."

Given Name: Henry Ford
Born: July 30, 1863
Married: Clara J. Bryant, 1888, 1 child
Highlights: Inventor, founder of Ford Motor Company, 1903. Put automobile within reach of common man with Model T and thus changed the face of America.
Died: April 7, 1947

Ford posed in 1915 with his first auto, invented in 1896.

SCIENCE, INDUSTRY AND MEDICINE

A few years later he met Clara Bryant at a New Year's Eve dance in 1886 and married her two years later. Clara was fascinated by a watch Henry had made himself and told her parents what appealed to her was the young man's serious-mindedness, his maturity and his originality. They settled on the farm for several years and then Henry decided to move to Detroit so he could learn something about electricity, knowledge he needed if he was to put together his long-planned gasoline engine. Henry had outlined, on the back of a sheet of organ music, his scheme for a horseless carriage and Clara believed in it as firmly as he did. On September 25, 1891 they packed their furniture into a haywagon and moved to Detroit.

Although he worked full time as the chief engineer for Edison Illumination Company, he also kept a workbench at the Edison plant in a basement room across the alley and a workshop at home where he could concentrate on his obsession. By Christmas Eve, 1893, he made his first working engine using house current to supply the electricity which, in a horseless carriage, would have to come from batteries. Then he pressed on for another three years to make camshafts, crankshafts, pushrods, bearings, piston rings and gears from scratch. Finally, on June 4, 1896 at 4:00 AM, Ford completed his first horseless carriage. The chassis of this four-horsepower "car" was a buggy frame mounted on four bicycle wheels. Its air-cooled motor had two handmade cylinders and a transmission consisting of a belt from the motor to the rear wheels. There was no reverse gear, nor any brakes.

Unlike other automotive inventors who held onto their creations, Henry sold his "quadricycle" to begin work on a second, more expensive, vehicle, backed by an old family friend. William Maybury, the mayor of Detroit, brought in three other men who agreed to provide a few hundred dollars in return for part ownership of Ford's patents. But in 1899 the arrangement collapsed because Henry wanted to perfect his model on the race track. Without brakes, and using a mere 26 horsepower engine, Henry Ford beat out Alexander Winton's 70-horsepower race car in a five mile event. Then in 1902 at the second annual Grosse Pointe race, Henry raced his famous "999" and broke all speed records. Satisfied, Ford turned to manufacturing his passenger car. Six years later he brought out his Model T, which was to be produced for the next twenty years. Henry Ford died in 1947. He was 83 years old.

In addition to his inventions and production miracles, Ford shared profits with employees (in the form of an unprecedented five dollars a day) and with customers (with annual price reductions and rebates on the Model T), and he set up the Ford Sociological Department which fed, housed, trained and educated employees and their families.

On his 79th birthday in 1942, Ford revisited his first car and the small shop in which he built it.

SCIENCE, INDUSTRY AND MEDICINE

Sigmund Freud

He invented the psychchoanalyst, the man with the couch, the listener with a note pad, the detective of dreams, always out of sight of his reclining patient but never really out of mind. His name was Sigmund Freud and his writings systematized the way we look at the mind.

Born May 6, 1856 in Freiberg, Moravia (Now Pribor, Czechoslovakia), the creator of psychoanalysis was the intellectually precocious son of Jakob Freud, a struggling Jewish merchant. The family moved to Vienna when Sigmund was four and by the time he was eight years of age Freud was reading Shakespeare. His literary gifts and insights into human motives and emotions were first apparent in letters he wrote during adolescence. In 1866 he married Martha Bernays and in order to support a wife he turned from research to the clinical practice of neurology.

By that time Freud's interest in hysteria had been stimulated by Josef Breuer's successful use of therapeutic hypnosis and he took up Breuer's "cathartic method." They published their findings in *Studies in Hysteria* (1895) which outlined their "talking cure". This is regarded as the beginning of psychoanalysis.

Breurer lost interest when sexuality emerged as central to Freud's view of neurosis and Freud discarded the cumbersome hypnosis and enlisted his patients' cooperation in "free association". The central discovery of this approach was transference, or the unconscious shift of feelings associated with persons in the patient's past to the therapist.

Breuer's defection and the death of Freud's father (1896) precipitated a crisis for Freud and he responded by entering a period of self-analysis with his friend Wilhelm Fliess, exploring his dreams and fantasies for clues to his childhood sexual passions—his Oedipus complex.

Freud was the first person to scientifically explore the human unconscious mind and his ideas profoundly influenced the shape of modern culture by altering man's view of himself. He wrote *The Interpretation of Dreams* (1900) which was at first all but ignored, then gradually attracted a number of interested followers, including Alfred Adler and C. G. Jung. Both eventually defected to form their own schools of psychology when they could not accept the infantile sexuality idea as pivotal.

With psychoanalysis, Freud added psychological treatment methods to the biological basis of psychiatry and his concepts, such as the powerful influence of the unconscious mind on conscious thought and behavior, have become part of our culture.

One psychiatrist, who uses Freud's techniques only sparingly, said, "If you were to remove this man from history it would have the same devastating effect as removing Thomas Edison." Almost all his enemies and disciples alike acknowledge psychiatry's debt to the goateed, white-haired wizard who first made sense out of the tangle of human emotions.

Three essentials in Freudian theory are the id, the ego, and the superego. The id, totally below the conscious surface of the mind, is the heartland of primitive drives which demand gratification, no matter what. The superego, some of it conscious, some of it unconscious, is the seat of our conscience, what we accept of social and ethical values, our personal judge over good and bad, whose verdicts are self-esteem or guilt. The ego, caught between id and superego, synthesizes our behavior from the drives of id and the frigid standards of superego and determines the way we finally appear to the outside world, the part that shows of our true personality.

Although recognition from the scientific community had not yet come, Freud was honored in 1930 with the Goethe Prize for Literature and in 1936 he was elected to the Royal Society. When the Nazi occupation of Austria threatened his life and work, he moved to England and died there on September 23, 1939, having added psychological treatment methods to the biological basis of psychiatry. Beyond that,

Freud boarding a plane at Tempelhof Field in Berlin in 1928 for his first flight.

Freudian concepts have become an important part of our culture and his insightful understanding of human emotions has pervaded American thinking and social action.

Given Name: Sigmund Freud

Born: May 6, 1856, Freiberg, Moravia (Pribor, Czechoslovakia)

Married: Martha Bernays, 1886, 2 children

Highlights: Generally acknowledged as "the father of psychoanalysis" and the first person to systematically explore the human unconscious mind.

Died: September 23, 1939.

SCIENCE, INDUSTRY AND MEDICINE

Princess George of Greece and U.S. Ambassador William Bull III greeted Freud (center) in Paris in 1938 when he left Nazi Germany.

Joseph Lister

Hospitals were viewed as places of death, not life, before the 'Father of Surgery', Joseph Lister's revolutionary work in the field of antiseptics. Because, by the end of 1866, more than 40 percent of all patients entering hospitals died there. Even treatment of a minor disability often resulted in suffering and death. A conscientious surgeon-to-be might have well been appalled at the unpredictable prospect for his patients, but Lister was undaunted.

Lister was born April 5, 1827 in Upton, Essex, England and as a child was introduced by his father to microscopy. He attended two private schools, then entered University College in London. Here Lister's painstaking system of learning and his naturally retentive memory became evident as he showed a talent for integrating and applying the knowledge he acquired. When he became a hospital resident he participated in the debating society and the hospital medical society and he attacked the homeopaths and read papers (never published) on hospital gangrene and on the use of the microscope in medicine.

Early in 1854 Lister became resident house surgeon to the household of James Syme, the brilliant, opinionated professor of clinical surgery at the University of Edinburgh and here he broadened his experience. The relationship was made even closer when in 1856 he married Syme's eldest daughter, Agnes. After a prolonged wedding tour at the renowned medical centers in Europe, Lister returned to take up his assistant surgeoncy at the Royal Infirmary. During the next four years he read reports of his research into inflammation to the Royal Society of Edinburgh and his reputation as an original and thorough investigator brought him election to fellowship in the Royal Society in 1860. He was only thirty-three years old. That same year he was appointed the Regius professorship of surgery at the University of Glasgow. But Lister worked even harder when elected in 1861 to take charge of the surgical wards at the Royal Infirmary.

Lister was dismayed by the high incidence of erysipelas, septicemia and hospital gangrene. The mortality from amputations, as in many other well-known hospitals, was around 40 per cent. The prevailing medical doctrine had it that organic substances in the moist state and in the presence of oxygen undergo a peculiar form of combustion, so misguided surgeons treated wounds on the supposition they should be shielded from atmospheric oxygen. Lister soon doubted oxygen's responsibility and published a paper declaring that when one patient's persistent sores became gangrenous the process was "checked by the application of carbolic acid..."

Having read the work and writings of Louis Pasteur which claimed putrefaction was a fermentative process caused by living microorganisms carried on dust particles and transported by the air, Lister realized the "spontaneous generation" teaching was a myth. These claims revealed startlingly to Lister the cause of wound sepsis and provided the key to banishing hospital diseases. Between August 1865 and April 1867 Lister worked out the main features of his antiseptic treatment: thorough cleansing of the wound with carbolic acid, and protection of the wound from airborne germs by a dressing soaked in the acid with dressings changed daily.

Lister described these remarkable advances in a classic series of reports in *The Lancet* and began to apply his antiseptic principle to surgical wounds. In August 1867, at the Dublin meeting of the British Medical Association, he announced that during the last nine months his wards—previously "amongst the unhealthiest in the whole surgical division of the Glasgow Royal Infirmary"—had been entirely free from hospital sepsis.

Many of Lister's university colleagues viewed his accomplishments with indifference, skepticism and even hostility, but as time passed favorable reports in medical journals began to counterbalance the opposition. Lister returned to spend the next eight years in Edinburgh and in 1871 he became surgeon in Scotland to Queen Victoria. Meanwhile, antiseptic surgery gained more adherents abroad than at home. Among the earliest of his enthusiastic disciples was J. Lucas-Championniere of Paris, author of the first manual of antiseptic surgery. In America antiseptic surgery made slow progress until Lister personally addressed the 1876 International Medical Congress at Phiiladelphia.

For the next 20 years Lister published papers on antiseptic surgery and lectured, but eager lecture audiences dwindled to a few restless students who feared examination penalties for airing antiseptic doctrines. Then advances in bacteriology strengthened his antiseptic doctrine, and his prestige at home became further enhanced by his celebrity abroad. At the 1879 International Medical Congress in Amsterdam he was acclaimed with great enthusiasm and he received honorary doctorates from Oxford and Cambridge in 1880.

Lister was raised to the peerage by Queen Victoria in 1897 when he assumed the title Baron Lister of Lyme Regis. During later years Lister's tributes multiplied tremendously. He died on February 10, 1912 in Kent, England. A medallion by Sir Thomas Brock, one of the finest of Lister's many portraits and busts, hangs in Westminster Abbey, acknowledging one of mankind's greatest benefactors.

Given Name: Joseph Lister
Born: April 5, 1827, Upton, Essex, England
Married: Agnes Syme, 1856
Highlights: Discovered and developed antiseptics and introduced antiseptic surgical procedures that multiplied patient's chances for post operative survival.
Died: February 10, 1912

Three portraits of surgeon Dr. Joseph Lister, in photography, wood engraving and line engraving.

SCIENCE, INDUSTRY AND MEDICINE

J. Robert Oppenheimer

The man who many call "the father of the atomic bomb" was as naive in his dealings with the government as he was brilliant in his work in physics.

Oppenheimer himself said, in a 1954 letter to the Atomic Energy Commission, that "I was deeply interested in my science; but I had no understanding of the relations of man to his society". By a 4-1 vote, the AEC denied him further access to secret government data because of its finding that "his associations with persons known to be Communists have extended far beyond the tolerable limits of prudence and self-restraint."

Following his suspension by the AEC, Oppenheimer said that he would continue his research in fundamental physics at the Institute for Advanced Study at Princeton, N.J. "I may not be able to move freely in laboratories, but that has nothing to do with thinking freely," he said. He added that the things which "stimulate my curiosity are pretty far removed from the practical and therefore from classification."

The tall, thin, chain-smoking Oppenheimer was little known to the public, but well recognized in scientific and academic circles. His brilliance was evident early in his life, and he attended Manhattan's Ethical Culture School, which was dominated by children of unusual intelligence. From there he went to Harvard and Cambridge, and earned his Ph.D. degree at Germany's Goettingen University. He read seven languages, including Sanskrit. One scientist who worked with him at Los Alamos said that "he is so smart no one can fool him even for a second. He knows more about our specialties than we know ourselves."

In 1943, Oppenheimer had been called to take part in secret wartime atomic research, and was put in charge of the group working at New Mexico's Los Alamos laboratory, which was built under his direction. Although many of the scientists working under him were older, and some were Nobel Prize winners, they had no trouble working with a man who had such a well-earned reputation for brilliance.

Under his leadership, the group achieved in two years of war-time pressure what might otherwise have taken decades to accomplish. Oppenheimer, always shy and modest, gave credit for the group's success to the entire staff, saying that it "was a real team effort." But many of his fellow scientists felt that the acclaim given Oppenheimer was well-deserved. One said: "The main decisions were made by Oppenheimer and all proved to be correct." Another said: "Without Dr. Oppenheimer, the United States might not have the atomic bomb."

Before the explosion of the atomic bomb at Hiroshima thrust him into the spotlight, Oppenheimer had been virtually unknown outside academia. He had been perfectly content, and totally engrossed in his work at two California universities at Berkeley and Pasadena, at which schools he led programs in graduate and post-doctoral study in theoretical physics. His contacts outside the academic community were limited, and as he said "I was almost totally divorced from the contemporary scene in this country . . ." For years he did not read a newspaper or current magazine; had no radio, no telephone. He even said that "I learned of the stock market crash in the fall of 1929 only years after the event."

Oppenheimer freely acknowledged his associations with known Communists during the late 1930's and early 1940's, and said that his wife had been a party member "for a year or two." But he said that "I never accepted Communist dogma or theory; in fact, it never made any sense to me." He did, however, continue to associate with Communist friends, even after he became active in secret research. And it was these associations that led to his removal from government research projects. No charges of spying were ever proved against him, but he was suspended nonetheless.

The brilliant scientist, devoted to turning abstract theories into proven facts, was undone by naive actions and others' perceptions.

Given Name: Julius Robert Oppenheimer
Born: April 22, 1904, New York City
Married: Katherine Harrison, 1940, 2 children
Highlights: One of the world's great physicists, he was "father of the atomic bomb".
Died: February 18, 1967

Oppenheimer at work in 1957 at the Institute for Advanced Study in Princeton, New Jersey.

Ivan Pavlov

Accidentally stumbling onto the principle of conditioning, Ivan Petrovich Pavlov laid the foundation for turning psychology away from study of the mind to the study of overt behavior. It was a key discovery and brought about a major step toward the study of human psychiatry in mental hospitals.

Pavlov described the genesis of his behaviorism theory "The time is ripe for the transition to experimental analysis of the subject from the objective, external side, as in all other natural sciences."

And the time, indeed, was ripe. By the beginning of the 20th century many physiologists, zoologists and psychologists had already undertaken experiments to study the function of the brain. But they had assembled only fragmentary data. Pavlov drew upon Darwin's theory of evolution, and Sechenov's reflexology to create his own theory of behavior and he made his first public statement on the conditioned reflex in 1903, in a paper presented to the Fourteenth International Medical Congress in Madrid.

For his research on digestion, Pavlov needed to collect saliva from his laboratory animals, dogs. He stimulated saliva flow by placing meat powder in the dog's mouth. He soon noticed the dog would begin salivating at the sight of the experimenter, in the expectation of receiving meat powder.

Then Pavlov tried to pair other stimuli, such as the ringing of a bell, when issuing the meat and found the dog did indeed salivate to this stimulus. Applying his model of a functioning system to human behavior, he perceived language as "a second system of signals" which developed out of the first system of conditioned reflexes. Applying this concept to mental diseases, such as schizophrenia and neurosis as an imbalance of the central nervous system, he also developed a classification of human temperament on a similar basis. The discovery of conditioning was born.

Pavlov found in the conditioned reflex a mechanism of individual adaptation which, he held, exists throughout the entire animal world. "A temporary nervous connection is a universal physiological phenomenon in the animal world and exists in us ourselves." Pavlov's hypothesis has been verified by more recent neuro-physiological data.

The greatest part of Pavlov's research is devoted to three major areas: the physiology of the circulation of the blood (1874-1888), the physiology of digestion (1879-1897) and the physiology of the brain and of higher nervous activity (1902-1936). During the time of his research he served as a professor of physiology at the Military Medical Academy, the Institute of Experimental Medicine and the Academy of Sciences. It was here that the Russian scientist investigated the physiology of the cardiovascular system, the digestive system and the central nervous system. Pavlov's scientific work received worldwide recognition. In 1904 he was awarded the Nobel Prize for his research on digestion. In 1907 he was elected an academician of the Russian Academy of Sciences. In August 1935 he presided over the Fifteenth International Physiological Congress in Leningrad and in Moscow.

Pavlov was a severe critic of all the schools of psychology—French, German, American—for their dualistic presuppositions and their simplistic misunderstandings of his work. His idea for "a legitimate marriage of physiology and psychology" was developed long before the modern concept of holistic medicine.

Born September 26, 1849, Ivan Petrovich Pavlov was educated at the Ryazan seminary and at the University of Saint Petersburg (now Leningrad) in science and medicine. He spent all his working life in Leningrad, receiving many awards and honors from the Soviet government and from foreign scientific societies until his death on February 27, 1936, but his work continued to be a major influence in physiology, psychology and psychiatry.

Given Name: Ivan Petrovich Pavlov
Born: September 27, 1849, Ryazan, Russia
Married: Serafina Vasilievna Karchevskaya, 1881
Highlights: Discovered the conditioned reflex and conducted other research important to the understanding of human behavior. Won Nobel Prize in physiology, 1904.
Died: February 27, 1936

Professor Ivan Petrovich Pavlov, undated.

John D. Rockefeller, Sr.

The American who became the first billionaire in history felt few impulses to indulge himself in money-spending. "I never had a craving for tobacco, or tea and coffee," said John D. Rockefeller, Sr. "I never had a craving for anything."

John D., Senior was a solemn young man; so grave, pious, methodical and unemotional that to some he seemed lacking in human qualities. But he had a business vision, the vision of a one-track genius, and he came upon the scene when the oil business needed organization. The organizer was the smart, 21-year-old bookkeeper from Cleveland, Ohio who had saved his pennies and become a junior partner in a produce commission firm.

In 1860 a group of money men in Cleveland sent John Davison Rockefeller off to Oil Creek to look the situation over and report on the long-range possibilities of the gushers. He was not well received by the wildcatters, one of whom called him "that bloodless Baptist bookkeeper." After his first survey he went home and blandly reported that oil had no commercial future. It is clear that he didn't believe this; his report was more likely an early sign of his gift of protesting a lack of evidence while holding back "something for the lawyers."

He had sensed, or been told, that the black glue was not necessarily an end in itself. The existence of petroleum had been known for some time but it was thought to have a medicinal use and had been peddled as Kiers' Rock Oil as early as 1850. Then just before the Civil War an American chemist, J.A. Bissell, discovered its use as an illuminant and lubricant, and in 1859 a well was sunk in western Pennsylvania. Rockefeller apparently guessed oil for lighting might become oil for heating, for steamships, for lubrication, for power. And the new word "refinery" appealed to a neat young city man.

Rockefeller and his partner heard of a candlemaker who had refined lard oil and was moving on to petroleum. With his responsibility to the Cleveland money men at an end, Rockefeller and his partner pooled their savings and invested all of $4,000 in the candlemaker's refinery. By 1863 Rockefeller had determined to devote himself exclusively to refining oil. His mode of approach was to accumulate capital as rapidly as possible. "Take out what you've got to have to live on, but leave the rest in," he said to his partners. "Don't buy new clothes and fast horses; let your wife wear her last year's bonnet. You can't find any place where money will earn what it does here."

Rockefeller's advice was particularly good because the banking community was conservative about this new industry and hesitated to lend to refiners on a large scale. Rockefeller built a monopoly by means both genteel and ruthless, and it was rudely hinted that he had in the palm of his hands the best state legislatures and United States Senators that money could buy. By the time he was thirty, Rockefeller had formed the Standard Oil Company of Ohio and had bought 25 refineries. He not only got the railroad to give him secret low rates because of the colossal business he could throw their way; they secretly guaranteed him a bonus from the regular rates that all the small producers had to pay. When the arrangement leaked it provoked a national outcry.

Between 1870 and 1879 Rockefeller and his friends acquired about 90 per cent of all American refineries, plus all the main pipelines and oil cars of the Pennsylvania Railroad. He was in his mid-thirties when he became the first billionaire in history.

Probably no industrial combination earned as much ill will as Standard Oil. Rockefeller appeared at all times indifferent to public opinion, and whether in each individual instance he was responsible or not, the business procedures of the trust awakened widespread indignation. In his heyday, the nation viewed Rockefeller as a ruthless money-getter, without heart or scruple.

Rockefeller was very much a Victorian in his capacity to rationalize his energy as the engine of God, but at age sixty penitence set in. And, as happened with many more of the money barons of that time, the onset of arthritis convinced him that he had made all his money for the public good. With complete sincerity he created a foundation in his name and gave $530,000,000 for worldwide medical research. It has been noted that Rockefeller is the only philanthropist who gave away his fortune with no strings binding its use.

Choosing able men to administer his gifts and the foundation, Rockefeller dispersed over $125 million to the General Education Board, $45 million to the University of Chicago and nearly $60 million to medical education.

For the next two decades Rockefeller was photographed everywhere doing folksy things—attending a county fair, teetering on the putting green, marrying off a couple of midgets for charity—and he began to be seen as one who was mortal. Though he was a kind of monarch, he too had the common touch.

As the twenties gave way to the thirties the era of the money barons had passed and Franklin D. Roosevelt was besieging the "economic royalists" during the longest and worst depression in American history. John D. Rockefeller, Sr. died on May 23, 1937 in Ormond Beach, Florida, at age ninety-eight, having become known more as a philanthropist than as an oil magnate.

Given Name: John Davison Rockefeller
Born: July 8, 1838, Richford, N.Y.
Married: Laura C. Spelman 1915, 4 children
Highlights: Industrialist, philanthropist, first billionaire in history. Founded Standard Oil Company of Ohio and at one time controlled over 90% of U.S. oil production. Later donated over five hundred million dollars to charitable causes.
Died: May 23, 1937

In 1932, young William Gebele Jr., received one of the famous dimes given away by John D. Rockefeller Sr.

Jonas Salk

A gifted high school student, Jonas Salk planned to be a lawyer but science courses he took his freshman year at City College of New York changed his mind, and helped him change the course of medical history when, in 1955, the by-then Dr. Salk developed a successful vaccine against the paralyzing disease poliomyelitis.

In 1944 28,000 Americans suffered in a polio epidemic that left thousands crippled. President Franklin D. Roosevelt, who wore metal leg braces and conducted World War II from a wheel chair, was its most famous victim. Young children were particularly susceptible to the disease—thus its other name, infantile paralysis. Salk, a medical researcher who had worked on a cure for influenza, had three young sons. His desire to conquer polio was a personal crusade. Confident and committed, he would work in the lab 18 hours a day and sometimes around the clock. Using an inactivated polio virus, Salk developed a vaccine that was tested on a million school children. His boys were among the first innoculated. Finally in 1955, when he was 40, Salk stood before a cheering crowd of his colleagues and pronounced the vaccine successful.

Massive immunization programs were begun, and ten years later, the number of polio cases in the United States had dropped dramatically to a mere 121. Today babies born here are routinely administered the Salk vaccine in the first months of life, and polio has been virtually eliminated in both the United States and Europe.

Although Salk didn't profit financially from his unpatented discovery, he has been the recipient of countless honors, as well as citations from Presidents Eisenhower and Johnson. A quiet and modest man, he always attributes the discovery of the Salk vaccine to the combined effort of countless researchers, lab workers and doctors who together had one goal, to wipe out polio. In 1963 The Salk Institute was established in California as a research center for work in the fields of immunology, virology and geneology. Dr. Salk was appointed president but he resigned after two years to return to the quiet world of the laboratory where he had achieved his great victory over one of the medical scourges of our times.

Given Name: Jonas Edward Salk
Born: October 28, 1914, New York City
Married: Donna Lindsay, 1939, 3 children
Married: Francoise Gilot, 1970
Highlights: Developed vaccine that prevented polio and has made the disease virtually unknown since 1956.

Dr. Jonas Salk takes time out from laboratory work to explain the making of polio vaccine to newsman in 1955.

SCIENCE, INDUSTRY AND MEDICINE

Orville Wright

From the day in 1878 when his father, a clergyman in Dayton, Ohio, brought home a flying toy made of cork, paper, screws and rubber bands, Orville Wright dedicated himself to fulfilling man's agelong dream of flying. As boys, he and his older brother Wilbur studied aeronautical literature and built themselves a wind tunnel where they experimented with gliders to learn about wing control and lateral balancing. The brothers turned aside their father's wish that they enter the ministry, started a weekly newspaper, then opened a bicycle shop where they continued their experiments. They tested their crude inventions at Kitty Hawk, North Carolina, where rolling sand dunes and constant winds provided ideal conditions. There, on December 12th, 1903, in a flimsy box-kite affair made of wood, wire and cloth, a sputtering motor and two crude propellers, Orville skimmed above the dunes travelling 120 feet in 12 seconds, in man's first powered flight in a heavier-than-air machine.

The Wright brothers success in the air where others, including their forebear Otto Lilienthal, who died in 1896 in a glider experiment, had failed, was attributed to their working as a team. Because of countless false starts which drew newspaper men onto the dunes to witness flights that never took off, their 1903 achievement was neither reported nor believed. It wasn't until 1908, when they had already received patents in France and were manufacturing aircraft commercially at the original Wright Company, that a reporter witnessed and reported on a 1000-foot flight. In 1909, their design was accepted by the U.S. Army. Early on, Orville was horrified at the destructive use of airplanes beginning in World War I.

Orville Wright was a shy man who said little, neither smoked nor drank, and when asked once if he didn't need a wife, pointed to his airplane and stated, "You can't support both." After his brother Wilbur died of typhoid fever in 1912 he sold his stock in the Wright Company and retired further into the laboratories and work shops where he continued his experiments. He seldom appeared in public, though he could be counted on by the Wright Company to help solve a particularly knotty problem, kept a clockwork schedule and responded to tributes to his world-shrinking breakthroughs with little more than "thank you."

In 1928, when the secretary of the Smithsonian Institution in Washington where the original Kitty Hawk machine was enshrined claimed a former Institution secretary had designed a successful flying machine prior to the Wright brothers', Orville took his pioneering contraption to London, installing it in the Science Museum there. In 1943, on the 40th anniversary of the Wright brothers' flight, President Roosevelt announced that the controversy was finally resolved and that the Wright machine would be returning to the Smithsonian where it belonged. He then saluted Orville Wright as the outstanding symbol of American genius, a dreamer who pursued his goal through failure and doubt until he finally triumphed.

Given Name: Orville Wright
Born: August 19, 1871, Dayton, Ohio
Unmarried
Highlights: Aviation pioneer and inventor. Made first heavier than air flight on December 17, 1903 in craft designed by him and brother Wilbur
Died: January 30, 1948

The Wright brothers, Orville (left) and Wilbur (right) relax outside their Dayton, Ohio home in 1910.

SCIENCE, INDUSTRY AND MEDICINE

ARTS

Louis Armstrong

He was born on the Fourth of July, and that was perhaps fitting. Because Louis Armstrong did more than any other man or woman to bring jazz, often called America's only original art form, to the world. Even his nickname, "Satchmo", short for "Satchelmouth", was supposed to have come from British fans when he made a tour of England and Scotland in 1932.

Armstrong started his musical career as a young boy on the streets of New Orleans, where he strolled as the tenor in a boy's quartet which sang and passed the hat for pennies. His first formal training was with cornetist Bunk Johnson, but was interrupted when he was sentenced as a "juvenile delinquent" to a year at the New Orleans Waifs Home. His "crime" had been setting off some blank cartridges on New Year's Eve. At the home, Armstrong was encouraged to pursue his music, and learned to play the bugle and cornet, but it was not until later that he began taking trumpet lessons from the legendary King Oliver. Finally his musical education was rounded out when, in 1921, he had a fellow musician teach him to read music while they were playing an engagement on a Mississippi River excursion boat.

The chunky, 5'8" Armstrong played with everything that was in him. At each of his performances, he would use up a stack of handkerchiefs wiping the sweat from his face. Before each performance, he would gargle and salve his lips with a special preparation to firm them up. "What's the good of havin' music in your mind if you can't get it past your pucker?" he asked.

Armstrong attracted vast crowds wherever he went, and he went almost everywhere. After the first tour in Britain, he played Denmark, Sweden, Norway and Holland in 1933-34; England again in 1934; then France, Italy and Belgium. In the 1950's, he made tours to Australia, Europe, Africa, New Zealand, South Korea and Japan, as well as giving concerts in Iron Curtain countries such as East Germany, Czechoslovakia and Hungary. He didn't always speak the language of his audiences, but he always communicated with them through his music and his upbeat, happy attitude. When playing for King George V, he started an encore by looking at the King and saying "This one's for you, Rex".

In the 1960's, Armstrong's gravelly-voiced recording of "Hello, Dolly" sold over a million copies, a feat that was then relatively rare. He made about 1500 recordings all told, many of which have become collector's items. One such record is "Ding Dong Daddy from Dumas". During the recording session, he forgot the lyrics, but just kept singing, and filled in the missing words with "Now I done forgot the words", in synch with the music, until he remembered the proper lyrics and picked up where he had left off.

Armstrong was at times troubled by his failure to physically participate in the Civil Rights marches of 1965, even though he supported the movement with donations. He explained his absence from the front lines by saying that "My life is music. They would beat me on the mouth if I marched, and without my mouth, I would not be able to blow my horn."

In addition to being a trumpeter and singer, Armstrong was also a composer and movie performer. But it was his music—now hot and frantic, now sweet and low—that made him the idol of millions. Armstrong once said that "When you play jazz, you don't lie. You play from the heart."

Armstrong did play from the heart. And that's what made people respond.

When Ella Fitzgerald appeared at the Waldorf-Astoria in 1971, Armstrong made a guest appearance.

ARTS

Louis "Satchmo" Armstrong and his group, seen at dress rehearsal for a 1967 television special.

Given Name: Louis Armstrong
Born: July 4, 1900, New Orleans, Louisiana
Married: Daisy Parker, 1917 (divorced)
Married: Lillian Hardin, 1924 (divorced)
Married: Lucille, 1942
Highlights: Leading jazz trumpeter, singer, recording star. Through his 1500 recordings and live concert performances, he brought jazz to audiences all over the world.
Died: July 6, 1971

In his Las Vegas dressing room, Armstrong relaxes before a 1970 appearance.

Armstrong at a 1948 recording session.

George Balanchine

"To see the music and hear the dancing" was the goal of George Balanchine, one of the greatest choreographers in the history of ballet. He believed that tradition was the base for renewal, and radical innovation could come only from those steeped in tradition.

George Balanchine, whose original name was Georgi Melitonovitch Balanchivadze, was born in St. Petersburg, Russia, on January 22, 1904. Young Georgi was enrolled by his parents at the Maryinsky Theater's (now the State Academic Theater) ballet school in 1914. In 1924 he joined Diaghilev's Ballets Russe. In the Diaghilev company a knee injury in 1927 sidelined him and then led him to give up dancing, except to fill in on an emergency basis, by 1930. At one time Balanchine toyed with becoming a pianist and he also became involved in the staging of avant-garde theatrical productions that were part of the artistic ferment swept in by the Russian Revolution.

In 1922, at age 19, he married Tamara Geva, a 16-year-old ballet dancer and later an American actress, and together they became part of a nucleus of young dancers from the ballet school. Like other young artists, Balanchine was in revolt against the past. A chief influence at the time was Kasyan Goleizovsky, whose choreography revealed the use of the unadorned human body in a fluent plastique of movement. The message that dance could be a self-sufficient art was impressed on him.

Balanchine said he found his true self in the 1928 Stravinsky "Apollo", whose uncluttered neo-Classic style pointed to the direction Balanchine's work would take. It was about this time Diaghilev died suddenly in 1929, but already the 25-year-old choreographer had made an international name for himself. With Diaghilev's death the members of the Ballets Russe faced an uncertain future. There were also changes in Balanchine's personal life. His marriage to Miss Geva had broken up and she was replaced in Balanchine's affections by another ballerina. The fact that Mr. Balanchine did eventually marry four times—each time to a dancer for whom he created ballets—became a part of ballet lore.

The years between 1929 and Balanchine's immigration to the United States in October 1933 were rootless ones, but he apparently relished the creative opportunities that came his way. The small ballet company Balanchine had organized folded, but not before the all-Balanchine repertory had convinced Lincoln Kirstein to invite him to the United States to found a school and a company. Lincoln Kirstein was the distinguished dance scholar who became Balanchine's patron and eventually co-founder of the New York City Ballet.

The first Balanchine-Kirstein company was named the American Ballet in 1925, but in a few months the troupe's first tour suffered financial collapse. To stabilize their fledgling company, the two men accepted an invitation to make the American Ballet part of the Metropolitan Opera. The unhappy associated ended in 1938 and, faced with this failure, Balanchine spent the next eight years mostly choreographing for broadway shows and films.

During the next decade financial worries continued to plague Balanchine's efforts to found a permanent company that could serve as his creative instrument. Financially pressed, the New York City Ballet which performed at the City Center from 1948 to 1964, was often obliged to present its ballets without scenery or costumes. Necessity became a virtue and a whole line of practice-clothes ballets developed center in the Balanchine repertory. Almost all were identified with his most avant-garde works to contemporary music. Balanchine began to achieve wider recognition and an astonishing number of ballets from the City Center period remained long or permanently in the repertory.

When the New York City Ballet moved to its new home in the New York State Theater at Lincoln Center in 1964, the Balanchine reputation was at its peak. He began to create elaborate works long on spectacle and even on story and his range was wide, going from the 1966 Stravinsky "Variations" to his 1980 Romantic masterpiece, "Robert Schumann's Davidsbundlertanze" and the popular "Vienna Waltzes."

Balanchine died in 1983 at age 79. As a choreographer and artistic director of the New York City Ballet, his ballets delighted audiences for years. "I think", he once said, "that . . . everything a man does he does for his ideal woman. You live only one life and you believe in something; and I believe in that." Balanchine's "ideal woman" was, of course, ballet.

Dancer Patricia McBride and Balanchine in a 1966 rehearsal.

Balanchine is hugged by dancer Ray Bolger as pianist Victor Borge watches following a 1980 award presentation.

Given Name: Georgi Melitonovitch Balanchivadze
Born: January 22, 1904, St. Petersburg, Russia
Married: Tamara Geva, 1922
Married: Three more times
Highlights: Perhaps the world's leading choreographer and long time director of the New York City Ballet. Staged over 100 ballets.
Died: April 30, 1983

In 1960, dancers Jillana and Francisco Moncian were shown the movements for a TV ballet sequence by Balanchine.

Balanchine (left) and Lincoln Kirstein drink a vodka toast in 1982 to honor composer Igor Stravinsky.

Balanchine and Vera Zorina after announcing they had married on Christmas Eve, 1938.

Ballerina Maria Tallchief listens to Balanchine's direction in 1965.

Béla Bartók

Béla Bartók lived a life of disappointment. He spent most of his life preserving his musical heritage in Hungary—and watched its towns torn apart in the '30s and divided among Czechoslovakia, Russia, Rumania and Yugoslavia. Regarded as one of the 20th Century's greatest composers he died unrecognized far from the land he loved.

A virtuoso pianist, Bartók studied in Budapest at the Conservatoire, where later he served for 30 years on the faculty, teaching such great conductors as Sir Georg Solti and Antal Dorati. He decided to become a composer after a performance of German composer Richard Strauss' 'Also Sprach Zarathustra" (a piece whose opening bars are linked in the public ear with outer space, having been used in the film "2001" as well as the film about Apollo's launching. His early efforts were unexciting. Then he and his lifelong friend, composer Zoltan Kodály, became interested in Magyar folk music. Until the '20s, folk music meant gypsy music played in cafes. But Bartók heard in it "the ideal starting point for a musical renaissance", and he and Kodály began recording peasant songs. Eventually they accumulated 8000 melodies.

Bartók began to write pieces with names like "Allegro barbaro" in reaction to the prettiness spilling over from 19th century musical influences. He preferred dissonance and avoided sentimentality. He was a master of orchestration, often pushing the orchestra to the very limits of its resources with special effects such as bow-tapping and wild pizzacatos. His famous "Concerto for Orchestra," unusual in that it calls upon the whole orchestra to perform as a solo instrument generally does in concertos, displays his preference for eerie harmonies and unusual rhythms which create an extraterrestrial effect.

In 1940 Bartók fled Hungary, now fallen into Hitler's hands, for America, where he hoped to find recognition and financial success. However, he fell into a life of dire poverty. In 1945 Hungary was liberated and Bartók was invited back to receive the honors he had formerly been denied. By then he was dying of leukemia and starvation. He never made the trip, but died in America.

Bartók's influence on a wide range of musicians and musical styles is strong on both sides of the Atlantic. While in the U.S. he wrote a piece for clarinettist-band leader Benny Goodman. Jazz musician Dave Brubeck has acknowledged his debt to Bartók in such pieces as "Blue Rondo à la Turque." The great Yehudi Menuhin commissioned a violin piece by Bartók. His six string quartets are regarded by many as the finest since Beethoven. His six-volume set of piano pieces, "Mikrokosmos", are standard text now for begining piano students. Their interesting harmonies and entertaining rhythms have replaced the more traditional exercise series, saving young musicians from the boredom that was formerly a given in learning to play the piano.

Three portraits of Hungarian composer Bela Bartok, above, opposite, and below, all undated. The one below is circa 1927.

Given Name: Bela Bartok

Born: March 25, 1881, Nagyszentmiklos, Hungary

Married: Twice. Second time to Ditta Pastory, 1 child.

Highlights: Leading modern composer who broke with tradition and adapted the sounds and rhythms of folk music for orchestra.

Died: September 26, 1945

ARTS

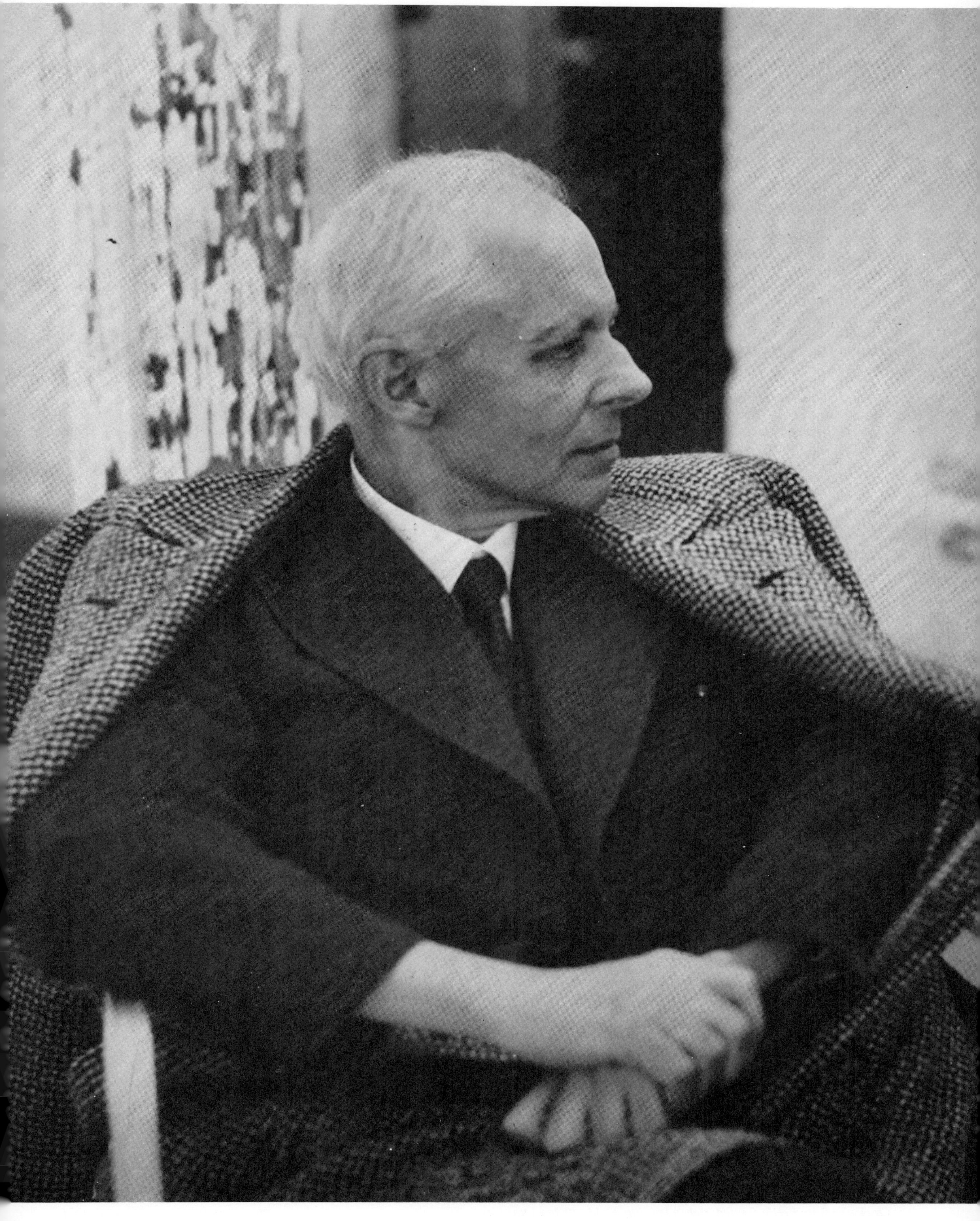

Irving Berlin

"Irving Berlin has no place in music", said fellow songwriter Jerome Kern. "He is American music."

Berlin, who played by ear and could never read harmony, wrote over 1000 songs on the "trick" piano he bought for a hundred dollars. The piano had a clutch, so he could switch out of the key of F sharp, the only key he could compose in, into other keys. In 1972 Berlin gave his piano to the Smithsonian.

An immigrant from East Russia where his father was a cantor in a synagogue, Berlin came to America with his family in 1893 to escape the pogroms. They settled on New York's teeming lower East Side. When Irving was eight his father died and the boy, who had only two years of schooling, went to work. One of his first jobs was as guide for a blind singing beggar. He plugged songs for a music publisher and worked as a singing waiter in Chinatown at a cafe where he wrote his first song—"Marie from Sunny Italy", which earned him 37 cents. In 1911 he wrote the words and music for "Alexander's Ragtime Band", a tune that ushered in the Jazz Age and made Berlin an international celebrity.

Over the years Berlin kept all the rights to his music, earning millions. When the wealthy father of his second wife (his first wife died after contracting typhoid on their honeymoon) objected to his daughter's marriage to an "East Side boy", Berlin retorted, "If you see fit to disinherit her, I'll probably have to make her a wedding gift of a couple of million dollars."

Besides music, Berlin's passion was his country. He wrote dozens of songs that praised America and sang of national trials. Drafted into the army in 1917 he wrote "Oh, How I Hate To Get Up In The Morning" for an army show. "Any Bonds Today?" and "I Left My Heart At The Stagedoor Canteen" were written during World War II. On Armistice Day 1939 Kate Smith introduced "God Bless America", whose royalties, totaling hundreds of thousands of dollars, Berlin earmarked for the Boy Scouts and Girl Scouts of America. President Eisenhower and the U.S. Army honored him with medals for his patriotism.

His huge hits "White Christmas" and "Easter Parade" became theme songs for holidays American-style. He once chose these songs to describe how he wrote. He did nothing, he claimed, but rewrite 7 or 8 songs over and over. "White Christmas" was nothing more than "Easter Parade" re-written in thirds. "Easter Parade", in turn, was based on a song he wrote in 1917. "All good songwriters have no more than half-a-dozen good tunes in their systems . . . if they have that many, they're liberally blessed."

Before World War I Berlin was an outstanding vaudeville performer. He also toured in "This is The Army" during World War II, travelling to most of the cities in the U.S. and military bases around the world. He had a thin, raspy voice of which a comedian once said, "You gotta hug him to hear him."

"Music and lyrics by Irving Berlin" seemed to guarantee hits for six decades; in musical revues in the '20's, film musicals, including several for Fred Astaire and Ginger Rogers, in the 30's, and in the 40's and 50's—"Holiday Inn", "White Christmas", "Blue Skies", "Easter Parade", "There's No Business Like Show Business". His stage hits included "Annie Get Your Gun" and "Call Me Madam."

Attempting retirement in the 50's, Berlin fidgeted with golf, fishing and painting, but soon went back to songwriting. "Other people may be able to retire gracefully', he said, "but not me. If you'll pardon my quoting my own line, 'There's no business like show business.'"

Clockwise from Berlin (seated, right): Dorothy Fields, Richard Rodgers, and Ethel Merman in 1966.

The songwriter at his "desk" in 1941.

Above: Berlin leads singing of "God Bless America," which he wrote, in 1942 ceremonies at New York City Hall.

Right: This 1920's photo shows Berlin at the upright piano he used to compose such tunes as "White Christmas" and "Easter Parade". He donated the piano to the Smithsonian Institute in 1972.

Right below: The composer in repose, 1938.

Below: Ginger Rogers and Berlin rehearse for a 1962 "Songs of Irving Berlin" TV special.

Given Name: Israel Baline
Born: May 11, 1888, Tyumen, Russia
Married: Dorothy Goetz, 1912
Married: Ellen Mackay, 1926, 3 children
Highlights: Leading American composer of popular music, including "Easter Parade", "White Christmas" and "God Bless America". Awarded Presidential Medal of Freedom, 1977.

Enrico Caruso

Legend has it that in the great San Francisco earthquake Italian tenor Enrico Caruso, roused from sleep after singing the role of Don Jose in the opera "Carmen", ran weeping down Market Street in his pajamas crying "Vesuvio si! San Francisco no!"

Recently historians came up with a different story. Celebrating in a North Beach cafe when the tremor hit, Caruso followed friends' urgings to open a window and sing to prove his voice hadn't been damaged. With buildings crashing and citizens screaming, the tenor sang out to assure himself his gift was unimpaired.

Early in his career Arturo Toscanni heard Caruso sing in "L'elisir d'amore". "If this Neapolitan continues singing like this", the great conductor prophesized, "he will make the whole world talk about him." Toscanni's words proved true—during the early part of the century Caruso's voice made him the most adulated and highest paid singer in the world.

His voice was powerful yet supple, possessing a superb "bel canto" quality for lyric parts as well as a richness in the lower registers. It was warm, vital, smooth, perfect for his specialty, the melodramatic roles in Italian opera. For dramatic effect he often resorted to the "coup de glotte", which became known as the "Caruso sob." When he interjected it into his famous rendition of "Vesti la giubba" from "I Pagliacci", critics sneered at his tiresome Italian mannerism—while audiences around the world jumped to their feet and cheered.

Caruso was the 18th child born into the family of a Neapolitan labourer. All 17 born before him died in infancy; two born after him survived. He made a lackluster debut in Naples in 1894. It was four years later, as the artist Rudolpho in Puccini's "La Boheme", a role which became his most celebrated part, that he caught critics' attention in Milan. He first became known outside Italy when he sang with the famous soprano Melba at Monte Carlo. From there he went on to triumphs at Covent Garden in London, Rome, St. Petersburg, Lisbon and South American, before arriving in America in 1903 to make his debut in Verdi's "Rigoletto" at the Metropolitan Opera House in New York. He met with immediate success, and sang at the Met until his death.

Caruso's interpretations of the tenor roles in "I Pagliacci", "Rigoletto", and Puccini's "Tosca" became models which every singer emulated. In 1918 he made a movie of "I Pagliacci". He was the first musical performer to recognize the importance of phonograph recordings. He began recording in 1902, eventually making over two million dollars from his records. Despite the poor quality of early recordings, th quality of his voice as preserved on records stands on a with such great tenors of today as Domingo and Pavor

Besides his gift for music Caruso had a gift for caricature and a volume of his drawings was published. He worked in charitable causes in his native Naples and during the first World War appeared at countless war bond rallies in America. His appeal was so great that once he raised $150,000 by singing only one song.

He loved conviviality and good food. A macaroni was named after him.

Everything Caruso did drew enormous publicity, especially in America, and it wasn't all good. He had a turbulent love life. Disagreeable publicity surrounded his divorce from his first wife, with whom he had two children. Late in life his marriage to Dorothy Park Benjamin was opposed by her New York industrialist father. In 1906 the publicity given the celebrated "monkey-house" case, in which the tenor was accused of improper behaviour towards a lady while viewing monkeys in the Central Park Zoo, threatened his continued success in America.

Caruso's last days had all the melodrama of an Italian opera. During a performance of "L'elisir d'amore", the opera that inspired Toscanni's prediction, he coughed blood. Suf-

Above and right: Two views of Caruso as Cannio in "Pagliacci"

fering acute pain, he sang one more time, Christmas eve 1920, his 607th performance at the Met and his last anywhere. Promised he would sing again after treatment for pleurisy and pneumonia, Caruso returned for a long rest to Italy, eventually beginnning to work with his voice. After a relapse, believed to have been caused by an unsterilized instrument used by an examining doctor, he died.

In 1950 a fictional movie—"The Great Caruso"—starring Mario Lanza was made based on his life.

Given Name: Enrico Caruso
Born: February 27, 1983, Naples, Italy
Married: Dorothy Park Benjamin
Highlights: One of the greatest operatic tenors of all time and one of the first recording stars.
Died: August 21, 1921, Naples, Italy

Enrico Caruso in costume for "Rigoletto"

Bass Josi Mardones (left), Caruso, and Rosa Ponselle in her 1918 debut in "La Forza del Destino"

Paul Cezanne

What is there in the works of Paul Cezanne that entitled him to become regarded as one of the most brilliant and revolutionary painters in the history of art, even though his art was misunderstood and discredited by the public during most of his life?

The answer is that Cezanne prepared the ground for the movement away from realistic representation toward abstraction.

Paul Cezanne was born January 19, 1839, in Aix-en-Provence in southern France. The son of a kind, but almost illiterate, mother and domineering and successful banker, Cezanne received an excellent classical education at the College Bourbon in Aix. After two years spent vacillating between law school and some kind of artistic career, he persuaded his father to allow him to study painting in Paris.

During his first stay in Paris (1861), Cezanne found he was not as technically proficient as some of the other students at Atelier Suisse, but he continued on, encouraged by his close friend, writer Emile Zola. He also met Camille Pissarro and others of the impressionist group of painters, though he remained outside their circle. From 1864 to 1869 Cezanne submitted his work to the official salon and saw it consistently rejected. Paintings in this early style, almost opposite to that of his mature works, were violent and dark and form what is usually called his "romantic" period.

Cezanne rejected this early approach of harsh and somber colors and extremely heavy paintwork and in July 1870, with the outbreak of the Franco-Prussian War, he moved to Provence and began to paint the landscapes that marked the begining of his "impressionist" years. He began seriously to learn the techniques and theories of impressionism from Pissarro and the two artists painted together intermittently through 1874.

In 1874, and again in 1877, Cezanne exhibited with the impressionists in Paris and although his works were the most severely criticized, he continued to work diligently.

He developed his mature style during this peirod of isolation, from late 1870 to early 1890. "L'Estaque" (Louvre c. 1888) is perhaps the first masterpiece of the classic Cezanne. Like all mature landscapes, this composition of grand and calm horizontals has the exciting and radically new quality of simultaneously representing deep space and flat design. He said, "I seek to render perspective only through color," and "When color is at its richest, form is at its fullest."

Applying techniques of the impressionists to create landscapes, portraits, and still lifes, Cezanne slowly achieved his purpose in painting; to express ideas and arouse emotions through pure form and color. His art was also deeply intellectual, a conscious search for solutions to problems of representation.

Cezanne's work attracted little attention during his lifetime, but a year after his death a retrospective showing of 56 paintings was held at the Salon D'Automne in Paris and won considerable acclaim. The exhibition had great impact on many leading painters of the 1900's, including Georges Braque, Fernand Leger, Henri Matisse, and Pablo Picasso.

Paul Cezanne's unique vision of the world and his conception of art were such a revelation to his contemporaries that he has been called the "father of modern painting."

Given Name: Paul Cezanne

Born: January 19, 1839, Aix-en Provence, France

Married: Marie-Hortense Figuet 1886, 1 child

Highlights: One of the great forerunners of modern painting whose works hang in major museums and private collections all over the world.

Died: October 22, 1906.

"Self Portrait" by Paul Cezanne.

Charlie Chaplin

He was the acknowledged master comic of the silent screen, a genius at pantomime who became one of the wealthiest men in the film industry. Yet, despite his professional success, his private life was filled with troubles. He had three unhappy marriages, suffered through a lurid paternity suit, and was charged with being a Communist.

In his autobiography, Chaplin wrote that "my prodigious sin was, and still is, being a nonconformist. Although I am not a Communist, I refuse to fall in line by hating them. In an atmosphere of powerful cliques and invisible governments, I engendered a nation's antagonism and unfortunately lost the affection of the American public." That statement may have been accurate for awhile in the 1950's, especially after the government, in 1952, barred his return to the United States from a trip to his native England on the grounds of moral turpitude and dangerous political affiliations. But twenty years later, Americans gave him back the affection he had known for so long, and the Academy of Motion Picture Arts and Sciences gave him an honorary Oscar. He was cited at the ceremony for "the incalculable effect he has had in making motion pictures the art form of the century."

Chaplin was more than the most successful comic of his time, or perhaps any time. He was also a writer, director and producer—one of the most creative and productive men in the film industry. His original production organization, the Charlie Chaplin Film Corporation, was started in 1918, and became a unit in the United Artists Corporation. The character he created, "The Little Tramp", evoked laughter and sympathy from audiences all over the world as he suffered all sorts of indignities but somehow always managed to rise above them.

His success as a producer and director almost matched Chaplin's greatness as a performer. He introduced Adolphe Menjou in "A Woman of Paris", Jackie Coogan in "The Kid", and Paulette Goddard in "Modern Times". Starting with his own debut in 1913, he went from one success to another as critics and public alike applauded his work.

When sound arrived in pictures in 1927, Chaplin insisted that he wanted no part of dialogue, and didn't think it was necessary. He insisted that the basis of his comedy was pantomime, and refused to jump on the sound bandwagon. In 1931, he produced "City Lights", which did use music and sound effects, but only to enhance his pantomimic comedy. Five years later, in "Modern Times", he sang for the first time on screen, and in 1941 he finally spoke on screen in "The Great Dictator", his first departure from the "Tramp" role that he had created and made so popular.

While Chaplin's film career was soaring, his private life was filled with troubles. Three marriages—two to 16 year old girls and the last to film protege Paulette Goddard—ended in divorce in the years between 1918 and 1941. Then he was tried, and acquitted, for violations of the Mann Act, and lost a drawn-out, lurid paternity suit, even though blood tests showed he was not the father of the child in question. In 1943, when he was 54 and she was 18, Chaplin married Oona O'Neill, daughter of playwright Eugene O'Neill, despite her father's opposition. The couple eventually had eight children, and lived in comfortable "exile" in Vevey, Switzerland, overlooking Lake Geneva.

Chaplin paid a high price for his success. But he left the world with a body of cinematic work that is unmatched for portraying the hopes and fears, strengths and weaknesses—in short, the humanity—that is in all of us.

In "Dog's Life."

Chaplin and wife, Oona O'Neill, after he was knighted in 1975.

Given Name: Charles Spencer Chaplin
Born: April 16, 1889, London, England
Married: Mildred Harris, 1918, 1 child, (divorced 1920)
Married: Lita Grey, 2 children, (divorced 1927)
Married: Paulette Goddard, 1935, (divorced 1942)
Married: Oona O'Neill, 1943, 8 children
Highlights: Actor and motion picture pioneer whose character, "The Little Tramp", brought joy to millions.
Died: December 25, 1977

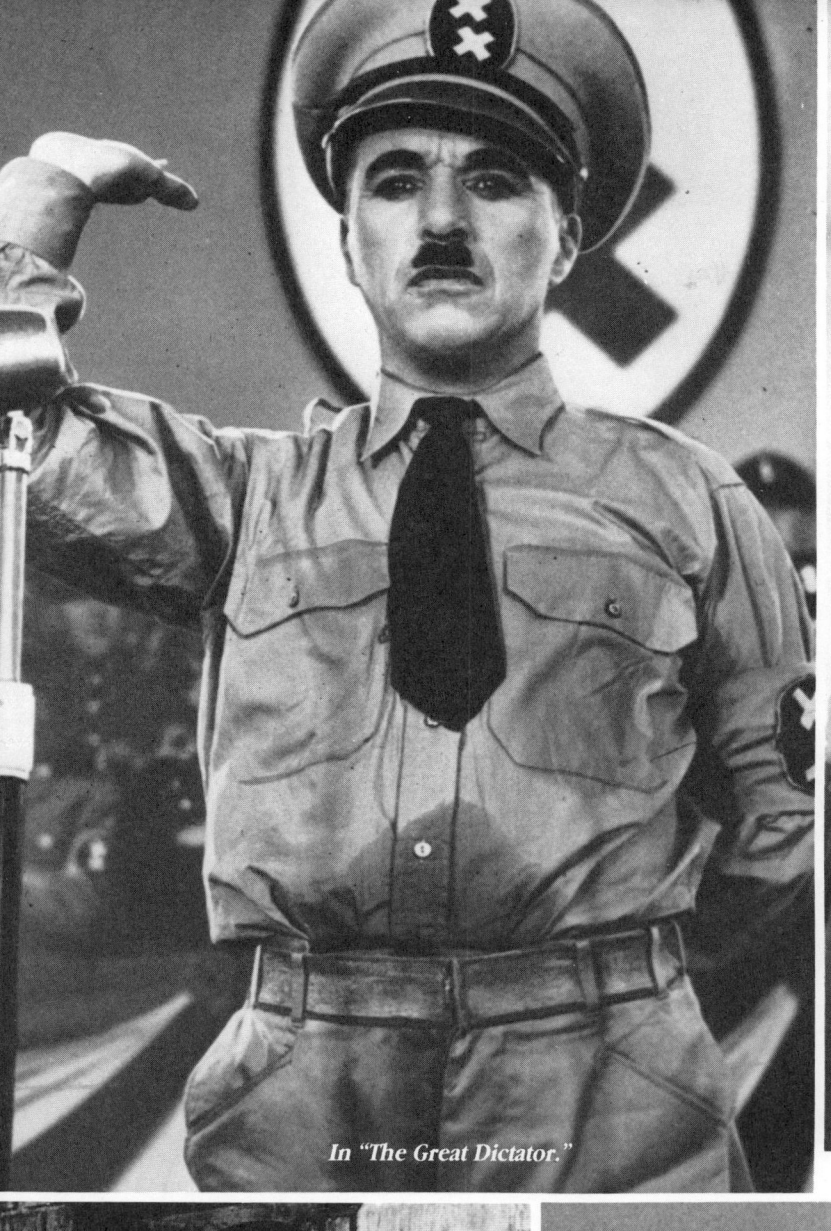

In "The Great Dictator."

Chaplin and brother Sydney as seen together in "Charlie's Aunt."

Chaplin and Jackie Coogan in "The Kid."

Ex-wife and costar Paulette Goddard with Chaplin in "Modern Times."

In "Gold Rush."

Anton Chekhov

Russian author Anton Chekhov wrote about such a vast variety of characters that his plays and stories could almost be used as a sociological study of his times.

Born to a serf who had bought his freedom, Chekhov grew up in the provincial center of Taganrog, where, while helping in his father's grocery store, he met the factory workers and commercial people who'd later appear as characters in his work. After high school he followed his family to Moscow, where his father had taken the family when his business failed. There Chekhov studied medicine, wrote humorous sketches for journals, and became the chief support of his family, a role he would cheerfully fill for the rest of his life. He beame a physician and wrote comic pieces that gained him a lowbrow audience, at the same time writing pessimistic, almost clinical, studies of the physically and mentally ill.

In Moscow he was a lively member of the intelligentsia. Assisting in the relief of the disastrous peasant famine in 1891 brought him close to the peasant class, who appeared in a sequence of short sketches titled "Peasant." His characters were not the sentimental figures familiar from Russian literature at that time, but were presented in a realistic, sometimes brutal light. Moving his family to a country estate outside Moscow, Chekhov got to know the landowning class whose pretensions and frustrations would haunt his great plays.

Chekhov is best known as a playwright. At school he wrote amateur theatricals. As a young man in Moscow he wrote "joke" plays, which always centered on a mix-up, such as "The Bear," in which the quarrel between a boorish landowner and sentimental widow ends in marriage. But it is his longer plays that give him a reputation as a major playwright. In them he balances pathos and humor, contrasts the real life of work, unspoiled nature and compassion, with the hollow life of self-delusion and boredom. "Uncle Vanya" is a study of aimlessness in a rural manor house. "The Seagull", a clash between the older and younger generation, was hissed off the stage when first performed in St. Petersburg but was later revived and became a hit. "The Cherry Orchard" protrays Russia's landowning class in decline. "Three Sisters" centers on the longings of a trio of provincial women.

Often criticized for too much mood and talk and too little plot and action, Chekhov's dramas weren't applauded by everyone. Leo Tolstoi, his revered contemporary, said he disliked Chekhov's plays even more than Shakespeare's. The plays were produced at the Moscow Art Theatre by the great Stanislavsky, who introduced a natural, non-declamatory style to the Russian stage. But even so, Chekhov wasn't satisfied with the productions of his plays—he intended them to be done with the lightest possible touch and felt even a hint of the tragic ruined them.

Chekhov is regarded as the greatest of all short-story writers. His stories have a haunting, lyrical quality that defies analysis. Usually centered on the trivial, they describe the pathos of everyday life, always with an underlying touch of humor. In a Chekhov story it is what is left unsaid that is often more important than what is said. Although in Russia many films are based on his stories they are difficult to transfer to cinematic treatment for Western audiences.

Chekhov didn't become famous outside Russia until after World War I, when his stories were translated into English. He is the father of the modern short form, with authors such as Ernest Hemingway and Katherine Mansfield acknowledging their great debt to him.

Besides plays and stories, Chekhov wrote a tract on penal reform after he took an arduous journey to the remote island of Sakhalin, on the other side of Siberia, a notorious penal settlement in Imperial Russia. He was staunchly unpolitical, adhering to no philosophical beliefs. Though for a time he espoused Tolstoi's theory of the simple life and non-resistance to evil, he later satirized these views in his stories. He came under attack from contemporaries who thought art and literature should serve a social purpose and carry a message. Chekhov's commitment to freedom was so fierce that he believed any alliance, even to an idea, was a menace to liberty.

Given Name: Anton Pavlovich Chekhov
Born: January 29, 1860, Taganrog, Russia
Married: Olga Knipper, 1902
Highlights: A leading dramatist and author, he was also a recognized master of the short story who poignantly depicted the lives of ordinary people.
Died: July 15, 1904

Anton Chekhov and his mother, Eugenia Yakovlevna at their home in Yalta in 1901.

Noel Coward

When King George VI of England offered Noel Coward a knighthood in 1947 Coward turned it down. "Noel Coward" looked better on theatre marquees than "Sir Noel", he said. This jack-of-all-theatrical-trades, and master of most, spent 60 years making news and making a name for himself with what he called his "talent to amuse". He did everything there was to do in the theatre except design scenery. Actor, singer, dancer, playwright, author, composer, librettist, lyricist and director, he created some of the best comedies in the English tradition—stage plays like "Hay Fever", "Design for Living", "Tonight at 8:30", "Blithe Spirit", and the romantic film hit "Brief Encounter", to name only a handful.

Coward's characters were rich, vain, spoiled, neurotic, snobbish and selfish, spoofs of the "smart set" he partied with during the '20's and 30's, when he was the toast of London. Somehow he made his characters bearable, even likeable, tossing them lines like the witty quips that someone once said fell from Coward's conversations like hailstones. One of his biggest and most-often performed hits, "Private Lives", was written for his adored and adoring British actress friend Gertrude Lawrence, with whom he starred in its first production.

Although he couldn't read music, Coward wrote hundreds of songs, including "Mad Dogs and Englishmen", "Mad About The Boy", and one of his best-known songs, "I'll See You Again", which he wrote in a taxi during a 20-minute traffic jam. A compulsive gadabout and globetrotter, Coward moved back and forth between the theatre worlds of London and New York and travelled the seas on freighters, but he never stopped writing. Once when a yacht he chartered shipwrecked and sank he lost all his money and clothing but managed to salvage the manuscript he was working on.

Son of a doting stage mother, the strongest influence in his life, and a musician-father who was forced to work as a piano and organ salesman to support his family, Coward made his first stage appearance in London at the age of 11. "I was a brazen, odious prodigy", he claimed in his autobiography "Present Indicative". One prestigious theatre figure, revolted by his stylistic manner, demanded that "someone take that boy out of my sight and never let me see him again." But "that boy", after a variety of stints on the London stage (and in a D.W. Griffith movie) set sail for New York in 1921 with a sheaf of manuscripts and 75 dollars in cash. Ten years later he was one of the highest paid playwrights of all times.

With his trademark tophat and glittering wit, Coward was always provocative. He was scorned by intellectuals for his highly polished style. A bon vivant with a jaded manner, he was also a friend of such powers as Winston Churchill, Franklin Roosevelt and Bernard Shaw. Although he kept houses in Jamaica and Switzerland in order to avoid paying British income taxes, he was a fanatical patriot. Until he was discharged because of illness he served in World War I, and entertained troops in Africa and Asia in World War II until he collapsed from exhaustion. His play "Cavalcade" glorifies the devotion Englishmen of his time had to their country. A 1943 song "Don't Let's Be Beastly To The Germans" aroused a storm of protest until he explained its ironic tone was a dead-serious warning against being too quick to forgive the Nazis, as Britain had forgiven the Germans and forgotten their own heroes after world War I. In 1970 Coward accepted a knighthood from Queen Elizabeth II.

Falling from disfavor in the 50's and 60's, the versatile Coward worked up a cabaret act which he played in, among other spots, Las Vegas. He died at 73 during a tremendous revival of his plays on both the New York and London stages.

Coward's advice to young actors was typical of his delightful wit: "Speak clearly, don't bump into people, and if you must look for motivation think of your pay packet on Friday."

Coward in Hollywood dressing room 1958.

Coward on a Riviera holiday in 1958.

Given Name: Noel Coward

Born: December 16, 1889, Teddington, Middlesex, England

Highlights: Prolific lyricist for popular musical theater. Knighted by Queen Elizabeth II in 1970.

Died: March 25, 1973

Above: Noel Coward (left) talks with Laurence Olivier at Coward's 70th birthday tribute in 1969.

Right: Another view of Coward on his 70th birthday.

Left: In Hollywood, 1932.

Below: In Jamaica, 1952.

Salvador Dali

Salvador Dali claimed he was destined to live up to his first name, which in his native Spanish means "saviour", and rescue modern art. Flamboyant in his life style as well as his artistic style, he said his "sublime craziness" began at an early age in Figueras, where he was born, spurning his father's wish that he follow in his footsteps and become a notary public, instead attending art school first in his home town, later in Madrid. There he not only studied artistic technique but commenced his career as an activist eccentric, twice being expelled from the School of Fine Arts. Before going to Paris, center of the European art world in the Twenties, he spent a month in prison for supporting a revolutionary movement in Catalonia.

It was due to the prodding of Spanish artists Joan Miro and Pablo Picasso that Dali's father allowed him to go to France. Miro's and Picasso's belief in Dali's talent was vindicated at once. He joined the surrealist movement and "incarnated the surrealist spirit", wrote French author Andre Breton. Picasso was both encourager and rival to Dali, who wanted to be the more famous of the two. In typical hyperbole, Dali once said that Picasso was "a brilliant painter but not a total genius like Dali. If one plays at being a genius", he added, "one ends up by being one." Putting their names in what he considered the proper order, he said, "After Dali and Picasso, nothing."

However, the two Spaniards had their differences, especially in politics. During the Spanish Civil War Picasso was an avid foe of Gen. Francisco Franco. Dali supported Franco until the dictator's death in 1975. In the 30's, Dali was expelled from the surrealist movement in Paris on the grounds that he was a pro-Hitler fascist.

In 1929 French poet Paul Eluard visited Dali at his Costa Brava home with his Russian wife Gala. At Dali's request, Gala never left. She became his muse, his model and eventually his wife. They were childless because, he said, "great geniuses always produce mediocre children . . . I am only interested in inheriting myself."

An outrageous exhibitionist, Dali's trademarks were a pointed waxed moustache, long hair and a walking stick—he had 30 of them, designed, he said, to provoke all feelings from laughter to indignation. He loved making headlines—in 1965 he staged a "sewerastic happening" in New York to attract attention to his retrospective show at the Gallery of Modern Art.

Blending super-realism and hallucinatory transformations of form and space, Dali's painting style was as shocking as his personal style. One of his best-known works, "The Persistence of Memory" (1931), which hangs in New York's Museum of Modern Art, is a painting of wet, limp watches. Although not a faithful Roman Catholic, he began painting religious subjects in 1949, and referred to himself as a mystic painter. During the war years he lived in the United States, doing more commercial projects than serious art—jewelry, fabrics, furniture, stage designs, decorations in shop windows on Fifth Avenue.

In 1974 Dali realized his ambition of establishing the Dali Museum in Figueras, in which he placed 621 works he and Gala had kept aside as insurance against hard times. But his main goal, he said, was to become so famous, through his antics as well as his art, that he lived up to the name he called himself—"the Divine Dali."

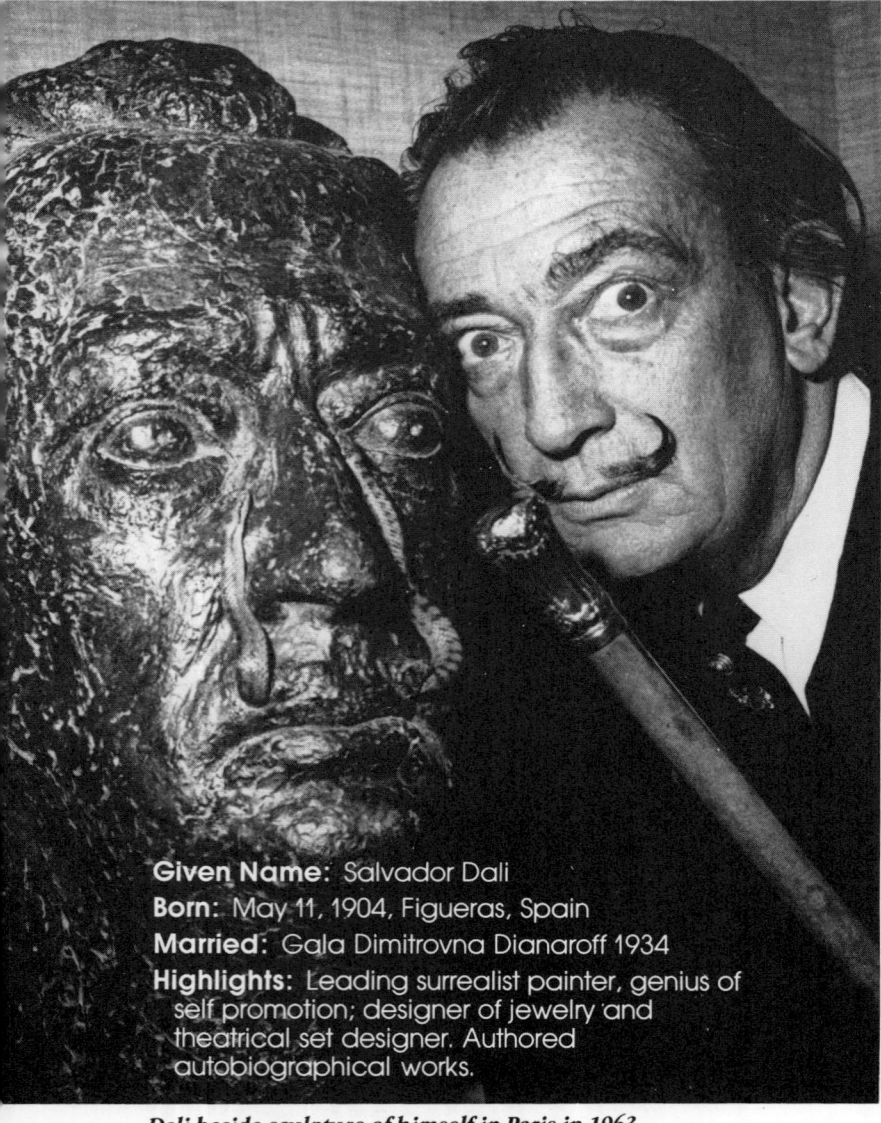

Given Name: Salvador Dali
Born: May 11, 1904, Figueras, Spain
Married: Gala Dimitrovna Dianaroff 1934
Highlights: Leading surrealist painter, genius of self promotion; designer of jewelry and theatrical set designer. Authored autobiographical works.

Dali beside sculpture of himself in Paris in 1963.

In 1964, Dali drew attention with his own version of the Venus de Milo.

ARTS 160

Dali unveils a new painting in 1975.

"The Faces of War" and its painter, 1941.

Dali exhibits his mustache and one of his Great Danes before opening of his 1954 show in Rome.

Dali at work in the Walt Disney Studio in 1946.

Volunteers escort Dali from a 1979 exhibition of his work closed by striking employees.

ARTS

Cecil B. DeMille

In 1956, near the end of his life, Cecil B. DeMille went to Egypt to oversee the second production of "The Ten Commandments." There the master of super-colossal epics broke his own crowd-scene record, filming the greatest number of extras in history—25,000. A master of detail, DeMille trudged up Mt. Sinai with camera crews—"I figured if Moses could do it, I could do it", he said.

His biggest crowd scene until then was in an earlier production of the same story—4000 extras and 6000 animals were used in the parting of the Red Sea. It was fitting that the producer who worked only in superlatives should win an Oscar for "The Greatest Show on Earth", his circus spectacular.

A DeMille production guaranteed spectacles—clashing battles, violent storms, lavish banquets, sweeping fires and of course, impassioned love-making. He had an unerring judgement of public taste, combining Victorian moral tone with graphic sexuality.

His movies also guaranteed huge profits. DeMille believed you had to spend money to make money. He spent it like water—with the judgement of a banker. Only 2 of his 70 films lost money. Often, he earmarked profits for charity.

DeMille was raised in a religious atmosphere. His father, who considered entering the ministry before he became a playwright, read from the Bible every evening. Biblical characters who were heroes of his childhood became super-heroes of DeMille productions. Evangelist Billy Graham called him "a prophet in celluloid . . . who has brought the word of God to more people in the world than any other man." At the time of the producer's death it was estimated that 5 billion people—twice the world's population—had seen his films.

The man who made more millions and developed more stars than anyone else in the film industry entered the business half-heartedly. Backed by New York showman David Belasco, he went West in 1913 to Los Angeles, where movie pioneers had begun to gather. He rented a barn in a lemon grove in a quiet suburb named Hollywood, riding to work each day on horseback, carrying his lunch in a pail. "Squaw Man" was finished in 1914, became a hit, and Paramount pictures was born. In 1915 he filmed "Carmen", with scores of extras and real sets, instead of painted flats. In 1923 he spent an unprecedented million and a half dollars making "The Ten Commandments." It held the Paramount box office record for 25 years until another DeMille epic, "Reap the Wild Wind", broke it.

The rest, as they say in Hollywood, is history.

Portrait of the 75 year old DeMille taken at his home in 1956.

DeMille played himself in the 1956 "Buster Keaton Story" starring Donald O'Connor (left). Keaton (right), advised on the film.

Given Name: Cecil Blount De Mille
Born: August 12, 1881, Ashfield, Massachusetts
Married: Constance Adams, 1902, 4 children
Highlights: Pioneer motion picture producer and director, master of the motion picture spectacular. Won Academy Award in 1953 for *The Greatest Show on Earth*. Producer of seventy films between 1913 and 1956.
Died: January 21, 1959.

Visiting niece, Agnes DeMille, in 1954.

Dancing with granddaughter at 1952 Golden Wedding Anniversary.

DeMille listens to the sound track for one of his films.

Egyptian Premier Gamel Abdel Nasser greets DeMille before 1954 location filming of "The Ten Commandments".

Behind the camera in 1932.

In his first office.

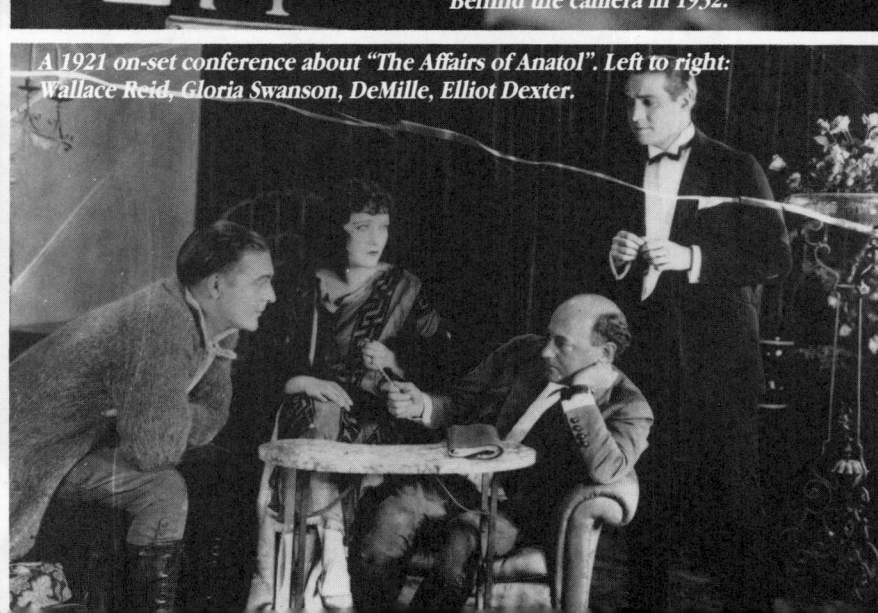

A 1921 on-set conference about "The Affairs of Anatol". Left to right: Wallace Reid, Gloria Swanson, DeMille, Elliot Dexter.

Walt Disney

Disney used a combination of talent, courage and vision to put together a vast entertainment empire. He brought smiles and joy to millions of families—adults and children alike—and made a fortune in the process.

The Disney empire was founded on a very unlikely cornerstone, a cartoon rodent called Mickey Mouse. At the height of his popularity, Mickey was one of the best-loved characters in the world. He was known as "Michel Souris" in France, "El Raton Miguelito" in Latin America, "Topolino" in Italy and "Miki Kuchi" in Japan. During World War II, his name was the password at Supreme Allied Headquarters in Europe, and later, Mickey had over a million members in his fan club in the United States alone. And all of that fame, as well as the character himself, was the results of Disney's observations, and what seemed at the time to be bad luck.

Early in his career, Disney had been producing a series of cartoons called "Oswald the Rabbit". After a disagreement with the distributor over money, Disney lost the series, and was forced to develop a new character. He thought of some mice that had lived in a commercial art studio in which he had worked in Kansas City, and one particularly bold and friendly mouse that he named Mortimer. That was the beginning of the mouse that roared, who was later renamed Mickey at the suggestion of Disney's wife, Lillian, who had once worked for him as a $15-per-week animator.

Disney and his brother Roy, with whom he had been running a small studio, believed in Mickey Mouse, and risked everything they had to bring him to the screen. They borrowed all they could on their homes, cars and life insurance to launch their good-hearted creation. The first two Mickey Mouse episodes didn't sell, because they were silent in a time when sound pictures were beginning to take over. But the third Mickey cartoon, "Steamboat Willie", had music and sound effects, and was well-received by the public when Disney released it himself. From that time on, the Disney studio grew almost geometrically.

Other characters, such as Donald Duck and Pluto the Dog, were developed and began to rival Mickey in popularity. Then Disney introduced feature-length animated films with "Snow White and the Seven Dwarfs", followed by "Pinocchio", "Fantasia" and others. In 1949, the studio began doing all-live action films, the first being "Treasure Island". Disney television shows followed.

In the 1950's, looking for new ways to bring his characters and their joy to the public, Disney conceived and developed "Disneyland", the vast amusement park complex in southern California that has become an attraction for visitors from all over the world. Later, "Disney World" was opened in Florida to make the world of fun and fantasy available to even more people.

The actions of one bold little mouse, seen by one struggling cartoonist who believed in himself, inspired a whole world of fun.

Mickey Mouse rides a fire engine with the boss at Disneyland.

Weeding out some of the 4 million drawings made for "Bambi".

Given Name: Walter Elias Disney
Born: December 5, 1901, Chicago, Illinois
Married: Lillian Bounds, 2 children
Highlights: Created "Mickey Mouse" and other popular cartoon characters, founded the studios that made film animation an art, and conceived and developed Disneyland and Disneyworld amusement parks.
Died: December 15, 1966

Young Walt Disney with his first camera in 1925.

Disney at his studio drawing board in 1955.

Live fawns were used as models for Disney's 1938 production, "Bambi".

Disney poses with some of his characters before a 1950 performance of Ice Capades.

T.S. Eliot

Even after he had been heaped with fame, financial independence and two Nobel prizes, T.S. Eliot remained the poet of grey melancholy. During the period between the two world wars, his verse chronicled the spiritual despair of his times, when his generation saw in the disintegration of Europe a symbol of their own discontent. His great epic poem, "The Wasteland", written in the '20's, was a haunting reflection of the wasteland of the spirit which seemed to afflict Eliot and his literary peers.

Born Thomas Stearns Eliot in St. Louis, Missouri, Eliot emmigrated to England after a Harvard education, ultimately becoming an English citizen once described as "more English than the English." The opposite of a Bohemian artist, Eliot, who once worked at Lloyd's of London, appeared to be the model British banker, precise in his habits, conservative of dress, speaking in a clipped British accent. A man for whom, his tailor reported, nothing was ever in excess, Eliot might have been a stand-in for the timid hero of his poem "The Lovesong of J. Alfred Prufrock", a 20th century man of little faith who has bold dreams of hearing mermaids singing, but is so anxious he isn't sure how to wear his clothes, or whether or not he dares eat a peach.

A voracious reader, Eliot packed "The Wasteland" and his other verse with references and quotes from a variety of myths and cultures. He was often accused, as was his friend and fellow ex-patriate Ezra Pound, of employing obscurity for its own sake. He dedicated "The Wasteland" to Pound. But his writing also evoked images of the contemporary urban scene—dehumanized crowds streaming across bridges over the Thames, brown fog, impotent men and despairing shopgirls. His bleak "The Hollow Men", which contains the most often quoted lines in 20th Century poetry, sums up his view of modern man's fate:

> "This is the way the world ends
> This is the way the world ends
> This is the way the world ends
> Not with a bang but a whimper."

Although Eliot wrote about spiritual despair and in "The Hippopotamous" compared the church to that awkward animal, he was eventually confirmed in the Church of England. His religious beliefs surface in his later works, especially his plays. "Murder in the Cathedral" (1935) was a grim account of the murder in 1170 of Thomas Becket, Archbishop of Canterbury. "The Cocktail Party", a search for spiritual salvation, won the New York Drama Critics' Award for the Best Foreign Play of 1950. He was perhaps best known for his plays, which also included "The Family Reunion". Writing then in verse, he hoped to restore poetic drama to an important place in theatre arts.

Eliot was married twice and had no children, but he was a devoted admirer of cats. His witty collection of cat poems, "Old Possum's Book of Practical Cats" ("Old Possum" was Pound's nickname for Eliot) became after his death the hit musical "Cats" and enjoyed long runs in both London and New York.

Besides his Nobel Prizes for "remarkable pioneering work in modern poetry", Eliot was honored by King George VI with the prestigious Order of Merit and by President Lyndon Johnson with the Medal of Freedom.

In a lecture on the theories of poetics, Eliot's contention that poetry "is not a turning loose of emotion but an escape from emotion" perfectly suited this restrained, prim giant of an age which, if it were to be labelled with one poet's name, might be called the Age of Eliot.

A 1956 portrait of T.S. Eliot taken in London.

Given Name: Thomas Stearns Eliot
Born: September 26, 1888, St. Louis, Missouri
Married: Vivian Haigh Haigh-Wood, 1915
Married: Esme Valerie Fletcher, 1957
Highlights: Leading poet whose work conveyed the hopelessness and despair of much of his generation. Won Nobel Prize for Literature in 1948.
Died: January 4, 1965

T.S. Eliot lecturing at the British Information Center in 1949.

United States Ambassador David Bruce (right) presenting the Medal of Freedom to T.S. Eliot in September 1964.

"Duke" Ellington

His nickname was a title earned for his appearance. But he had more important titles earned for his talent—titles like "Composer", "Conductor", "Arranger", "Performer". The always elegant "Duke"—a nickname he acquired as a boy for his careful attention to dress—stayed at the top of the jazz world for decades and had a musical career that lasted over half a century.

There were few musical challenges that Ellington did not accept. And few areas in which he did not excel. He composed for movies, the stage, and television, as well as for recording and live performances. His compositions totalled almost a thousand, and included such classics as "Mood Indigo", which became one of his trademarks, as well as "Solitude", "Sophisticated Lady", and "Take the A Train". He wrote the background score for the movie "Anatomy of a Murder", and also composed several extensive jazz tone poems, including "Black, Brown and Beige" and "Liberian Suite". Much of his work, particularly the more extensive pieces, was devoted to a musical exploration or celebration of the black man in America. In 1959, the National Association for the Advancement of Colored People gave Ellington its Spingarn award for "the highest or noblest achievement by an American negro during the preceding year or years."

Ellington had written his first piece when he was 14, but his big break didn't come until 14 years later, when his five-man combo was engaged to play at Harlem's famous Cotton Club. (Six other bands had been scheduled for auditions, but Ellington's group was so impressive it was hired on the spot, and the other auditions were canceled.) He immediately ex-

Ambassador Jacques Kosciusko Morzet (right) joins Ellington at the piano in 1973 after presenting him with the French Legion of Honor.

Ellington and Louis Armstrong rehearse for their first recording together in 1946.

Ellington leads a 1968 concert at the Cathedral Church of St. John the Divine in New York in 1968.

panded the group to 11, and started playing music unlike anything heard before. The crowds loved it, and continued to fill the Cotton Club for five years, the length of Ellington's stay.

"We didn't think of it as jazz," Ellington said later. "We thought of it as Negro music." But it was jazz, with all the guts and soul the word implies, but with a new sophistication, discipline and interdependency among the players and their instruments. To a form that had often been a joyous but unbridled musical free-for-all, Ellington had brought new order and purpose. He also brought new concepts, and new adaptations of existing forms. He pioneered in the use of wordless voice as an instrument in orchestration and in the use of a miniature concerto form in building jazz arrangements around a soloist.

His innovations brought him worldwide acclaim, and he led his band on many international tours that generated ovations wherever it performed. And no matter how hectic his schedule, Ellington kept his composure, and kept on composing. Sometimes he would get out of bed to bang out a new tune, or dash off a theme in a taxi. Any event, any occasion, any observation could become the basis for a new piece. When asked how he could compose, run a band and keep up with his public, Ellington replied "Why, man, ideas are free. They're all around you. All you gotta do, you know, is reach up there and grab them."

Ellington did grab them, by the bushel. Then he gave them to audiences all over the world. And to generations of music lovers to come.

Danny Kaye (right) presents an award to Ellington in 1945 at the Los Angeles Philharmonic Auditorium.

Given Name: Edward Kennedy Ellington
Born: April 29, 1899, Washington, D.C
Married: Edna Thompson, 1918
Highlights: Leading jazz composer, conductor, performer and recording artist. Created over 1,000 compositions from single songs to extensive suites.
Died: May 24, 1974

Erte

Erte, born Romain de Tirtoff, had an exclusive contract with Harper's Bazaar for 22 years, beginning in 1915. During that time the artist-designer also created theater sets and costumes for the Folies Bergere and the Ziegfeld Follies. In his later years, Erte became known for his intricate art deco-style sculptures and jewelry.

Some of the famous who were his old friends and clients are Liz Taylor, Andy Warhol, Barbra Streisand and Claudette Colbert. The Russian-born artist, turned fashion designer, won two important French awards; Officer of Arts and Letters, and the City of Paris' medal for the arts.

In 1982, at 90 years of age, artist Erte still turned out drawings like hot cakes and lifted 5½ pound weights every day. The pink-cheeked nonogenarian cheerfully said, "I also walk about four miles a day, eat and drink what I want and smoke at times."

He talked about his love for all natural forms, all living creatures and lived with his majestic Burmese cat and eight glass-caged turtle doves in an apartment in Paris from which he has a view of the Eiffel Tower.

Born in St. Petersburg in 1892, Erte began to draw at age four with colored pencils and he speaks of designing a dress for his mother when he was only five years old. He came from a long line of naval officers but refused to become a sailor, instead moving to Paris and pursuing his art. Later, his parents and sister followed to escape the Russian Revolution.

In his early days Erte speaks of working for a second-class dressmaker who said he was hopeless and proceeded to throw all his sketches into the wastebasket. But when he sent his portfolio to couturier Paul Poiret, he was hired instantly. Then came the long stint for Harper's Bazaar, a job he performed while remaining in Paris. He produced every cover for Harper's from 1915 to 1935 and also designed costumes for legendary dancer Anna Pavlova and actress-dancer Norma Shearer. And he created opulent and fanciful show clothes and sets for the Ziegfeld Follies, George White's "Scandals" and the Folies Bergeres. In addition, he designed costumes and sets for operas and films and Erte graphics became collector's items.

Later, in 1986, his art deco designs of the 1920's were applied to knitwear and issued in a limited edition clothes collection in which each piece was numbered and signed by the artist. His backer in this venture, entrepreneurial Italian Paul Magit, wanted the art knitwear to appeal to the afffluent, to a collector of Erte's works and to fashion-conscious women.

A French citizen, who was better known in America than in France, Erte divided his time between Paris, Barbados and Majorca where most of his sculptures were executed. He also designed costumes for Debussy's "Pelleas et Melisande," Racine's "Phaedre" and "Der Rosenkavalier" for England's Glyndebourne Festival. He loved showing his glass-framed designs for the Poulene opera, "Les Mamelles de Tiresias." In this ambiguous work, a woman wearing a tight top and slinky skirt finally turns into a man. And the male character shown in Erte's panel wears a dressing gown painted with voluptuous nude women.

As an artist who contributed much to the world of theatre, fashion and magazine design, Erte watched and participated in all vagaries of fashions from flappers to minis and viewed the new fashion freedom of choice as a good thing for women

Erte at Dyansen Gallery in New York with "Aments" sculpture behind him.

An unidentified well-wisher and Singer Diana Ross (right) congratulate Erte at his 90th birthday exhibit in 1982.

Given Name: Romain de Tirtoff

Born: 1892, St. Petersburg, Russia

Highlights: Prolific and influential artist and designer. Created every *Harper's Bazaar* cover from 1915 to 1935, designed costumes and sets for ballet, theater and cinema.

Fellow designer Gabriole Van Bryce congratulates Erte at a party celebrating his 92nd birthday.

Actress Lillian Montevechi also brought birthday greetings.

William Faulkner

Faulkner country, the setting for William Faulkner's often violent novels and stories, isn't the South of moonlight and magnolias. It is a region haunted by memories of a life gone forever and threatened with a bleak, commercialized future in which greedy country yokels seize land and power from faded aristocracy. It is Yoknapatawpha County, whose chief town is Jefferson, a fictional replica of Oxford, Mississippi, where the author was born, lived and died. The Sartoris family, degenerating relics from a dead past who are set upon by the money-grubbing and amoral Snopes clan, are very much like Faulkner's own family.

Yet Faulkner contended that in the novels viewed by some as powerful tragedies and others as slabs of depravity he was concerned not with mere regional problems but with human problems. With the publication in 1929 of "The Sound and The Fury" it was obvious the author was a major figure struggling with major themes. In 1931 he wrote the shocking "Sanctuary", a gothic horror story written, he said, to make money. Although many found the themes of sadism and rape in "Sanctuary" offensive, the novel gained Faulkner a popular following.

Faulkner was taken seriously abroad before he found fame in the U.S. "The writer in America isn't part of the culture", he once said bitterly. "He's like a fine dog. People like him around, but he's of no use."

During the next 30 years this writer "of no use" made Yoknapatawpha County world famous and earned the Nobel Prize with such novels as "As I Lay Dying", "Light in August", "Absalom Absalom!" "The Fable", which won him a Pulitzer Prize, and "The River", published the year he died to great critical acclaim.

A high school drop-out, Faulkner joined the Canadian Air Force during World War I. The youth from Oxford, Miss., was sent for training to Oxford, England, where he discovered Shakespeare and the Elizabethan poets, whom he regarded as the greatest writers in the English language. He worked briefly in New York, but returned home because, he said, he missed hunting and fishing. He served as Postmaster at the University in Oxford until he was dismissed for playing bridge on the job. He then settled down to writing, composing the endlessly winding sentences that made him often difficult to read, capturing the rhythms of poor white and black speech. He spent some time in Hollywood writing scripts, one of which was the movie version of Hemingway's "To Have and Have Not".

Although his writing style was eccentric and complex, Faulkner himself was a gentle, plainspoken, often taciturn man. Once when he was teaching at the University of Virginia President Kennedy invited him to dine at the White House. "Why, that's a hundred miles away", he said. "That's a long way to go just to eat", and he declined. He was reluctant, also, to travel to Stockholm to receive the Nobel Prize in 1950 but decided he could work the trip in with a visit with his only daughter in Paris. Though hailed by the Swedish Academy as the "unrivaled master of all living British and American novelists as a deep psychologist", Faulkner retreated to his 366-acre farm back home and contended he was really just a farmer, not a literary man. Of his work in general, he said "If I could write again I'd do it better. I've never been completely satisfied with what I've done." Faulkner then stated that writing must concern itself with "the old verities and truths of the heart—love and honor and pity and pride and compassion."

In a statement that has become as much a part of his legacy and legend as his novels, this writer famous for tales of depravity and violence celebrated the nobility of man: "I believe man will not merely endure. He will prevail . . . because he alone has a soul and a spirit capable of compassion and sacrifice and endurance."

Given Name: William Faulkner
Born: September 25, 1897, New Albany, Mississippi
Married: Estelle Oldham Franklin, 1929
Highlights: Leading American novelist whose work described the decay of the Old South. Won Pulitzer Prize in 1954, Nobel Prize for Literature in 1949.
Died: July 6, 1962

F. G. Strachan, Consul of Sweden (left) looks on as Consul Lionel Vassey awards the French Legion of Honor to William Faulkner in 1951.

King Gustav VI (left) of Sweden hands William Faulkner the 1949 Nobel Prize for literature.

Faulkner at the typewriter in his Oxford, Mississippi home in 1950.

The pipe-smoking author in his Rome hotel on the way to Egypt in 1954.

Faulkner at his newer typewriter in 1956.

Wearing tweeds and carrying his pipe, Faulkner strolls the Oxford campus of the University of Mississippi.

Ella Fitzgerald

Few people in the performing arts or, for that matter, in the public eye in any way, can maintain the level of their performance for a couple of decades, let alone five. But Ella, as she has been known affectionately to generations of fans, has gifts that are given to very few. She also has an innate shyness and a quiet dignity which are rare in popular figures, and which have probably contributed much to her success and longevity as a performer.

Ella is "on stage" only when she is on stage. And even then, listening to her, one still gets the sense of her humility and wonderment. Even after all she has achieved, all the world-wide acclaim that has come her way, one can still hear her asking herself "Did all these people really come to hear me?" Despite having received enough awards to fill a concert hall, she remains shy and uneasy in public, especially when being praised.

Her shyness could even be said to be the cause of her incredible singing career.

The "First Lady of Song" actually wanted to be a dancer. But when she had her first chance, at a Harlem amateur contest in 1934, she was too scared to dance. So she sang instead. Her tremulous rendition of "The Object of My Affection" won her first prize. More importantly, it won the raves of some professional musicians in the audience, who brought her to the attention of band leader Chick Webb. He then gave her a chance to prove her popularity, which she did at a 1935 Yale dance, so Webb kept her on.

Her first record, "Love and Kisses", was recorded with Webb's band on June 12th of that year. But the first hit for Ella, and for Webb's band, didn't come until 1938. That was the year she recorded "A-Tisket A-Tasket", a song she had written with friend Al Feldman. That was also the year in which her popularity exploded, as her talents became loved by the public at large as well as by the jazz lovers who had adopted her almost instantly three years before.

Decades later, The Rolling Stone Record Guide would call her "The most perfect pop-jazz voice on record.... Guided by musical form instead of lyrics, she brought an unparalleled sense of classicism to everything she did, from scat to pop ballads. Blessed with perfect pitch and perfect diction, she was mistress of the long-lined narrative phrase."

After recording on the Decca label for 20 years, she switched in 1955 to the Verve label of Norman Granz, with whose "Jazz at the Philharmonic" tours she'd begun traveling in Europe in 1946. That association helped broaden her appeal even farther beyond the jazz audience, both in America and abroad. She recorded the songs of Jerome Kern, Johnny Mercer, Rodgers and Hart, Harold Arlen, Irving Berlin and Duke Ellington. After appearing with Ellington in 1958, she toured Latin America in 1960, Europe in the early 1960's with the Oscar Peterson Trio, and Japan and Hong Kong in 1965.

Announcing her songs in a girlish voice, wiping nervous perspiration from her brow with her trademark large handkerchief, Ella Fitzgerald literally brought her music to the world. When she returned to the stage following eye surgery in 1971, she was wearing glasses, which just added to her unique charm. They gave her a look of a dignified grandmother about to say something worth listening to. And that's only fitting. For, as long as people love music, Ella Fitzgerald will always be worth listening to.

Given Name: Ella Fitzgerald
Born: April 25, 1918, Newport News, Virginia
Married: Bennie Kornegay 1941 (annulled 1943).
Married: Ray Brown, 1949, (divorced 1953) 1 child.
Highlights: The "First Lady of Song". One of the world's leading female vocalists since 1935. Winner of numerous awards.

"The First Lady of Song" performing at Rome's Circus Maximus.

Leaving the courtroom in 1943 after the annulment of her 1941 marriage to dancer Bennie Kornegay.

ARTS

Frank Sinatra (left) and Placido Domingo introduce Ella Fitzgerald at a 1986 benefit concert.

Performing in Munich in 1967.

Ella Fitzgerald at 1974 funeral services for jazz great Duke Ellington.

At a 1952 concert in Stockholm.

F. Scott Fitzgerald

Francis Scott Key Fitzgerald said about his novel, *This Side of Paradise,* published in 1920, that he spoke for "all the sad young men" who had "grown up to find all Gods dead, all wars fought, all faiths in men shaken." Fitzgerald had brilliant writing talents and at his best attained real eminence, but he wrote unevenly, and the dissipation and inner struggle characterizing his career were often the enemy of his best literary achievement.

A master of the short story and the novel of manners, Fitzgerald was called the "laureate of the Jazz Age". Both his life and his works offer an acute commentary both on the life of the twenties and the disillusion and depression of the 1930's. He was born in St. Paul, Minn. on September 24, 1896 and his work spanned the years between World Wars I and II. Educated at St. Paul's Academy, he was sent East to a Catholic prep school, Newman School, Hackensack, N.J. in 1911. He went on to Princeton University in 1913 but did not return after his junior year because of ill health and low grades due to his inattention to academic work. Instead, he entered the army as a second lieutenant in 1917.

Nevertheless, Fitzgerald's Princeton years were important. They provided a foundation for his writing talent, introduced him to more and better literature than he had known before, and brought him together with other literary young men, notably Edmund Wilson. Princeton also furnished most of the material for *This Side of Paradise,* the success which launched his career.

Once the novel was published, Fitzgerald left his job as an advertising copywriter for Barron Collier Agency in New York and married Zelda Sayre, the Alabama girl who occupied much of his fiction. The central characters of *The Beautiful and Damned* (1922), his second novel, are a couple like the Fitzgeralds, who lead a life of drinking, partying and endless talk. But while the Fitzgeralds' disorderly lifestyle both mirrored and created the pattern for others of the 1920's generation, it was increasingly damaging to Fitzgerald's work.

Going to Europe, first in 1921, was both an adventure and an escape, but during their second period there, 1924-25, he completed what many consider his best work, *The Great Gatsby* (1925). As the 1920's advanced, Fitzgerald's drinking became regarded as alcoholism, while Zelda's erratic behavior was diagnosed as schizophrenia in 1930. His difficulty in organizing *Tender Is the Night* (1934) was largely due to the strain that his own, and Zelda's, conditions placed on him. Yet, his struggle to understand and utilize the conflicts created by these conditions became the substance of the novel. Not many people read the novel at the time it was

The only known portrait of F. Scott Fitzgerald was acquired by the National Portrait Gallery in Washington.

F. Scott Fitzgerald, daughter "Scotty" and wife Zelda at sea in 1926.

ARTS

published; it sold less than 13,000 copies in its first two years.

Fitzgerald's life reached a low point in 1935 when he suffered the nervous collapse that he later described so brilliantly in three essays called *The Crack-Up* (1945). The events of his stories are nearly always events in which Fitzgerald himself participated with all his emotional energy: "My own happiness . . . often approached such an ecstasy," he wrote in *The Crack-Up*, "that I could not share it even with the person dearest to me but had to walk it away in quiet streets and lanes with only fragments of it to distill into little lines in books. . ."

"He had," as John Peale Bishop put it, "the rare faculty of being able to experience romantic and ingenuous emotions and half an hour later regard them with satiric detachment. Even the breaking of his own heart was a sound to be listened to and enjoyed like the rest." To some readers, this experience is a revelation, the opening of a door for the first time into the world of imagination.

Fitzgerald "really created for the public a new generation," as Gertrude Stein said, by quite innocently being it; he was as surprised as anyone else to discover that in *This Side of Paradise* "he had written a 'bible of flaming youth.'"

In his biography on Fitzgerald, Arthur Mizener said, "Fitzgerald failed the critics . . . and they were uncertain whether to take him as a serious writer who was sometimes popular or as a popular writer who was occasionally serious." He estimated that of Fitzgerald's 160 stories, at least 50 are serious and successful stories and perhaps half of these are superb.

Fitzgerald's work, off and on, as a movie scriptwriter marked his last years; at his death he was working on a novel about Hollywood, *The Last Tycoon* (1941). Not long before he died on December 21, 1940 at age 44, every one of his books was out of print; the novel he wanted so desperately to complete was unfinished; the reputation in which he found his justification was only a faint echo. But a phenomenal revival that began in 1950 restored interest and the Fitzgerald's lives have made a permanent claim upon the American imagination

Given Name: Francis Scott Key Fitzgerald
Born: September 24, 1896, St. Paul, Minnesota
Married: Zelda Sayre, 1920, 1 child
Highlights: Leading American novelist of the 1920s and 1930s whose work accurately conveyed the behavior and feelings of the economic elite in the "Jazz Age"
Died: December 21, 1940

The Fitzgeralds in their Paris apartment in 1925.

Fitzgerald at work, 1934.

Robert Frost

"Nobody takes up poetry", said Robert Frost when he was 80. "You drift into it by little things." It was writing about "little things"—a chimney, a door, simple country people, that made Frost the most popular American poet of the 20th century.

Brought East by his mother from San Francisco when his father died, Frost kept a farm in Derby, New Hampshire "less as a farmer than as a fugitive from a world that seemed to 'disallow' me", he said. There he raised a family, did some school-teaching and writing, and in 1912 set out for England to seek his fortune as a poet. With encouragement from expatriates T.S. Eliot and Ezra Pound he published two books, "A Boy's Will" and "North of Boston". Containing some of Frost's most enduring poems, the books were well-received, and when World War I drove Frost back to the U.S. he found himself established as a poet, with an offer to teach at Amherst College, one of the many colleges with which he was connected all his life. Frost received numerous honorary degrees throughout his long life but since he never graduated from college he said none of them were "honest ones."

A rarity among the so-called modern poets, Frost used what he called "unliterary" language in his verse, and the colloquial rhythms of everyday speech. He believed a poem's power was in the "saying", not its placement on a page, and was an early "performance poet", reciting his folksy creations on university campuses around the U.S. Near the end of his life he reached his peak as a public poet when John Kennedy asked him to read at his inauguration.

Frost believed that any subject matter is as good as any other; it's the treatment that makes the difference. He was intensely interested in people and said only two of his poems had no person in them. New England was the setting for his poems—its snowy woods, lonely roads and farmhouses—and his characters were rugged North Country folk. But he was not a regional poet. His people—a neighbor mending a fence, a hired man—and his themes—choosing which of two roads to travel—were transformed by his imagination into mythic figures and universal truths.

The Frost family was plagued with a series of harrowing tragedies. The poet's first child died of cholera. His beloved sister, and later his daughter Irma, were committed to mental institutions. His wife Elinor, his childhood sweetheart, died suddenly. His only son Carol committed suicide. Only his daughter Leslie survived the extremities of suffering that hounded the family, suffering which is not directly revealed in Frost's poetry. He believed that a poet's worth should be judged by what he holds back, but his background of tragedy had led some critics to see beyond the homey tone of most of the poet's work. To some a "dark Frost" exists in such works as "Acquainted With The Night."

Many of Frost's poems have become almost anthems to America's spirit of frontiersmanship and rugged individualism. "Stopping by Woods on a Snowy Evening" is one, as is "The Road Not Taken", with its last two lines:

> I took the one less travelled by,
> And that has made all the difference.

Frost was the winner of four Pulitzer Prizes and countless other honors. Even as an old man he was a familiar figure, tall, stooped, with his shock of white hair, "speaking" his poems to college audiences. At 90 he was sent to visit Nikita Khrushchev by President Kennedy. "I don't call myself a poet yet", he said near the end of his life. "It's for the world to say whether you're a poet or not. I'm one-half teacher, one-half poet and one-half farmer. That's three halves."

Frost expressing himself on the eve of his 80th birthday in 1954.

Given Name: Robert Lee Frost
Born: March 26, 1874, San Francisco, California
Married: Elinor Miriam White, 1895, 6 children
Highlights: Leading American poet who used simple language and simple subjects to convey important themes. Won the Pulitzer Prize for poetry 4 times (1924, 1931, 1937, 1943).
Died: January 29, 1963

The poet on the eve of his 1957 trip to England to receive honorary degrees from Oxford and Cambridge.

In 1948, the four-time winner of the Pulitzer Prize for Poetry was photographed in his garden near Bread Loaf Mountain in Vermont.

"The Dean of American Poets" as he looked in March 1962.

Greta Garbo

By dodging publicity all her life, legendary film star Greta Garbo became one of the most publicized women in the world. Solitary and elusive even at the height of her career, the Swedish-born beauty famous for the statement "I want to be alone" once complained that she had really said, "I want to be left alone." Yet since her retirement from films in 1941 glimpsing Garbo has been a favorite activity on New York's Upper East Side where she lives and in Europe, where she often visits.

Born Greta Gustafsson, Garbo went to work at 14, when her father died, in a barber shop. Typically terse, she described her early life in a 1931 biography: "I was born, I had a father and mother. I lived in a house. I went to school. What does it matter?" She won a scholarship to drama school when at 17 her goddess-like looks came to the attention of an actor-director and she was admitted to the Royal Dramatic Theatre School in Stockholm. There she became a protegé of film director Mauritz Stiller, and in 1925 when he won a 3-year contract with MGM, Stiller took the 20-year-old Garbo to Hollywood with him. A publicity team went to work to create a star image for Garbo, billing the shy introvert who spoke little English as "a mysterious stranger", an image that would describe Garbo all her life.

Garbo starred in 10 silent films in the '20's, playing seductive, sultry women in such movies as "The Torrent" (her first film, in 1926), "The Temptress" and "The Flesh and The Devil". Her romance with John Gilbert, with whom she co-starred in "The Undying Past", a 1927 box office hit, as well as "Love", based on Tolstoi's novel "Anna Karenina", became Hollywood's hottest love affair, both on and off the screen.

When sound came to Hollywood films Garbo's voice, a deep, husky contralto often described as "smoky", enhanced her mysterious, glamourous image. Her 1930 appearance in the film version of Eugene O'Neill's play "Anna Christie" was advertised by MGM with the slogan, "Garbo Talks." (Over 50 years later Hollywood brought out a film titled "Garbo Talks" in which a son tries to fulfill his dying mother's last wish to see and talk with the elusive Garbo.)

Among Garbo's great roles were "The Divine Woman", in which she portrayed Sarah Bernhardt; "Mata Hari", in which she co-starred with Ramon Novarro, playing the famous dancer and spy; "Grand Hotel", voted the best film of 1932; and "Queen Christina", for which she returned to Sweden to research the queen's life, and which was regarded as the height of her dramatic performances. In 1935 she co-starred with Frederic March in "Anna Karenina", which won the New York Film Critics' Award and was regarded as superior in every way to the silent version of the same novel. In 1936 she won the same award for her portrayal of Marguerite Gautier in Dumas' "Camille". "Ninotchka", a 1939 satire on Bolshevism directed by the famed Ernst Lubitsch in which Garbo played the title role, was her first comedy part. The film, regarded as an all-time classic, broke attendance records in Europe, where Garbo was already adored.

Her last film was "Two-Faced Woman", another comedy and her only unsuccessful picture. After bad reviews and at the age of 36 Garbo retired from the film industry.

Living in seclusion since 1941, Garbo has become a phantom-like figure, spotted now and then dressed in long coats, hiding behind floppy hats and dark glasses, taking long, lonely walks in New York. Repeated rumors about her return to the movies have proven unfounded. In a rare interview granted in 1977 to a West German magazine Garbo broke her apparent vow of silence and finally talked: "I have messed up my life", she said, "And it's too late to change it."

Robert Taylor shared the screen with Garbo in "Camille" in 1938.

Given Name: Greta Louisa Gustaffson
Born: September 18, 1905, Stockholm, Sweden
Unmarried
Highlights: Leading actress and film star of the 1930s. Won Special Academy Award in 1954.

The elusive Garbo made a rare public appearance to attend a debut in Los Angeles in November 1974.

Basil Rathbone and Freddie Bartholomew starred with Garbo in 1935's "Anna Karenina".

A scene from "Two-Faced Woman", in which Garbo created a dance called the "Chica Choca" in 1940.

The beautiful Swede adds something to an Italian Seascape, circa 1940.

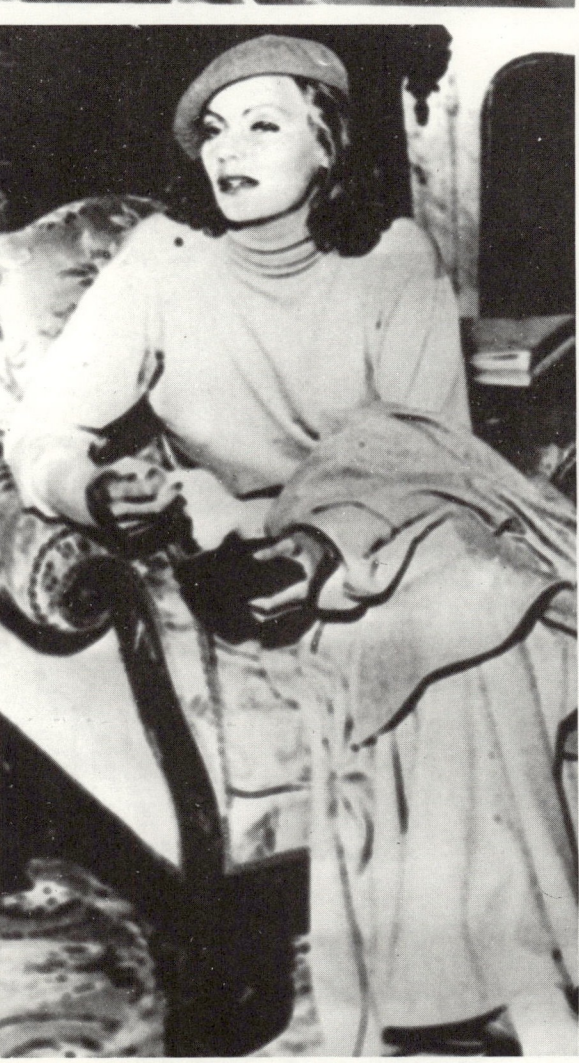

The originator of the "Garbo Bob" haircut on the liner "Gripsholm" bound for Sweden in 1932.

Even in 1985, Garbo was still avoiding photographers, but was snapped here in Klosters, Switzerland.

Gilbert & Sullivan

"A frothy production destined soon to subside into nothingness." This excerpt is taken from the London Daily Telegraph, May 27, 1878. It refers to the opening night performance of *H.M.S. Pinafore* written by the most successful collaborators in all music: Gilbert and Sullivan.

There was, however, a time when it looked as if the critic had hit the nail on the head for *Pinafore* gave no indication of being an immediate smash hit. Luckily, Sullivan had just been appointed conductor of the justly famous Queen's Hall Promenade Concerts and decided to include a selection from *Pinafore* in one of the proms. The result was staggering and the following morning the theatre box office was besieged and a near failure became a smash hit overnight.

William Schwenk Gilbert, born November 18, 1836, died May 29, 1911, wrote drama criticism, verse and stage pieces before working with Sullivan. Even before collaborating with Gilbert, Arthur Seymour Sullivan, born May 13, 1842, died November 22, 1900, had composed prolifically: hymns, cantatas, oratorios, piano pieces, songs and orchestral works.

The *H.M.S. Pinafore* was the fourth comic opera produced in the perfectly matched association between Gilbert and Sullivan. Their first, *Trial by Jury* (1875), was not an immediate success, but it did bring the team together. An impresario was looking for a curtain raiser to proceed Offenbach's *La Perichole* and the name of Gilbert occurred to him. Gilbert hauled out a script that had been turned down once before and the impresario was delighted and decided to produce it. This time the name of Sullivan was suggested as being the perfect composer. The producer was Richard D'Oyly Carte and it was this operetta that brought Gilbert, Sullivan and Carte together.

Their second production, *The Sorcerer* (1877), marked a milestone in the history of theater. Never before had a librettist and/or composer been given so much authority regarding a production. At one rehearsal, going over one of the duets, Sullivan told his principals that he wished them to imagine themselves singing grand opera, and to use all the flamboyant gestures that Italian grand opera singers indulged in. During rehearsal, actor George Grossmith carried out Sullivan's instructions of exaggerated flamboyance and, "nearly fell over the footlights into the orchestra."

The Pirates of Penzance (1879) was the only opera of the series that had its world premiere outside of England. The reason was that *Pinafore* had been pirated in many versions in the United States and Mr. Carte and Gilbert and Sullivan were determined to put a stop to it. Litigation had already been started and the court ruled that versions of the libretto and vocal score placed the work in the public domain. At that time the U.S. was not a signatory to the then-existing International Copyright Agreement.

So, to protect their literary property, the three partners decided to produce their next opera, *Pirates,* in New York.

Sir William Schwenk Gilbert.

They would not publish any printed versions and would allow no one in the theatre during rehearsals. But in spite of the rule, piratical producers managed to get spies into the opening—people versed in taking musical dictation rapidly—and obtained enough material to produce their own versions of this successful opera. The British copyright was safe, but the authors and producer never again tried to open one of their operas in the United States.

Patience was staged in 1881, followed next by *Iolanthe*. On the day of the opening night of *Iolanthe* (1882), Sullivan's bankers went bankrupt. When he entered the pit to conduct the first performance he was a financially ruined man. But once again the Gilbert and Sullivan magic worked. Although *Iolanthe* was not unanimously hailed as a smash hit it did run for 14 months and Sullivan's fortunes again began to rise. It was also during the run of this play, in May 1883, that Sullivan was knighted. Gilbert was not. Although it has not been suggested that Gilbert was so jealous of this honor that the seeds of their final breakup were sown then, there is no doubt the snub rankled. Additionally, Sullivan's knighthood was not conferred on him for his work in collaboration with Gilbert. Queen Victoria had little sympathy with those "frivolities". The accolade was given "in recognition of distinguished talents as a composer" and "promotion of the art of music generally in this country". Gilbert was knighted 24 years later, in 1902, by Edward VII.

The quarrels, or at least incidents, were beginning to occur more frequently and less than two months after *Princess Ida* (1884) had been produced Carte wrote each of the collaborators a letter stating that they would be liable for any losses incurred if they defaulted in providing a new piece. March of 1884 saw the beginnings of an impasse. Both Sullivan and Carte once again rejected Gilbert's new plot and Gilbert countered by saying that the length of their association had perhaps turned him stale. But as Gilbert fumed at the impasse, pacing his study while trying to come up with a new plot, a Japanese ceremonial sword that hung on the wall fell near his feet. His mind turned to the Japanese exhibition recently opened in London and by dawn he had written the outline of a plot. He immediately sent his notes to Sullivan whose reaction was relief and bubling excitement. The upshot of the near break was the 1885 production of *The Mikado,* one of the operettas which consolidated their success.

It was followed by *Ruddigore* (1887), . *The Yeomen of the Guard* (1888), and *The Gondoliers* (1889) but, much to the public's dismay, a serious quarrel between them halted their production for three years. Reconciled, they attempted two more operettas, *Utopia Limited* (1893) and *The Grand Duke* (1896), but without their earlier deftness. Sullivan did write more, and so did Gilbert, but not in collaboration. The famous partnership was finally and irrevocably at an end.

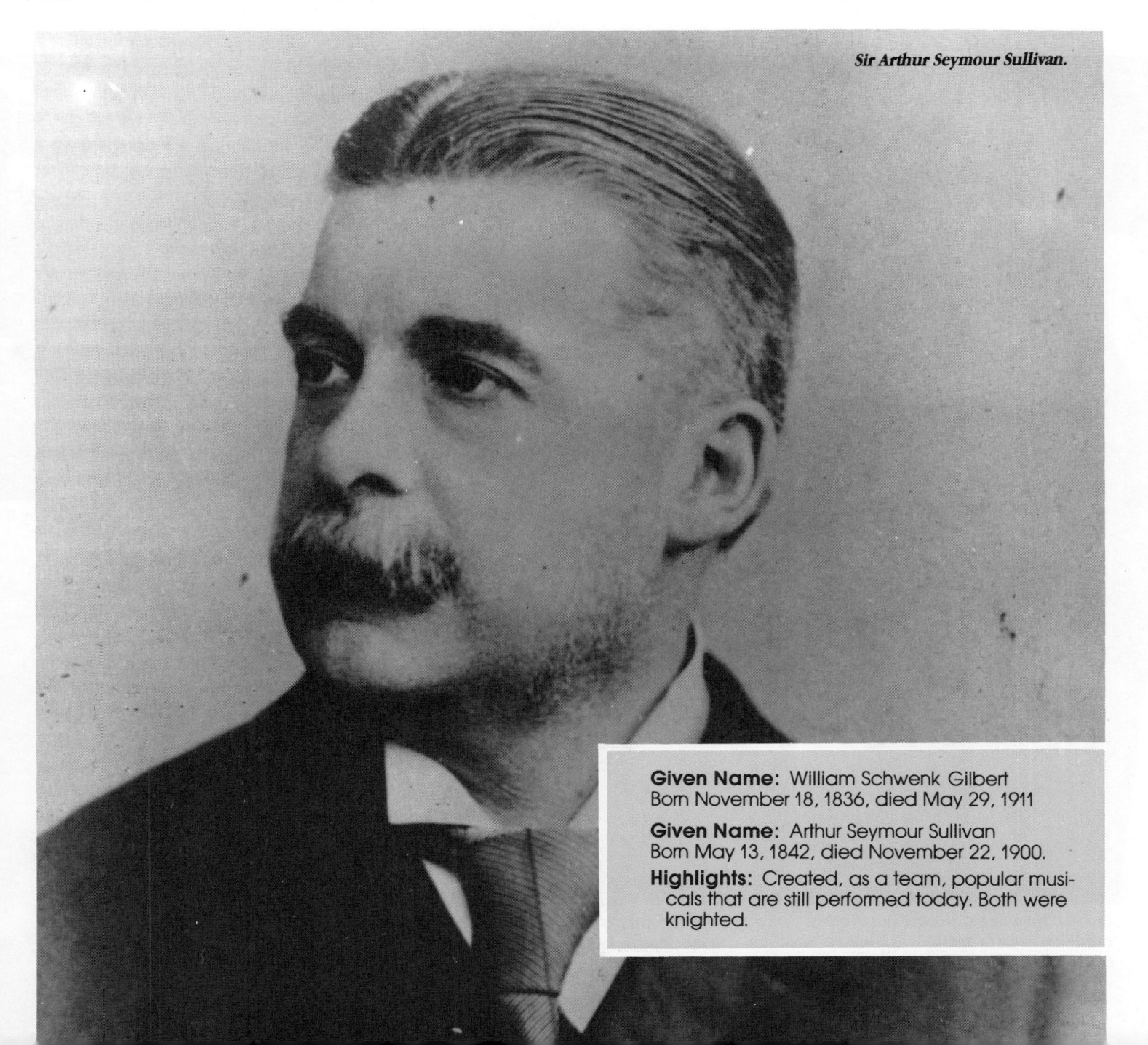

Sir Arthur Seymour Sullivan.

Given Name: William Schwenk Gilbert
Born November 18, 1836, died May 29, 1911

Given Name: Arthur Seymour Sullivan
Born May 13, 1842, died November 22, 1900.

Highlights: Created, as a team, popular musicals that are still performed today. Both were knighted.

Ernest Hemingway

He was a man of action who wrote action-filled stories, most of them based on his own lusty, often dangerous, experiences as soldier, correspondent, bull fighter and big-game hunter. He used death, violence and abortive love affairs as favorite themes, and was a master of dialogue. Few writers could match his talent for writing the way people think, talk, and act.

Hemingway risked his life in three wars, and had several narrow escapes from death on other occasions. He was also married four times.

While serving with an Italian infantry regiment in World War I, he was wounded and twice decorated. (He said later that one of the medals was simply for being an American, and the other was simply a mistake.) He served as a front-line correspondent in both the Spanish Civil War, and in World War II. During that war, he was injured in an accident during a London blackout. In 1954, he was in two plane crashes on successive days while on a trip to Africa. The first came in a chartered sightseeing plane which had to crash-land in the bush to avoid a river full of crocodiles. The next day, the plane which had been hired to take him and his wife to Nairobi crashed on takeoff.

When Hemingway returned to civilization, clutching a bunch of bananas and a bottle of gin, he was asked if he would write a book about his experiences. He answered that "I don't write books, books write me."

Hemingway's style—direct, simple, gutsy—was a result of his reportorial experience. He never attended college, but instead started as a cub reporter at the Kansas City Star right out of high school. After a short stint there, and his service in Italy, he became European correspondent for the Toronto Star, based in Paris. His literary career started there with the publication of "Three Stories and Ten Poems" in 1923. From that time on, he continued to produce works that were filled with action, and reflected many of the attitudes of the "Lost Generation" of the era between world wars.

"A Farewell to Arms", "The Sun Also Rises", "The Snows of Kilimanjaro" and "For Whom the Bell Tolls", which became a widely acclaimed film, were among his more famous works. In 1953, his "Old Man and the Sea", a rough but compassionate tale of an aged fisherman's struggle to land a giant fish, the climactic catch of his life, earned him the Pulitzer Prize for fiction.

Until his death by suicide, the hard-drinking, hard-living Hemingway worked almost every day. He would usually write from dawn until just past noon, then go fishing or hunting. He worked hard at his craft, writing and rewriting again and again. "Nobody but fools ever thought it (writing) was an easy trade," he said.

His work paid off. His prose style became the model for literally scores of writers, among them the best, and he probably exerted more influence on the world's literature than any modern American author.

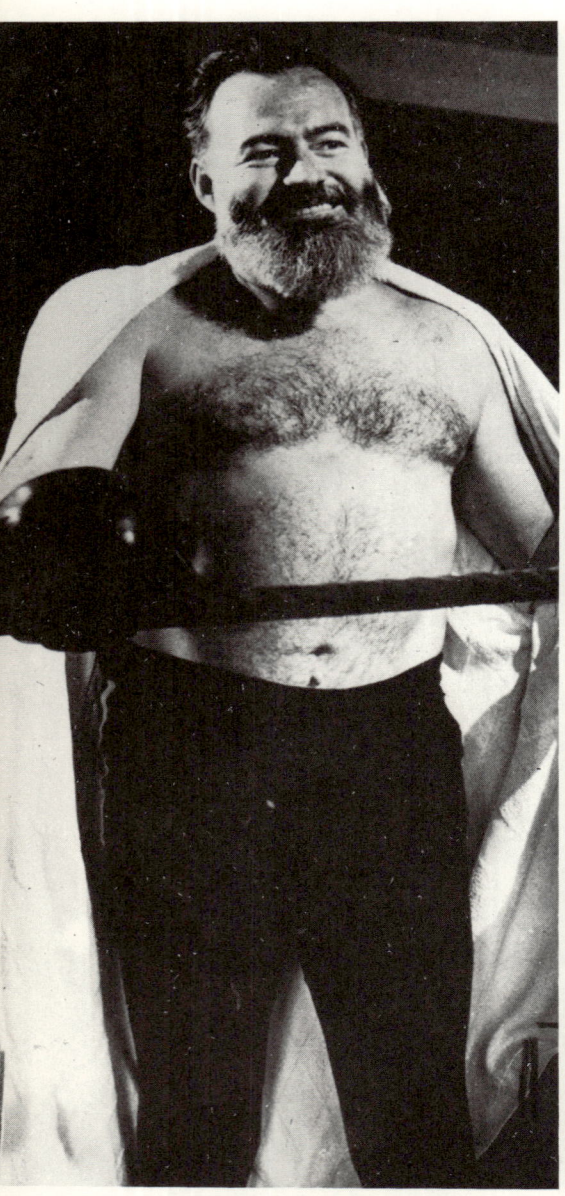

In 1944, Hemingway worked out to get in condition to go to the front as a war correspondent.

Hemingway checks a just-killed pronghorn antelope in 1940.

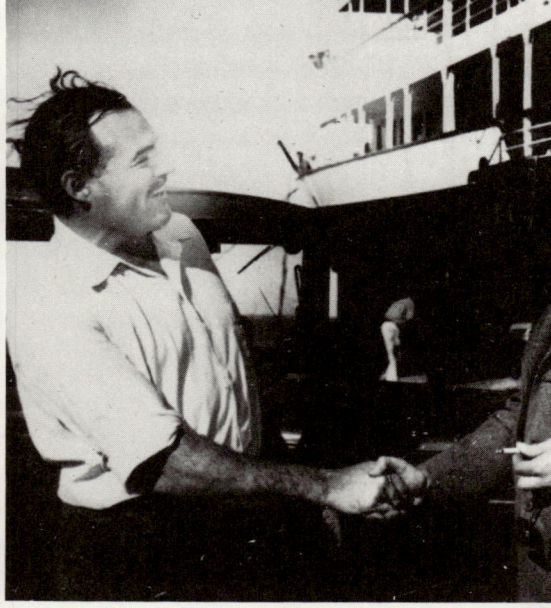

"Papa" greets Sinclair Lewis at dockside in Key West, Florida in 1940.

At Sun Valley Lodge, Hemingway works on "For Whom The Bell

Hemingway congratulates Cuba's Fidel Castro after the Prime Minister had won the 1960 Hemingway Anglers Tournament.

Hemingway and friend Gary Cooper hunt in Sun Valley, Idaho in 1940.

Given Name: Ernest Miller Hemingway

Born: July 21, 1888, Oak Park, Illinois

Married: Hadley Richardson 1921, 1 child
Paulene Pfeiffer, 1926, 2 children
Martha Gelhorn, 1940
Mary Welsh 1946

Highlights: One of the most widely read and translated American authors. Pulitzer Prize for Fiction 1953. Nobel Prize for Literature 1954.

Died: July 2, 1961.

Alfred Hitchcock

For more than 50 years, and more than 50 films, Alfred Hitchcock amused, thrilled and terrified audiences all over the world. His work made women afraid to shower, and men suspicious of themselves.

Hitchcock was the master of using photographic technique to create terror and suspense. "To me, the language of the camera is the important thing," he said. "I believe a real artist could make an interesting picture in a phone booth." His cinematic sense was amazing, and he never bothered to look into the camera to size up a scene. Instead, he would first visualize it for himself, and then sketch it. "The next shot," he once told an actor," will show you from the second coat button upward, so don't worry about your shoes."

His fascination with the cinema began when he was 17, in his native London. At 23, after university, he was employed by the famous German director Emil Jennings as a writer/assistant director. Soon after, he directed "The Pleasure Garden", and during the filming, married his assistant director. For the next 18 years, before coming to America, he made classic after classic, including "The Man Who Knew Too Much", "The 39 Steps" and "The Lady Vanishes".

Although he was nominated for four Oscars in his career, he never won one. But in 1969, he was awarded the Irving Thalberg Award for "consistent high level productions" by the Academy of Motion Picture Arts and Sciences. In 1979, the American Film Institute presented him with its Lifetime Achievement Award. At the awards ceremony, Ingrid Bergman called him "a gentleman farmer who raises gooseflesh," and John Forsythe said that "Hitch's genius is that he can put so much life in death." Hitchcock often said that "the one subject of most fascination to the general public appears to be murder," and he handled it with a skill unmatched by any of his colleagues.

Hitchcock had neither the physique nor the demeanor of a man who made his living by finding interesting ways to kill people. He was short and portly, with an egg shaped profile that later became a trademark on his television series, which also featured sly, wry introductions and closing remarks from the witty filmmaker. Although he enjoyed a quiet life away from his work, and lived his private life out of the public eye, he did enjoy playing a game with his audiences, and often put himself in his films as a background character.

The maker of "Spellbound", "Rear Window" and "Psycho", to name just a few of his brilliant films, was, by his own admission, "afraid of going to see any of my pictures with an audience present. I only tried that once . . . I'm afraid of seeing the mistakes I might have made." He also said that "I'm really quite sensitive and cowardly about many things. You'd never believe it, but I'm terrified of policemen and entanglements with the law, even though I make my living dramatizing such situations."

Despite his years of success, and his outward arrogance and self-assurance, Hitchcock never forgot that fame is fleeting. He enjoyed telling the story of his second picture, "The Lodger", the story of Jack the Ripper which was made in 1926. The opening shot was a full-face close-up of a woman screaming, and later in the film, he photographed the Ripper through a glass floor, nervously pacing up and down. Both of these scenes were departures for their time, and the producers almost didn't release the film. But they decided to show it to the press and it was acclaimed an overnight success. Said Hitchcock: "One day I was a flop, all washed up at 26. The next day I was a boy genius. So you can see I have had some experience in the field of suspense."

Hitchcock shared that experience with audiences all over the world. And left the world richer for it.

The American Film Institute Life Achievement Award went to Hitchcock in 1979.

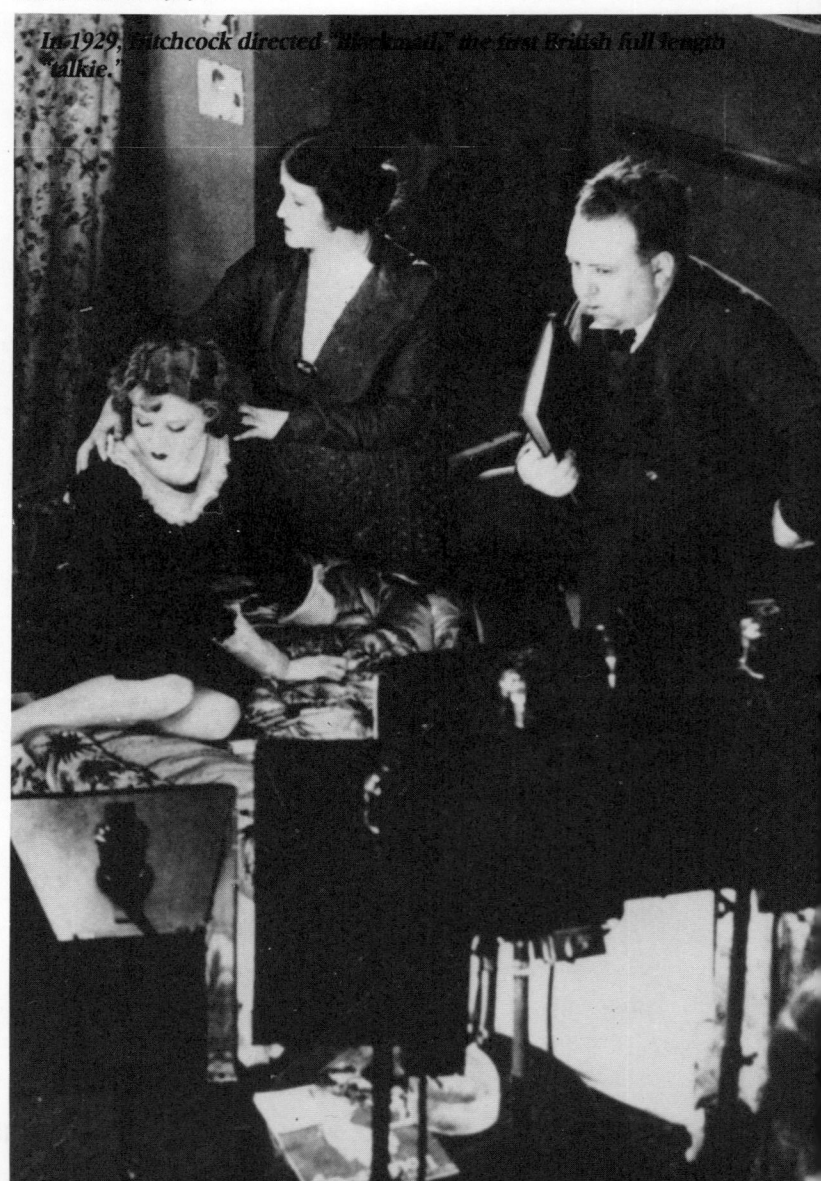

In 1929, Hitchcock directed "Blackmail," the first British full length "talkie."

ARTS

Given Name: Alfred Joseph Hitchcock
Born: August 13, 1899, England
Married: Alma Reville, 1922, 1 child
Highlights: Outstanding motion picture and television director who pioneered in the use of cinematic techniques to further the feelings of horror or suspense in his productions.
Died: April 29, 1980

Cary Grant (left) and Jimmy Stewart (right) present Hitchcock with the 1965 Screen Producers Guild Annual Milestone Award.

Princess Grace of Monaco (Grace Kelly) who starred in Hitchcock's films, joined the director at the 1972 Cannes Film Festival.

Hitchcock and wife at the 1956 premiere of "The Man Who Knew Too Much".

Henry James

In his letter to H.G. Wells, Henry James expressed his feelings on what writing meant to him. "I live, live intensely and am fed by life," James said, "and my value, whatever it may be, is in my own kind of expression of that. Art *makes* life, makes interest, makes importance and there is no substitute for the force and beauty of its process."

Henry James, born in New York City, April 15, 1843, has long been regarded as a writers' writer. His work is not only psychologically penetrating but also technically innovative and he achieved international status as a writer during his long and productive career. During his lifetime he wrote 22 novels, 113 tales, 15 plays, the equivalent of about 10 books of criticism, 7 travel books, 3 autobiographical volumes, and 2 biographies.

James's long apprenticeship may be dated from 1864 to 1875. At 21 he published his first works, an anonymous short story and an unsigned book review. He wrote more reviews and easily found magazine outlets for his early short fiction. After publishing his first two books of short stories and travel essays, both in 1875 and completing his first mature novel *Roderick Hudson* (1876), he moved to Paris. Here he met other writers: Ivan Turgenev, Gustave Flaubert, Guy de Maupassant and Emile Zola. During this phase, James wrote *The American* (1877), about a man whose Yankee dollars fail to buy him admission to French society.

Feeling unwelcome in Paris, James moved to "the great grey Babylon," London, where he soon met Alfred Lord Tennyson, Robert Browning, George Elliot, William Morris, Leslie Stephen and many others. James gained fame with his immensely admired short novel, *Daisy Miller* (1878), a story about an innocent, socially naive American girl destroyed by European mores. He also published the first book length treatment of Nathaniel Hawthorne and began his first masterpiece, *Portrait of a Lady* (1881).

In January 1885 James left London to take his ailing sister, Alice, to Bournemouth where she could recuperate from an illness. There he spent hours in happy talk with another Bournemouth invalid, Robert Louis Stevenson. Stevenson was 35, seven years younger than James and although disabled physically, he remained extraordinarily prolific. And when Stevenson left the seaside resort for the South Seas he continued corresponding with James. It was at Skerryvore in 1886 that Stevenson gave James a copy of *Kidnapped,* inscribing it "And I wish I had a better work to give as good a man."

From 1886 until World War I, when the Anglo-French cultural community he revered was shattered, James was extremely active. He bought a house south of London where he wrote and entertained and produced streams of fiction. Three long novels of this major phase of his career would alone assure the author's fame: *The Wings of the Dove* (1902), the *Ambasdsadors* (1903) and the *Golden Bowl* (1904).

Early in the summer of 1915, Henry James, friend of the Prime Minister and a singular figure in England's literary establishment, discovered to his deep chagrin that he was officially considered an alien. This gave James some troubled hours and the upshot was his decision to apply for British citizenship. He found out that he needed to surrender his American passport and, to his great amusement, have four persons testify to his literacy as well as to his good character. To James's delight, two of the persons who eventually testified were the librarian of the House of Lords, Mr. Gosse, and Prime Minister of England, Herbert H. Asquith. The news that Henry James had become a British citizen brought James the avalanche of mail from Englishmen that he had expected. But it also brought him acute American resentment. In the end James simply shrugged his shoulders. The American reaction seemed to him highly irrational, coming from a country which measured its own aliens by the speed with which they became naturalized Americans.

Henry James, who is idolized as "the Master" by readers who admire his superb craftsmanship, died in London on February 28, 1916. In the 1930's an unstoppable James boom started and gained momentum during and just after World War II. James ignored too many elements of workaday American life ever to be popular with the masses. He has, however, influenced literary geniuses such as Joseph Conrad, Edith Wharton, James Joyce, Virginia Woolf, William Faulkner and Graham Greene.

Given Name: Henry James
Born: April 15, 1843, New York City
Unmarried
Highlights: Prolific author of novels, plays and criticism and acknowledged master of the short story.
Died: February 28, 1916

Henry James: author, playwright, and master story teller.

James Joyce

James Joyce spent his lifetime in flight. As a child growing up in Dublin he moved with his family from place to place to avoid creditors. At the age of 22, chafing under the narrow conventions of his times and the teachings of the Roman Catholic Church, he fled Ireland to live and work in permanent exile in Europe, saying that to remain in Ireland would be to rot. Yet he wrote almost exclusively about Dublin, the "gallant and venal city" in which he grew up. They used to ask Joyce, "When are you coming back to Dublin?" "Have I ever left?" he'd say.

Joyce's stories scandalized the literary establishment in Ireland. He was asked to stop submitting them to magazines due to their unsavory content. His *Dubliners,* published after great difficulties, is a series of interrelated stories in which ghosts of the past and present-day convention suffocate ordinary Dublin citizens, whom Joyce wanted to free from the chains of church, state and tradition. The book was banned, as were all his works during his lifetime, in his native city where a publisher to whom he submitted it destroyed the sheets for fear of libel.

In Joyce's autobiographical *Portrait of the Artist as a Young Man,* the hero Stephen Dedalus—Joyce got the name from the Greek myth about the man who flew to freedom from a prison—tries to free himself from Mother Ireland, religion and history.

One of the conventions Joyce avoided was marriage. When he left Ireland he took with him a country girl, Nora Barnacle. She was his lifetime companion and bore him two children but it wasn't till the end of his life he married her, for reasons of inheritance. They spent long years living in poverty in Trieste and Zurich, where Joyce wrote and taught English. He never made any money off his works but received early encouragement from the great Irish poet William Butler Yeats and American ex-patriate Ezra Pound, who published *Portrait* in his magazine "The Egoist."

Joyce's great masterpiece was *Ulysses,* which was published in 1922 in Paris. Based on Homer's epic poem about Greek hero Ulysses' wanderings in the ancient world, it presents a thick slice of daily life in Dublin in which an ordinary citizen, Leopold Bloom, wanders the streets of his city, visiting pubs, the butcher's, a newspaper office, his experiences described through his thoughts rather than in his actions. Joyce's use of this "stream of consciousness" technique revolutionized the form and structure of the novel.

Besides its rich mix of myth, Irish folklore, puns, Catholic ritual and the plain grits of daily life, *Ulysses* had a bawdy tone and words and passages, including Molly Bloom's erotic monologue that ends the book, that created a scandal. It was banned in the U.S. until 1933 when a Supreme Court decision judged it a new literary genre, by turns "brilliant and dull, intelligible and obscure"—not pornography, but a tour de force.

Although hailed as a genius who wrote the greatest fiction masterpiece of the 20th Century, Joyce's complex novel makes him an author more talked about than read. His last work, *Finnegan's Wake,* was published two years before his death, with no explanation as to the meaning of its often gibberish style which confounds even Joyce's admirers.

Although there are still groups like Housewives for Ireland who protest Joyce's literary presence, today the author is celebrated as Ireland's illustrious son and grand literary exile. Each year on June 16th, known world-wide in literary circles as Bloomsday, the day in 1904 when Leopold Bloom wandered the streets of the city Joyce both loved and hated, Joyce pilgrims flock to Dublin to retrace Bloom's footsteps and visit sites used in *Ulysses,* sites now preserved as monuments to the author's great stature.

Joyce (left) and French poet Phillippe Soupault, who is supervising the translation of Joyce's work.

Given Name: James Augustus Joyce
Born: February 2, 1882, Rathgar, Ireland
Married: Nora Barnacle, 1931, 2 children
Highlights: Author of major novels—shocking for their time—in which he introduced the "stream of consciousness" form to convey the thoughts and feelings of the major characters.
Died: January 13, 1941

Joyce in Paris in 1931 before leaving for Zurich for operations on his eyes. Note the thick left lens on his glasses.

Joyce with his wife, daughter and son in Paris in 1924.

Man Ray

A painting by artist Man Ray brought three-quarters of a million dollars in 1979 at the Sotheby Parke Bernet Gallery in New York City and set a record as being the most money ever paid at auction for a surrealist painting.

The artist, a rare individual possessed of an endlessly fertile imagination, was a pioneering painter and photographer in the Dada, surrealist and abstract movements of the 1920's and '30s. He was the only American Dadist to earn a major international reputation.

Man Ray was born in Philadelphia, Pennsylvania on August 27, 1890, the son of Russian-Jewish immigrants. When he was seven the family moved to Brooklyn, New York. He wrote, in his autobiography, *Self Portrait* (1963) that in boyhood he "considered the painting of a picture the acme of human accomplishment." His favorite classes in high school were in drawing, both freehand and mechanical, and when he graduated he was awarded a university scholarship to study architecture. But after he had spent the summer painting, he decided against continuing his formal education.

To support himself in his apprenticeship as a painter, Man Ray took a job preparing layouts for an advertising firm and then for a technical publishing house, and he later worked in the drafting department of a map and atlas publishing company. In 1908 he attended evening classes at the art school of the National Academy of Design in Manhattan. But he was not satisfied with an academic approach to art. He became a frequent visitor to "393", the Fifth Avenue Photo-Secession Galleries of the famed photographer Alfred Stieglitz. This stimulated Man Ray's interest in both photography and in the works of modern European and American artists exhibiting at the gallery: Cezanne, Picasso, Brancusi, Rodin, Marin, Arthur Dove, and others.

Man Ray's own painting took a more experimental direction and in 1912 his work was exhibited for the first time at the Ferrar Center. The next year was one of many changes. The history-making Armory Show of modern art in New York in 1913 encouraged him toward more ambitious canvases in cubism, and he moved to an art colony in Ridgefield, New Jersey. The following spring he married the French poetess, Donna (Lacour) Loupov.

Man Ray's enjoyment of his rural surroundings was reflected in a series of colorful, somewhat cubistic, but also romantic landscapes, such as *The Village* (1913). But by 1915 he had changed his style, "reducing human figures to flat-patterned disarticulated forms", which he exhibited that fall in the Daniel Gallery in New York. One visitor to the gallery, the well-known Chicago art collector Arthur J. Eddy, picked out six paintings at random and paid Man Ray $2,000 for them. Tired of woodchopping in the winter, the artist moved from Ridgefield to Manhattan to open his own studio. He became further acquainted with a visiting painter from France, Marcel Duchamp. Duchamp had just startled the art world with his *Nude Descending a Staircase* in 1913. In his iconoclasm, his use of an irrational and "anti-art" idiom to ridicule the materialism and mechanization of society, Duchamp anticipated in spirit and purpose the Dada movement. His association with Duchamp, Man Ray has said, crystallized his own views.

After participating in radical art activities in New York, Man Ray moved to Paris in 1921 and supported himself as a portrait photographer. In 1922 he published Les Champs Delicieux (Delightful Fields), an album of abstract photographs he made without use of the camera. He called these Rayographs. Later he experimented with solarization techniques and negative prints. He turned to film-making in 1923, producing Le Retour a la Raison (Return to Reason, 1923), Anemic Cimena (1925-26) with Marcel Duchamp, and L'Etoile de Mer (Star of the Sea, 1928).

Successful both commercially and artistically as a portrait photographer, Man Ray assembled what has been called "perhaps the most complete record in existence of the *haut monde* in Paris" during the 1920s and early 1930's. Among the more renowned subjects of the psychologically revealing photographs were Ernest Hemingway, Gertrude Stein, James Joyce, Brancusi and Erik Satie. He also specialized in photographing the works of other artists.

But soon after the German invasion of France in 1940, Man Ray fled to the United States and settled in Los Angeles, and, although he came to know many people in the motion-picture industry, he concentrated on painting rather than photography. Then in March of 1951, Man Ray returned to France to make a permanent home there. He continued to seek adventure in painting and developed an automatic technique of making pictures, which he called "Natural Paintings". His method was to spread colors according to impulse and apply pressure with other surfaces. Man Ray has said there are no two things alike in his work and in her review of the 1963 retrospectives in *Art News* (Summer, 1963) Eleanor C. Munro noted the agility with which he kept pace with every evolving 'ism' of his time "and made a mockery of it almost before it was worked through."

The versatile artist died on November 18, 1976, having made major contributions to painting, sculpture, film and photography. In his autobiography he wrote that the motives that directed his artistic efforts were "the pursuit of liberty" and "the pursuit of pleasure". His love for freedom and his contempt for the orthodox and self-rightous characterize not just his art, but his entire life.

Given Name: Emmanuel Rudnitzky
Born: August 27, 1890. Philadelphia, Pa
Married: Donna (Lacour) Loupov, 1914
Highlights: Pioneering painter and photographer in the DADA, surrealist and abstract movements of the 1920's and 30's.
Died: November 18, 1976.

Given Name: Vladimir Vladimirovich Nabokov
Born: April 23, 1899, St. Petersburg, Russia
Married: Vera Slonim, 1925, 1 child
Highlights: Leading novelist whose works conveyed a poignant sensuality.
Died: July 2, 1977

Nabokov and wife, Vera, at home in Ithaca, New York in 1958.

Laurence Olivier

"Acting is a kind of lunacy", declared Laurence Olivier. "I don't really enjoy it. I just can't stop doing it", and for seven decades the Englishman regarded by many to be the greatest actor of his time played every kind of role on stage, in film and on television, from Shakespeare's Othello to Nathan Detroit, a crapshooter in the musical "Guys and Dolls."

The son of a Church of England clergyman, Olivier attributed his early passion for theatre to the high drama of the church that dominated his childhood with its ritual, gorgeous vestments and fire-and-brimstone sermons. At 15 he was playing girl's roles in plays at his all-boys school with an almost religious fervor that caused British stage great Ellen Terry to pat his head and urge him to keep acting. His "over-gesticulatory" style stood him in good stead when the young actor played Hamlet at the Old Vic in London, or a raging, ranting King Lear late in life on television. But in the 30's when Olivier went to Hollywood to star as Heathcliff in the film "Wuthering Heights", Director Sam Goldwyn threatened to shut down the studio if "Larry doesn't stop overacting."

During World War II his grand style came in handy when, frustrated because he was too old to fight, he made rousing speeches at war rallies. Becoming the first director to translate Shakespeare onto the screen, he infused "Henry V" with the immediacy of a contemporary war story.

The smouldering quality that haunted his best work, including his film "Hamlet", which won him an Oscar in 1948, came from, he said, the loss of his mother at an early age.

A master of tragic intensity as well as comic subtlety, Olivier believed that great acting parts are cannibals—they devour you. He constantly complained about acting, yet he never slowed down, even after, at age 60, a near-fatal bout with cancer and other ill health plagued him. "They'll have to kick me out," he said. "As long as I can stand I'll do my job." Still, he claimed he would rather direct than act. In 1963 he realized a lifelong dream, creating a National Theatre at the Old Vic where years before he and another British theatre giant, Ralph Richardson, had once been co-directors. The theatre's chief responsibility was to train new stars, he felt, and presided ("a sometimes dreadful task") over the building of the National Theatre Center, where he directed many of the early productions.

Olivier had three wives, all British actresses. The first was Jill Esmond. In Hollywood in the '30's, he met and married Vivien Leigh, who was in America to play Scarlett O'Hara in "Gone With the Wind." During their 6-year marriage they were Britain's theatre royalty. Olivier said the beautiful and troubled Miss Leigh gave him some of the happiest and most terrible moments of his life. He later wed Joan Plowright with whom he lived a simple life in Brighton, on the coast an hour south of London, taking care of their children, worrying about money, and studying scripts.

When in 1970 Queen Elizabeth II made Olivier a Lord and he became the only theatrical Baron in the world, he said, "I would prefer to be known as Larry. I won't use Lord on the theatre billboards but it might help the British public to stop regarding actors as 'rogues and vagabonds'".

Olivier's favorite role was that of the doctor in Russian playwright Anton Chekhov's "Uncle Vanya." Despite the vast variety of the roles he played, which earned him prestigious honors not only in America and Great Britain but also in France, Sweden and Italy, the epitaph Olivier requested for his gravestone was a one-liner from John Osborne's play "The Entertainer", in which he starred: "He's Funny."

Actors Ben Kingsley (left) and Dustin Hoffman (right) congratulate Olivier for winning the 1983 Cecil B. DeMille Award.

Given Name: Laurence Kerr Olivier
Born: May 22, 1907, Dorking, Surrey, England
Married: Jill Esmond, 1930, 1 child (divorced 1940)
Married: Vivien Leigh, 1940 (divorced 1960
Married: Joan Plowright, 1960, 3 children
Highlights: Recognized as one of the finest actors in the English language. Knighted by King George VI, made Lord by Queen Elizabeth II.

Olivier starred with Marilyn Monroe in 1957's "The Prince and the Showgirl".

Sir Laurence and Lady Olivier (Vivien Leigh) arrive at a London Theater in 1948.

Sir Laurence chats with friend Spencer Tracy on the set of "Carrie" in 1950.

Olivier as Hamlet in 1948.

A scene from "A Little Romance", 1979.

Olivier pedals Jennifer Jones on the set of "Carrie".

Merle Oberon was Olivier's costar in 1939's "Wuthering Heights".

Sir Laurence Olivier and Sir Malcolm Sargent just after they were knighted, July 8, 1947.

Eugene O'Neill

He was one of the most prolific of modern playwrights, and the winner of the 1936 Nobel Prize in Literature. But O'Neill himself felt that his greatest contribution as an American dramatist was to help bring international recognition to American theater.

As he expressed it, he helped bring about the realization that "an adult American drama existed which could be considered as something beyond mere theatrical entertainment and criticized as an art, as the work of the best European playwrights was criticized." He added that he considered it important for American drama that "an American dramatist did manage to break through the old European snobby superior attitude toward the American theater and awaken an interest in the work of our serious playwrights which had not existed before."

O'Neill's work was based on his own vast and varied experience. Over the years, he roamed South America, Africa and Europe, as well as the United States. After a try at gold prospecting in Honduras netted nothing but malarial fever, he was assistant manager for a touring theatrical company, and then went to sea for two years and spent one round-trip voyage tending mules on a cattle steamer from Buenos Aires to South Africa. His last seagoing job was with the American Line between New York and Southampton. He then toured the Far west as a vaudville actor, and worked as a cub reporter in New London, Connecticut.

It was while on this last job that he developed lung trouble and had to go to a sanitorium for six months. He later said that "It was in this enforced period of reflection that the urge to write came upon me." That "urge" must have been very strong, for in 15 months, he wrote eleven one-act plays and two long ones.

Although many of his characters and settings were drawn from his own specific experiences, O'Neill's themes were universal, and his plays were translated into many languages and produced all over the world. One, "The Hairy Ape", was even translated into Bantu and played in South Africa by a company of Zulus.

"Mourning Becomes Electra", "Anna Christie", "Long Day's Journey Into Night" and "The Emperor Jones", which also became an opera, were some of his more famous works. About forty of his works were produced for the stage, but he never did write for the screen. He turned down many offers to do scripts for Hollywood, saying that "This doesn't mean I have any prejudice against pictures. It merely means that the screen has never interested me as a medium." O'Neill also commented on the reaction to his refusal to write for motion pictures. "Some people seem to regard it as a mad—and even inexcusable—eccentricity", he said.

O'Neill won the Pulitzer Prize four times, and later recalled that he almost refused to accept the first one, in 1920. "I had honestly never heard of the Pulitzer Prize, or if I had, I hadn't listened. When a wire reached me, saying I had won it, my reaction was a disdainful raspberry—'Oh, a damned medal. And one of those presentation ceremonies'. Then a wire from my agent arrived which spoke of a thousand dollars and no medal and no ceremony. Well, I practically went delirious!"

His reaction to that prize was the same as audience reactions to many of the works of the man who, more than any other, was responsible for having serious American drama taken seriously all over the world.

O'Neill relaxing in his Seattle home in 1936.

O'Neill shakes hands with a canine friend at his chateau in Tours, France in 1930.

Given Name: Eugene Gladstone O'Neill
Born: October 16, 1888, New York City
Married: Kathleen Jenkins, 1909, 1 child (divorced 1912)
Married: Agnes Boulton, 1918, 2 children (divorced 1929)
Married: Carlotta Monterey, 1929
Highlights: Leading American dramatist whose work brought new credibility to American theater. Won Nobel Prize for Literature in 1938, Pulitzer Prize for Drama 4 times.
Died: November 27, 1953

Unlike many playwrights, O'Neill attended all rehearsals of his plays. Here he joins the cast of "The Iceman Cometh".

Seen here in 1936, shortly after the announcement was made, O'Neill was the second American to win the Nobel Prize for Literature.

George Orwell

As a young man Eric Arthur Blair, an Anglo-Indian born in Bengal and educated in England, returned to Burma to serve in the Imperial Police. He didn't stay long, resigning because he couldn't keep serving "an Imperial system I had come to regard as a racket." Eric Blair's experiences in India laid the groundwork for the works of "George Orwell", the name Blair signed to his biting satires on life under authoritarian governments.

Fighting in Spain as a volunteer for the Republicans in the Civil War, Orwell was badly wounded—and further disillusioned about politics and causes. He wrote about his disillusionment in "Homage to Catalonia."

George Orwell was the conscience of his generation, a generation which watched in horror as fascism and communism spread like fatal diseases across Europe. His fast, clear, grey, bitter prose seemed more suitable to political tracts than to novels. In fact, he wanted to make political writing an art, and said he was forced by his age to become a sort of "pamphleteer".

At first reading his "Animal Farm" appears to be an amusing story about life in the barnyard. Instead, it is a bitter satirical fable about the development of the Russian Revolution under Stalin. The animals on Mr. Jones' farm decide to stage a revolution. Their motto is "all animals are equal—but some are more equal than others." Leadership lands automatically on the pigs, Napoleon and Snowball, who fight about who'll be boss. The pigs could be Trotsky and Stalin.

But it was with "1984" that Orwell created his most sensational work and a worldwide furor. The author wrote it while he was dying of tuberculosis—he'd suffered from the disease since he was a young man—on a gloomy, rugged island in the Scotch Hebrides. At the time he conceived his projection of a futuristic totalitarian state, the superpowers were digging in to the depths of the Cold War; Stalin was having his last, mad power-fling and anything seemed possible. The book's title, said to have been chosen by the simple reversal of the last digits in the year Orwell completed the book, came to stand for the destruction of the human spirit by the all-powerful State.

"1984" takes place in Oceania, a nation made up of what's left of Britain and America after a global war. The hero works in the Ministry of Truth, destroying history, issuing propaganda in the new language, Newspeak. Big Brother is always watching from the telescreen. The Thought Police are everywhere, making sure people don't think for themselves—or make love: love is prohibited.

Orwell was never satisfied with his book, and died a year after it was published, in 1950, before his novel became a worldwide bestseller, read by every schoolchild in the Western world as a cautionary tale, as well as a creation of genius. When the real year 1984 arrived the world paused to consider how much it had come to resemble Orwell's prediction. A friend of his said it "wasn't meant to be a prophecy, but a kind of cartoon." Orwell himself said just before he died, "The moral to be drawn . . . is a simple one: Don't let it happen. It depends on you."

As a wax likeness of the gaunt and ailing author was unveiled at Mme. Tussaud's museum in London, a new movie based on the novel opened in theatres, and a symposium in Washington considered just how to close to Orwell's imagination real life had become. British critics drew parallels between the book and present times. One said that television, advertising and education have produced their own kind of newspeak, doublethink and thoughtcrime; that the wisdom of society is now based on the consensus. Another saw in Orwell's links between a decline in the physical fabric of life and moral decay parallels to Britain's growing tolerance for violence and graffitti-smeared ugliness. The clearest prediction come true, it was pointed out, is in the field of electronic surveillance—Big Brother *is* watching, through computer-stored data, the entire 1.5 million population of Northern Ireland.

In Russia, as in most Communist countries, Orwell's books are banned. A Communist newspaper article stated that America is the real Oceania. It claimed the FBI is "Big Brother", and President Reagan embodies Oceania's motto—"Ignorance is Strength."

Meanwhile, a dissident Latvian, found "guilty" of owning "1984" and other books, was sent off to seven years hard labor.

Given Name: Eric Arthur Blair
Born: 1903, Motihari, India
Married: Eileen O'Shaughnessy
Married: Sonia Mary Brownell, 1949
Highlights: Author of several important novels, including "1984", which warned against the loss of personal freedom to all-powerful governments.
Died: January 21, 1950

George Orwell, undated. His novels included "Animal Farm", and the frighteningly prophetic "1984".

Pablo Picasso

No twentieth century artist received more praise than Pablo Picasso. And no artist was more often damned. His work generated extreme reactions with critics and the public alike, and he was called either the greatest of modern painters or the least effective. But there was one point on which almost everyone agreed: Picasso was the most prolific artist of modern times.

In 70 years, he produced thousands of paintings, drawings, sculptures, prints and ceramics. He restlessly moved from one medium to another, one style to another, one subject to another, always pressing against the boundaries of comprehension and, some would say, often crossing them. He strove to paint thoughts and feelings that would touch the viewer. But many viewers didn't get the idea and found his work just meaningless collections of colored daubs. Audiences often had a difficult time comprehending the meaning of people with, for example, five ears, all in unusual places.

Perhaps Picasso's outstanding innovation was cubism, which he introduced to a startled art world in Paris in 1907, with "Young Ladies of Avignon". It was an abstract, distorted, angular image of five girls which, like so much of Picasso's work, drew both positive and negative reactions. Ignoring the negative, Picasso continued to do what pleased him, and continued along the cubist road for several years.

The cubist period had been preceded by what were known as his "blue" and "rose" periods, during which almost all of his paintings were dominated by single colors. Some speculated that the blue mirrored his poverty and hopelessness in the early days, and the rose a change for the better in his fortunes. "The Two Sisters" "The Woman with a Jackdaw" and an etching of a hungry couple at an almost empty table, "The Frugal Repast", are among his best known "blue period" works. His "rose period" was characterized by "The Woman with a Fan" and "The Harlequin's Family", among others.

Picasso's private life was as restless as his artistic life. Seven different women were important to him at various times and for various periods, several serving as models for some of his controversial paintings. In 1969, at age 79, he married Jacqueline Roque, a 35-year-old divorcee who put some order into his private life, but was careful never to touch the magnificent disarray of his several studios. Even in his later years, he would start working in late afternoon and continue until midnight or later. This was a pattern he had developed a a struggling artist in Montmartre, where he had shared an apartment with a poet. There had been only one bed, so Picasso had slept days, while the poet worked, and painted at night.

An avowed Communist for much of his adult life, Picasso nevertheless was prohibited from displaying his works in Russia during the reign of Joseph Stalin. Picasso had become a Communist during the Spanish Civil War, both out of respect for the bravery of the Communists in that conflict, and because communism stood for certain ideals in which he believed. His experiences in the Spanish war later led to the creation of "Guernica", which may be his most famous painting. In searing, violent strokes it portrays the slaughter and horror of war.

His talent, his passion and his energy all seemed endless. And for all these reasons, as one professor said, "Picasso dominates his century as Michelangelo dominated his."

In 1953, Picasso posed for this photo, surrounded by his work, in his studio in Vallauris on the French Riviera.

Ezra Pound

An eccentric, an enthusiast, a cynic, poet Ezra Pound was one of the most influential and controversial figures of 20th Century literature, flamboyant and famous for three things—his work, his encouragement of aspiring writers, and his 1945 indictment by the U.S. government for treason.

Pound travelled far from his Quaker heritage and birthplace in Idaho to an expatriate life in Europe where, before World War I, he was the dominant influence among Anglo-American writers. In London he founded two experimental schools of poetry, Vorticism and Imagism, publishing avant-garde verse in esoteric magazines. He urged the young writers who clustered around him, both in England and in postwar Paris, to break with the restrictions of 19th century form and "Make It New"! Among those he helped achieve recognition were Irish giants James Joyce and William Butler Yeats; Americans Robert Frost and Ernest Hemingway; and T.S. Eliot from St. Louis, Missouri, like Pound, a permanent expatriate.

Pound himself published his first volume of poetry in Venice in 1908. His mammoth life's work, "The Cantos", loosely inspired by Dante's "Divine Comedy", was composed over a period from 1915 to 1959. Chronicling the cultural rot and materialism Pound saw afflicting Western society, "The Cantos" contain references to everything he had ever learned about anything, from Confucianism, Japanese Noh plays, Homer, and Jeffersonian economics, to Italian Renaissance painting and myths from every culture. Nearly unreadable without footnotes, "The Cantos" were viewed by some critics as being purposely obscure. Others regarded them as the masterwork of the greatest poet of his time.

During World War II, which Pound blamed on international bankers and munitions interests, he developed an admiration for Italy's Benito Mussolini and made radio broadcasts favorable to the Fascist regime. After the Allied victory he was seized as a traitor and returned to his native America under federal indictment. Declared unfit to stand trial, Pound was incarcerated for 13 years at St. Elizabeth's Hospital in Washington, D.C. There, visited daily by his wife, the former Dorothy Shakespeare (a descendant of the William Shakespeare family) as well as students and fellow writers, Pound continued work on his Cantos. In 1958 he was pronounced "permanently and incurably insane" and returned to Italy to live with his daughter Mary.

While at St. Elizabeth's Pound was nominated for the prestigious Bollingen Prize for poetry for "The Pisan Cantos", written while he was confined to a U.S. Military prison in Pisa, Italy. This touched off a heated debate between politicians and others who objected to the award going to a pro-fascist (and, many contended, anti-Semite) and intellectuals who thought Pound deserved the award on the merits of his achievement. Eventually he received this and many other distinguished honors.

At the end of his life, however, a ghostly, increasingly silent figure wandering his old haunts in Italy, Pound was disturbed by feelings of persecution and disappointment that he had been deprived of the Nobel Prize because of his political activities. His comment on his prodigious life's work was, "I botched it." Pound died in Venice, where he had published his first pioneering verse, embittered and virtually silent.

Given Name: Ezra Loomis Pound
Born: October 30, 1885, Hailey, Idaho
Married: Dorothy Sheakespear, 1914
Highlights: Leading expatriate American poet.
Died: November 1, 1972

Pound passing through customs with other passengers from the Italian liner "Christoforo Columbo" in 1958.

Italian composer Giancarlo Menotti (left) and Pound shaking hands at the 1971 Festival of the Two Worlds in Spoleto, Italy.

Pound in Merano, Italy in 1960.

In 1947, Pound was escorted to jail in Washington, D.C. under indictment for treason.

Pound gave a Fascist salute on his return to Italy in 1958.

An emaciated Pound in Spoleto, Italy in 1968.

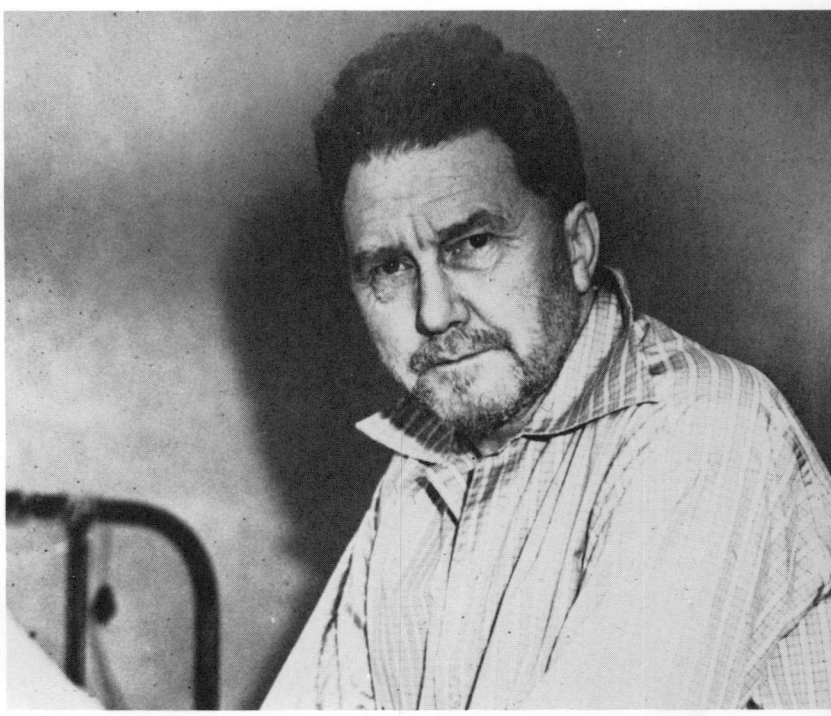

Pound in Rome in 1941.

George Bernard Shaw

His talent was exceeded only by his egotism. He was universally recognized as one of the greatest dramatists of modern times, yet held an even higher opinion of himself than critics and the public did.

Shaw delighted in knocking idols from their pedestals and said that "the secret of success is to offend the greatest number of people." America was one of his favorite targets, as was the educational establishment. He claimed that "I have been particularly careful never to say a civil word to the United States." He was also the author of "He who can, does; he who cannot, teaches." With tongue only partly in cheek, he attributed his success to his lack of formal education. "Schools are a prison for children," he said. "I was locked up in one many hours, but never learned anything there. That is how I preserved my brain. Otherwise, I'd be an imbecile, like other education people."

He wrote a number of novels, and many essays that covered a wide range of subjects—from music criticism to world politics. But his greatest love was the drama and that was the primary source of his fame. He wrote more than 50 plays, among which were "Pygmalion", "Man and Superman" and "Caesar and Cleopatra". In 1925, he received the Nobel Prize for Literature.

Shaw lived well into his nineties, and gave much credit for his longevity to his teetotalism and vegetarian diet. He said that he hoped to live well past 100 because "man cannot hope to reach anything like intellectual maturity in less than 150 years." In his later years, with typical wit, he listed his favorite recreation as "being past ninety".

Born in Dublin, of Protestant parents, Shaw moved to London at age twenty to join his mother, who helped support him for a long time, since his writings brought him a total of just $50 in nine years. His own people long denied him recognition, and he achieved stature in Berlin and Vienna long before he was accepted in London. But that didn't dent his ego. When Viennese producers objected to his dictatorial behavior at rehearsals for one of his plays, Shaw told them "Politically, your emperor is emperor of Austria, but dramatically I am the emperor of Europe."

A self-described Communist who often praised Joseph Stalin, Shaw nevertheless freely volunteered his opinion that Karl Marx's "Das Kapital" was ponderously unreadable. Parts of it, he said, were "quite unbearable, and its discussion a waste of time". "G.B.S.", as he was known through most of his career, also was interested in simplified spelling. He advocated a 42-letter English alphabet that would represent all speech sounds in the language, and said that he used it to save time in his own writing.

Shaw's works covered a wide range of economic, social and political issues, and he often seemed genuinely disappointed that his suggestions were not immediately adopted. "I have solved practically all the pressing questions of our time," he said, "but they keep on being propounded as insoluble, just as if I had never existed."

Although the world did not always do as Shaw wanted, nor satisfy his insatiable ego, the world did, and does, recognize that it is better for his having been part of it.

A 1928 portrait of playwright George Bernard Shaw.

Given Name: George Bernard Shaw
Born: July 26, 1856, Dublin, Ireland
Married: Charlotte Frances Payne-Townshend, 1898
Highlights: Author, playwright, gadfly to the political and educational authorities. Won Nobel Prize for Literature in 1925. Invented 42 letter English alphabet.
Died: November 2, 1950

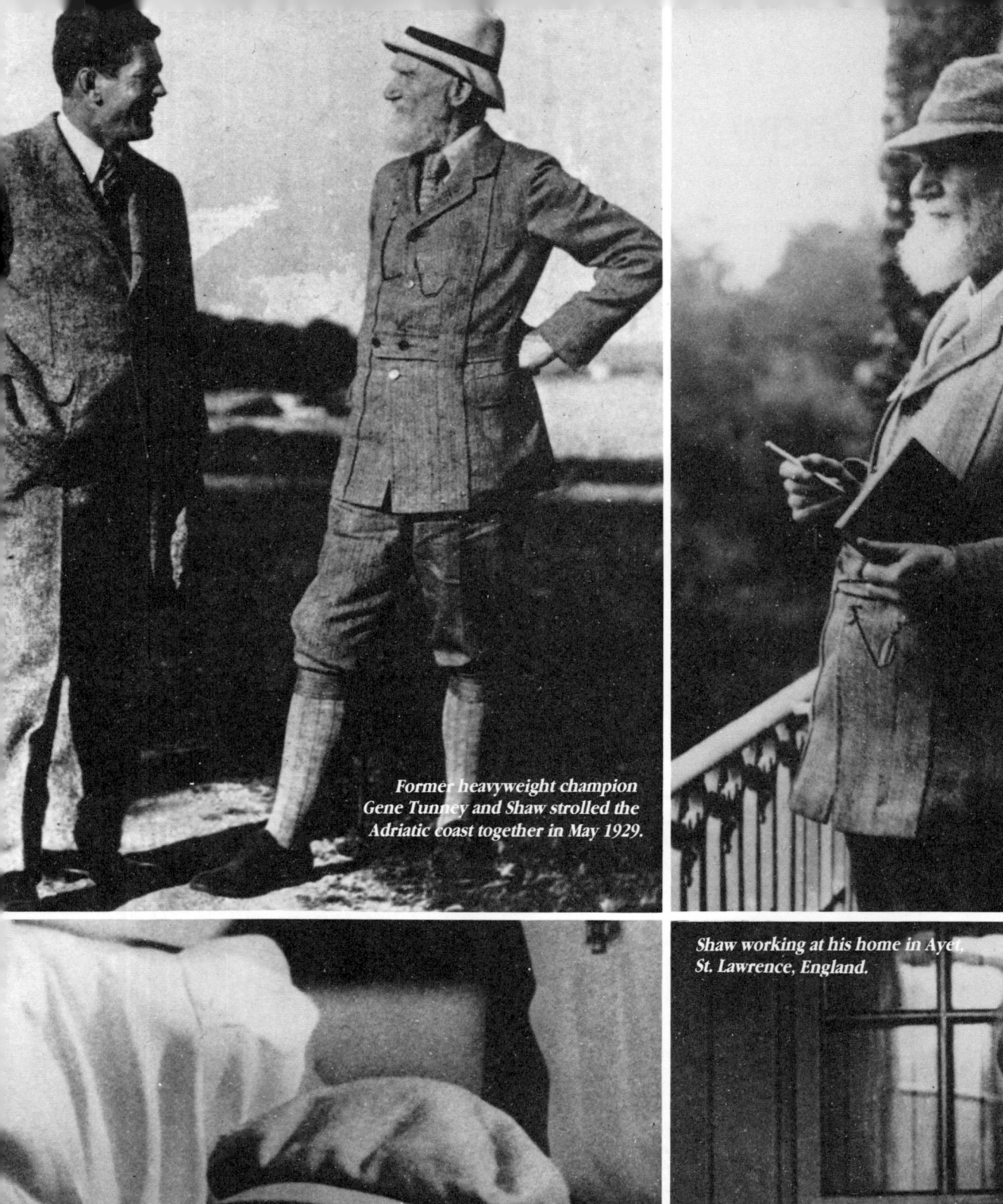

Former heavyweight champion Gene Tunney and Shaw strolled the Adriatic coast together in May 1929.

Shaw in August 1929.

Shaw working at his home in Ayot St. Lawrence, England.

One of the last photos of Shaw, taken just 17 days before his death on November 2, 1950.

Alexander Solzhenitsyn

In *The Cancer Ward,* one of 20 books which earned him the Nobel Prize for Literature in 1970, Russian author Alexander Solzhenitsyn wrote, "A man sprouts a tumor and dies. How then can a country live that has sprouted camps and exile?"

Solzhenitsyn knows about camps, and about exile. Near the end of World War II, he sent a letter to a friend from Leningrad, where he was a commander in the Red Army. In the letter he made a derogatory remark about "the whiskered one"—obviously Soviet leader Joseph Stalin. The letter fell into the hands of counter-intelligence agents and Solzhenitsyn was sent to a labor camp for eight years. Ironically, he was released the day of "the whiskered one's" death—March 5th, 1953. But that wasn't the end of his punishment. He was forced into exile in Soviet Central Asia for three more years. While there he taught, and wrote down some of the stories he'd composed while he was in prison.

One of the stories Solzhenitsyn wrote was *A Day in the Life of Ivan Denisovich.* The first published work to describe in detail life in one of Stalin's bleak camps, it tells the story of a simple farmer serving 10 years on trumped-up espionage charges. Soviet Premier Nikita Kruschev encouraged its publication in 1962, as it strengthened his anti-Stalinist campaign. When the book came out, it immediately sold 96,000 copies in Russia. Published worldwide, it won Solzhenitsyn international acclaim and instant recognition as Russia's greatest living author.

Solzhenitsyn's other great novels—*The Cancer Ward, The First Circle, Gulag Archipelago*—were not allowed to be published in Russia. Their publication without his consent in the West fueled accusations against him that he was a willing tool of the West's anti-Soviet propaganda. In 1964 Kruschev was removed. A return to ideological orthodoxy contributed

Solzhenitsyn (left) receives honorary degree in 1984 from President Rev. John E. Brooks of Holy Cross College.

The author autographs books for admirers.

Nobel laureate Solzhenitsyn does research at Stanford University library in 1976.

to growing disapproval of Solzhenitsyn by Soviet officials. The celebrated author became a non-person, with no mention of him or his works in the press.

In 1967 Solzhenitsyn wrote a letter demanding an end to Soviet censorship, which he said Russian literature had suffered under for decades. He was denounced by officials, declared unbalanced and schizophrenic. When he heard in 1970 that he had been awarded the Nobel Prize he was afraid to go to Stockholm to receive the prize for fear he would not be allowed to return. In 1974 Solzhenitsyn was arrested, put on a plane and sent to Zurich and into exile.

Today Solzhenitsyn lives in a small Vermont town on a farm with his three sons and his wife, who divorced him during his prison term to remarry someone else, then divorced her second husband to remarry Solzhenitsyn when he was released. She followed him into exile and became a U.S. citizen. In Vermont the author leads an almost monastic life of peace and quiet, and uninterrupted work. He is writing an 8-volume history of the Russian Revolution.

Solzhenitsyn is passionate about two things—Russia and freedom. He loves Vermont and wouldn't live anywhere else—except a "free" Russia. The author decries the West's failure to confront communism, saying that in 1919 Lenin proclaimed a death sentence for the West and it has never been rescinded. He sees the West sinking into materialism and self-destruction, with rosy unrealistic visions of a detente with Russia. Solzhenitsyn disagrees with the statement British pacifist Bertrand Russell once made—"better Red than dead." He believes that the West, which brought nuclear weapons into existence, has a responsibility to be fully armed against Russia. To be "Red", he says, "is to become dead gradually."

Solzhenitsyn got in some tennis during a 1975 visit to Norwich University in Northfield, Vermont.

Given Name: Alexander Solzhenitsyn
Born: December 11, 1918
Married: Natalya Reshetovskaya
Highlights: Author of several major novels depicting life in Soviet Russia and its forced labor camps. Won Nobel Prize for Literature in 1970.

At 1978 Harvard commencement, Solzhenitsyn said he has concluded that Western society is suffering "spiritual exhaustion".

The bad old days—Solzhenitsyn as Captain in Soviet Army in 1944, during deportation in 1946; after liberation in 1953.

ARTS

Igor Stravinsky

Stopped at the French border during World War I and asked to state his profession, Igor Stravinsky responded, "Inventor of Music". In the 20th Century no musical figure so personifies the avant garde as the Russian-born composer.

Born near Leningrad, Stravinsky was the son of a noted basso with the Imperial Opera who chose law as the career for his son to follow. Recalling his childhood as "a period of waiting for the moment when I could send everyone and everything connected with it to hell", Stravinsky did just that, quitting law school to study music with the father of a fellow student, the great composer Rimsky-Korsakov. His works soon gained notoriety bringing him to the attention of Sergei Diaghilev, head of the Ballet Russe, who commissioned him to write a series of ballet scores for his dancers. Their association produced the most colorful period in Stravinsky's career. In such works as "The Fire Bird" and "Petrouchka" Stravinsky blended Russian folk themes with eccentric and often erotic rhythms that seemed to be made for dancers. Years later in New York fellow Russian-born George Ballanchine would choose Stravinsky's music for some of the New York City Ballet's most dazzling productions.

In 1913 "Sacre du Printemps" ("Rite of Spring") exploded onto the music scene in Paris, creating protests and a wild scandal with its almost barbaric eroticism. Critics stated that this work shocked music out of the Romantic period for good. Overnight Stravinsky was looked at as the century's most significant composer and an international personality.

After World War I Stravinsky veered sharply away from his Russian musical heritage towards an unsentimental classic style which he constantly redefined in such works as the oratorio "Oedipus Rex" and Symphony of Psalms, written for

Given Name: Igor Fedorovich Stravinsky
Born: June 17, 1882, Oranienbaum, Russia
Married: Catherine Nossenko, 1906, 4 children
Married: Vera de Bossett, 1940
Highlights: Composer credited with the birth of "modern music". His use of atonality, dissonance and sensual rhythms broke new ground.
Died: April 6, 1971

Composer Igor Stravinsky relaxes at rehearsal for a 1966 concert with the Portland Symphony Orchestra.

the 50th anniversary of the Boston Symphony Orchestra. He never ceased experimenting with atonality, in such works as the ballet "Orpheus" and a completely abstract "Mass", performed at La Scala in Milan in 1948. Many of his late works were criticized as being bloodless and "thin".

Much of Stravinsky's music was written for and based on the church and church ritual. Raised in the Russian Orthodox Church, he believed you had to have religious faith in order to write religious music. However, he left the church during various periods in his life, once because the priest in the confessional asked for his autograph.

The composer never bought the "starving artist concept" and vowed to "earn every penny he could extract from a society that would let Mozart and Bartok die in poverty", writing most of his works on commission. The revolutionary musician whose works created uproars and controversy didn't match his image at all. A dapper little man, he kept banker's hours and three times, on stage to perform his own piano concerto, he was so nervous he forgot the music.

Stravinsky never returned to Russia after he left in 1914. He lived in France for a time, where he was friends with Debussy, Ravel, Picasso and Nijinsky. In 1945 he became a U.S. citizen, settling in California.

Although he allowed "Rites of Spring" to be used in Walt Disney's "Fantasia", the composer shunned the movies as an arena for his music. However, he was by no means against popular culture. He arranged "The Star-Spangled Banner" for a Boston performance—and police were summoned to accuse him of tampering with the national anthem. He composed the "Ebony Concerto" for Woody Herman's swing band, and a polka for the dancing elephants in the Ringling Brothers Barnum and Bailey Circus.

Stravinsky conducts a 1960 rehearsal of the New York Philharmonic.

Violinist Samuel Dushkin confers with Stravinsky before 1937 concert

Stravinsky conducting a 1947 rehearsal.

H. G. Wells

A fascination with man's place in time and space, the vistas of astronomy, the death of the world and the vastness of interstellar space provided the English writer H(erbert) G(eorge) Wells with the material for his science fiction novels. Along with Jules Verne, Wells is regarded as the inventor of this new genre.

His first novel, *The Time Machine* (1895) is a social allegory set in the year 802701, describing a society divided into two classes; the subterranean workers called Morlocks, and the decadent Eloi. More science fiction novels followed and by the time Wells was 32 he had written and published *The War of the Worlds* (1898), a powerful and apocalyptic vision of the world invaded by Martians. These novels, along with *The Wonderful Visit* (1895), *The Island of Doctor Moreau* (1896), *The Invisible Man* (1897), *The Time Machine,* and *The Invisible Man,* combine, in varying degrees, political satire, warnings about the dangerous new powers of science, and a desire to foresee a possible future, as in *A Modern Utopia* (1905). Wells's preoccupation with social progress, as well as scientific progress, distinguishes his science fiction stories from the fantasies of Jules Verne.

H. G. Wells was born in Bromley, Kent on September 21, 1866. His father was a shopkeeper, his mother a lady's maid. Wells left school at age 14 but four years later won a scholarship to the Normal School of Science in South Kensington where he studied under Thomas Henry Huxley. Another grant took him to London University and he graduated with a degree in biology in 1890. By the time he was 30, he had already embarked on his famous series of scientific romances.

Another group of several first-rate comic novels have become minor classics: *Love and Mr. Lewisham* (1900), the story of a struggling young teacher; and *Kipps* (1905), a tale of an aspiring draper's assistant undone by an unexpected

Given Name: Herbert George Wells
Born: September 21, 1866, Bromley, Kent, England
Married: Isabel Mary Wells, 1891 (divorced 1894)
Married: Amy Catherine Robbins, 2 sons
Highlights: Author of many novels of science fiction that often foresaw events, such as space travel, that have since become reality.
Died: August 13, 1946

Author H.G. Wells in his cabin aboard the Queen Mary.

Wells was smiling and relaxed on his 1937 visit to the United States

inheritance and its consequences. *Tono-Bungay* (1909), one of Wells' most successful works, is a picture of English society in dissolution, and of the advent of a new class of rich, embodied in Uncle Ponderevo, an entrepreneur intent on peddling a worthless patent medicine. Then in 1910 Wells published *The History of Mr. Polly,* which recounts the adventures of an inefficient shopkeeper who liberates himself by burning down his own ship and bolting for freedom.

His other novels include, *Ann Veronica* (1900), a feminist tract about a girl who, fortified by the concept of the 'New Woman', defies her father and conventionial morality by running off with the man she loves. *The New Machiavelli* (1911), about a politician involved in sexual scandal, is regarded as marking a decline in Wells's creative power.

In other novels, Wells outlined his socialist and internationalist solutions to civilization's ills in several books of analysis and speculation: *A Modern Utopia* and *New Worlds for Old* (1908). He continued to reach a huge audience, notably with his massive *The Outline of History* (1920) and its shorter offspring, *A Short History of the World* (1922), which was written in collaboration with his son, George Philip Wells, and Julian Huxley. These works, along with *The Shape of Things to Come* (1933) confirmed Wells's position as one of the great popularizers and one of the most influential voices of his age.

One of the great novelist's last statements, made after Hiroshima, was an exhortation to man to confront his 'grave and tragic' destiny with dignity and without hysteria. He died in 1946, having been one of the first writers to sense the great need to probe in the novel the growing social and moral unrest brought on by applications of new scientific and technological advances. In doing so he discovered and discussed many of the major social, psychological and moral questions which continue to plague us today.

Paulette Goddard, then Charlie Chaplin's fiancee, and Chaplin join Wells at a dinner in his honor in 1937.

Goddard and Chaplin's sons welcomed Wells to Hollywood.

Henry Ford (left) and Wells examine an electric motor at Detroit's Edison Institute in 1937.

Frank Lloyd Wright

He was a man of unquestioned talent and insatiable ego. Perhaps because of that ego, and his constant, open and aggressive challenges to the architectural establishment and the status quo, Wright lived in the center of a storm of controversy.

In both his professional and personal lives, he insisted on breaking new ground and refused to accept the standards of his time. The results were those that usually come to trailblazers: He reaped much praise and acclaim, yet suffered much pain and frustration.

Wright's designs were different in structure as well as appearance. In fact, because of his often unorthodox engineering concepts, he was frequently forced by building authorities to submit to tests to prove the safety of his ideas. Once, to prove the strength of mushrooming, tree-like support columns he had designed for the S.C. Johnson Wax Company headquarters, he erected a single column in a field and had a steam shovel dump sand on top of it. Even Wright was surprised when the column supported more than sixty tons.

Alexander Wolcott said that if he could apply the word "genius" to only one living American, he "would have to save it up for Wright." And Wright probably would have agreed. He himself said "Not only do I intend to be the greatest architect who ever lived, but the greatest who will ever live. Yes, I intend to be the greatest architect of all time."

Wright felt that he achieved his goal. But not all agreed. There were those who considered him an impractical visionary, his work half-baked and out-of-touch with the real world. There were also those whose opinions of Wright's work were colored by his unconventional life style.

In an age when divorce was uncommon, Wright was divorced twice and married three times. He also had a long, and open, relationship with Mrs. Mamah Borthwick Cheney,

A 1953 photo of Wright and the model for the Guggenheim Museum, his first permanent building in New York.

who was the wife of an Oak Park, Illinois neighbor when they first met. Wright took her to Europe with him in 1909, while she was still married. On their return, her husband obtained a divorce on the grounds of desertion, and Wright and "Mamah" lived together at "Taliesin", a home Wright designed and built at Spring Green, Wisconsin. In 1914, Mrs. Cheney, her two children, and four others were slain by a crazed servant, who also burned down the house, all while Wright was away working in Chicago.

Wright later married Miriam Noel, a woman with whom he had already been living, after he finally obtained a divorce from his first wife and the mother of his six children. When the stormy marriage to Noel broke up, after an acrimonious and financially ruinous divorce, he married Olga Lazovich, a young divorcee who bore his seventh and last child. They lived in "Taliesin II" until it, too, was destroyed by fire. He built a third.

His buildings, unlike his personal relationships, stood up to every kind of pressure. For earthquake-prone Tokyo, he designed an Imperial Hotel that used a non-rigid structure, the walls and floors of which were capable of shifting with the movement of the earth. The soft mud beneath the structure was used as a cushion for shock-absorbing frames resting on short-tapered concrete piling. The hotel went through one earthquake even before it was finished, and when Tokyo suffered one of the worst earthquakes in history in 1925, the Imperial Hotel stood. When the quake was over, more than 100,000 people had died and much of Tokyo was leveled, but Wright's building was the only major structure left upright.

His egotism, outspokeness and unconventionality offended many. But Wright left a body of work (over 550 structures) and important basic concepts (such as the idea that buildings should fit into their surroundings) that make him impossible to ignore.

Wright listens to Fiorello La Guardia at the Herald-Tribune Forum in 1940.

Wright in 1966, before testimonial dinner at which he was given $10,000 to help pay taxes on his estate.

Wright works with 4 apprentices at his estate, Taliesin, in Spring Green, Wisconsin.

In 1945, Wrights' model for New York's Solomon R. Guggenheim Museum caused surprise and controversy.

Given Name: Frank Lloyd Wright
Born: June 8, 1869, Richland Center, Wisconsin
Married: Catherine Tobin, 1890, 6 children
Married: Miriam Noel, 1923
Married: Olga Lazovich, 1928, 1 child
Highlights: Perhaps the greatest architect of his time, he designed well over 500 buildings, many of which introduced radically new structural or design concepts.
Died: April 9, 1959

ARTS

William Butler Yeats

In trying to construct a system which would provide a place for everything in man's history, Yeats tried to account for the way man's desires interact with circumstance. For such a man, the world was bound to be a theater of conflict.

William Butler Yeats, born in Dublin on June 13, 1865 is regarded by some as the greatest English-language poet of the 20th century. At 19 he "lived, breathed, ate, drank and slept poetry." By the time he was 20 his interest in the occult led him to found the Dublin Hermetic Society (1885) and two years later to join the London Lodge of Theosophists. A meeting with nationalist John O'Leary, in 1885, prompted Yeats's discovery of Ireland as a literary subject and his commitment to the cause of Irish national identity. These major defining elements of his poetic career were visible by his 24th year. In 1889 he fell in love with Maude Bonne and published *The Wanderings of Oisin* and he enshrined his unrequited love for the lady in the stylized, erotic symbolic verses of *The Wind Among the Reeds* (1899). His poem, *The Rose* (1893), is filled with Irish myth and landscape.

In 1902 he became President of the Irish National Theatre Society (later the Abbey Theatre) for which he had written many plays. Yeats wanted to raise national consciousness by cultural means as well as extending himself as not only a poet but as a shaper of the world.

The National Theatre encountered bitter opposition from its nationalist Catholic audience. Padraic Colum, who met Yeats during this time said, "At this time Yeats was still the youngish man of the velvet jacket and the flowing tie. To the Catholic intelligentsia who had a few years before picketed his play, *The Countess Cathleen,* he was subversive. But that did not recommend him to the other side, the Ascendency side, the side of his father's friend Professor Dowden... But the fact that two sides of the Irish public was hostile to him made this thirty-year-old man interesting..."

The body of poet William Butler Yeats, who died at Menton, France in 1939, is taken aboard an Irish corvette for return to Ireland.

Given Name: William Butler Yeats
Born: June 13, 1865, Dublin, Ireland
Married: Georgie Hyde-Lees, 1917
Highlights: Leadign poet who won Nobel Prize for Literature in 1923. Also became one of the first senators in the new Irish Free State.
Died: January 28, 1939

From the days of his youthful campaigning for the National Literary Society, Yeats had hoped and worked for an Irish literature that should be heroic. That hope he abandoned in 1912, coincidentally the same year he met Ezra Pound. Encouraged by his friendship with Pound, Yeats was to undergo a toughening of style that broke the grip of earlier romantic and Pre-Raphaelite influences on him. Pound also influenced the refinement of Yeats's drama, *Plays for Dancers* (1916).

Yeats married Georgiana Hyde-Lees in 1917 and her automatic writing and speech gave Yeats the raw material for *A Vision* (1925), a work containing part history, part philosophy, part mysticism, part psychology, and which crowned his pursuit of mystical knowledge.

Two events confirm Yeats's dual role as poet and public man: in 1922, at the end of othe Anglo-Irish war (1916-22), he became a senator of the Irish Free State. In 1923 he received the Nobel Prize for poetry.

Despite illness and approaching old age, Yeats's last 15 years bristled with astonishing energies. True to the principles of a lifetime, he refused to abandon the attempt to bend the world and himself to his imaginative pattern. He published *Essays* (1824), *Collected Plays* (1934) and volumes of poetry. His completed *Autobiographies* appeared in 1938. His final play, *The Death of Cuchulain,* and his last poems all dealing with heroic resolution in the face of death and were completed only days before he died on January 28, 1939.

Yeats's lifework was an attempt to "hammer into unity" the evolving areas of his experience and it has been said that Yeats's willed coincidence between his life and work guarantees his stature as the greatest modern poet in the English language.

Yeats' grave at Drumcliff, County Sligo, Ireland.

ARTS

INDEX

Ali, Muhammad	78
Anthony, Susan B.	6
Armstrong, Louis	142
Balanchine, George	144
Bannister, Roger	80
Bartok, Bela	146
Begin, Menachem	8
Bell, Alexander	108
Berlin, Irving	148
Caruso, Enrico	150
Carver, G.W.	110
Cezanne, Paul	152
Chaplin, Charlie	154
Chekhov, Anton	156
Chiang Kai-Shek	10
Churchill, Winston S.	12
Clemenceau, Georges	15
Comanici, Nadia	83
Coward, Noel	158
Curie, Marie	112
Dali, Salvador	160
De Gaulle, Charles	17
De Mille, Cecil B.	162
Disney, Walt	164
Edison, Thomas A.	114
Einstein, Albert	116
Eisenhower, Dwight D.	19
Eliot, T.S.	166
Ellington, Duke	168
Erte	170
Faulkner, William	172
Fitzgerald, Ella	174
Fitzgerald, F. Scott	176
Fleming, Alexander	119
Ford, Henry	121
Frost, Robert	178
Freud, Sigmund	123
Gandhi, Indira	22
Gandhi, Mohandas	24
Garbo, Greta	180
George, Lloyd	27
Gilbert & Sullivan	182
Gretzky, Wayne	85
Hemingway, Ernest	184
Hillary, Edmund	87
Hirohito	29
Hitchcock, Alfred	186
Hitler, Adolf	32
Ho Chi Minh	35
James, Henry	188
Joyce, James	190

Keynes, John	37
King, Martin Luther	39
Laver, Rodney	89
Lenin	41
Lindberg, Charles A.	44
Lister, Joseph	125
Louis, Joe	91
MacArthur, Douglas	46
Man Ray	192
Mao Tse-Tung	49
Mother Teresa	127
Mussolini, Benito	52
Nabokov, Vladimir	194
Navratilova, Martina	93
Nehru, Jawaharlal	54
Nicklaus, Jack	95
Nightingale, Florence	129
Olivier, Laurence	196
O'Neill, Eugene	198
Oppenheimer, J. Robert	131
Orwell, George	200
Owens, Jesse	99
Pavlov, Ivan	133
Pele	97
Picasso, Pablo	202
Pope John XXIII	56
Pound, Ezra	205
Renoir, Auguste	207
Rhodes, Cecil J.	58
Robinson, Jackie	101
Rockefeller, John D.	135
Rodin, Auguste	209
Roosevelt, Eleanor	60
Roosevelt, Franklin D.	62
Ruth, Babe	103
Sadat, Anwar	65
Salk, Jonas	137
Shaw, George Bernard	211
Solzhenitsyn, Alexander	213
Stalin, Joseph	67
Stravinsky, Igor	215
Sun Yat-Sen	70
Truman, Harry S.	72
Wells, H.G.	217
Wilson, Woodrow	75
Wright, Frank Lloyd	229
Wright, Orville	139
Yeats, William Butler	222
Zaharias, Babe	105